Harvard Film Studies

The World Viewed, Enlarged Edition

Also by Stanley Cavell

Must We Mean What We Say?

The Senses of *Walden*

The Claim of Reason

The World Viewed

REFLECTIONS ON THE ONTOLOGY OF FILM

Stanley Cavell

Enlarged Edition

Harvard University Press
Cambridge, Massachusetts
and London, England
1979

Library of Congress Cataloging in Publication Data

Cavell, Stanley, 1926–
  The world viewed.

  Includes bibliographical references and index.
    1. Moving-pictures—Philosophy.   I. Title.
PN1995.C42   1979   791.43'01   79–16670
ISBN 0–674–96196–X (paper)
ISBN 0–674–96197–8 (cloth)

Printed in the United States of America

To my mother and father

"Why do precisely these objects which we behold make a world?"
—THOREAU, *Walden*

Contents

Foreword to the Enlarged Edition

It is gratifying to know that "More of *The World Viewed*" will exist within the same covers as its parent work. Because both were written before I became involved, even to the limited extent I now am, with the apparatus of film study, especially with the metamorphoses of moviolas, slowing or repeating or freezing the progress of a film; because, that is to say, I wrote primarily out of the memory of films, though between the time of the parent book and the time of its offspring I had begun the practice of taking notes during and after screenings, thus altering my preparation for future writing about film, thus altering what *could* be written by me about it; I was always aware that my descriptions of passages were liable to contain errors, of content and of sequence. I have not attempted to correct such errors in this reprinting, wanting neither to disguise the liabilities of the spirit in which the work was composed nor to disguise the need for a study of what may be remembered in any art and for a study of how using an analyzing machine may modify one's experience of a film. The absence of both such studies helps to keep unassessed the fact that in speaking of a moment or sequence from a film we, as we might put it, cannot *quote* the thing we are speaking of. The fact is not merely that others might then not be sure what it is we are referring to, but that we ourselves might not know what we are thinking about. This puts an immediate and tremendous burden on one's capacity for critical description of cinematic events. The question of what constitutes, in the various arts, "remembering a work," especially in light of the matter of variable quotability, naturally raises the question of what constitutes, or expresses, "knowing a work" (is recognizing it enough? is being able to whistle a few bars necessary? does it matter *which* bars?). These questions in turn lead to the question of what I have called "the necessity to *return* to a work, in fact or in memory," an experience I try hitting off by speaking of "having to remember" ("The Avoidance of Love" in *Must We Mean What We Say?*, p. 314). (If you express this wish by whistling, you will have, unlike the former case in which you are expressing knowledge, to *mean* the whistling, which is not something everyone who can whistle can do.)

What I do about errors of memory in *The World Viewed,* having apologized in its Preface for whatever off memories crop up, is to offer a brave confession "that a few faulty memories will not themselves shake my conviction in what I've said, since I am as interested in how a memory went wrong as in why the memories that are right occur when they do." I should like to make good here on this claim in a few instances that have come to my notice.

I begin a description of the ending of *Mr. Smith Goes to Washington* as follows: "On the floor of the Senate, Jean Arthur kneels beside Mr. Smith's prostrate, rejected form, supporting his head in the ambiguous birth-death posture of a Pietà" (p. 54). I knew the minute my eye fell on that passage in the finished book that the Jean Arthur character never appears on the floor of the Senate, but has to remain in the gallery in a Capra passage of anguish into elation. What seems to have happened to me is that while my words captured a Christ reference that the film, and especially these concluding moments of the film, certainly calls for, I transposed the imagery in question from some other film (a reasonably sheer guess would be that it is from Fritz Lang's *The Return of Frank James,* made a year later).

Rather different explanations occur to me for such self-confident errors as speaking "of an opening shot of Katharine Hepburn in *The Philadelphia Story* walking abstractedly through a room, cradling a sheaf of long-stemmed flowers, saying aloud to no one in particular, 'The calla lilies are in bloom again' (see *Stage Door*); of Cary Grant's response, upon being introduced to Ralph Bellamy in *His Girl Friday,* 'Haven't we met someplace before?' (they had, in the same juxtaposition of roles, a couple of years earlier in *The Awful Truth*). No doubt these lines were improvisatory . . ." (p. 124). I can imagine, responding to the depth of the improvisatory or the contingent in the nature of film, that I displaced the moment at which Cary Grant fingers the character played by Ralph Bellamy by telling a conspirator that "he looks like that movie actor, you know, Ralph Bellamy"—displaced this rather funny gag forward onto the hilarious early routine in which, as Grant is to be introduced to Bellamy, he greets heartily, as if in innocent error, an old-timer who just happens to be standing nearby. But no explanation short of a dream would seem to explain how I could have made up Katharine Hepburn's reference to *Stage Door.* Perhaps she did this in some film other than *The Philadelphia Story* (though I can't think which it might be). It remains possible—and I'd bet a pre-War dollar on it—that the film was initially released with this improvised line left in, at least in some prints.

A more galling error occurs in my reading of the final frames of *Rules of the Game,* forming the concluding part of "More of *The World Viewed,*" where I remember the gentle homosexual rather than the reactive heterosexual cad to have attempted a final conspiratorial moment of gossip with the general. Here I was still incapable of letting Renoir's sensibility provide me with a peripheral but distinct piece of learning (p. 220).

So far these errors, however annoying, or hateful, have not seemed to vitiate the interpretations based upon them, perhaps because while certain images may have been tampered with, the ideas and feelings in them have not been. A more problematic case presents itself in the course of those remarks about *Rules of the Game*. I say twice that Schumacher, the game keeper, has his gun, the tool of his trade, strapped to his back during the tracking shot of the beaters as the shoot begins (p. 222, p. 227). I also claim, having identified the gun as a kind of metaphor for the camera, that we are to take Schumacher in that sequence as "not so much guiding the action as following it, tracking it, filming it" (pp. 227–28). But as a matter of fact Schumacher's shotgun is *not* in its place on his back during the shoot; even, it now seems to me, *obviously* not in its expected place. One kind of unfriendly critic is apt to say: "The idea of Schumacher as some kind of surrogate for a film director or for his movie camera thus need not be thought about. And, in general, let us be sensible and speak and teach not about the *reading* of films (whatever that is supposed to mean) but about *seeing* them." What is a friendly critic to say? I hope something along the following lines.

The mistaken memory of the presence of the gun turns out to have been a response to an assertion about the gun all right, to a difference in its placement; namely a response to the absence of the gun, to its complete displacement. Of course such an explanation can be entered irresponsibly, as an excuse, with no intention of going on to test its seriousness and validity. But the best alternative to irresponsibility is not pedantry. Reading is not an alternative to seeing but (as its root in a word for advising suggests) an effort to detail a way of seeing something more clearly, an interpretation of how things look and why they appear as, and in the order, they do. In the case at hand, the absence of the gun-camera may be taken all the more emphatically to declare that it is in its proper place, shooting *this* sequence. This is in line with my claim that "Octave-Renoir's absence from [the] concluding scene means . . . [that he] has taken his place behind the camera . . . [and] declares his responsibility for what has happened . . ." (p. 223). The director's implication in the figure of Schumacher is thus made as explicit and fundamental as his implication in the figures of Octave and of Jurieu, which I was more careful to detail. While this is implicit in what I wrote, I was evidently not then prepared to think its consequences through, to face more unsparingly that the most human of filmmakers still has at his command the murderous power of the movie camera, and that the measure of his humanity may be taken not alone by his identification with the heroes and workers of romance but as well by his identification with the villains of romance, those who would cast aside the romance of the world as romance has cast them aside. A reading, like any recitation, is by all means to be checked for its accuracy. It should also be thought of as an argument, something requiring a response.

When I claim that the way I was trying to read my way into the concluding frames of *Rules of the Game* "shows that facts of a frame, so far as these are to confirm critical understanding, are not determinable apart from that understanding itself" (p. 224), I am picking up a theme of *The World Viewed* that is explicit and guiding in all my subsequent thinking about film, namely that giving significance to and placing significance in specific possibilities and necessities (or call them elements; I sometimes still call them automatisms) of the physical medium of film are the fundamental acts of, respectively, the director of a film and the critic (or audience) of film; together with the idea that what constitutes an "element" of the medium of film is not knowable prior to these discoveries of direction and of criticism. This reciprocity between element and significance I would like to call the cinematic circle. Exploring this circle is something that can be thought of as exploring the medium of film.

This is a way of specifying what at the beginning of this Foreword I spoke of as "the immediate and tremendous burden" on one's capacity for critical description in accounting for one's experience of film. Such description must allow the medium of film as such and the events of a given film at each moment to be understood in terms of one another. Because the value of such an ambition is tied to its usefulness in reading films as a whole, and because in the present pieces I for the most part read only fragments, I will append a bibliographical note of some later writing of mine that, in various ways, does something you might call attending to films as wholes. I conclude these remarks not exactly with a reading of a film fragment but rather with a fragmentary reading of a whole film, or rather with a prescription of such a reading.

It concerns Terrence Malick's *Days of Heaven*. I assume that anyone who has taken an interest in the film wishes to understand what its extremities of beauty are in service of; and not just its extremities but its successions of beauty. Whatever its subject will be understood to be, no one could have undertaken to explore it without the confidence that his or her capacity for extracting beauty from nature and from the photographic projection or displacement of nature is inexhaustible, which is of course a confidence at the same time in nature's and in film's capacities to provide it. This ranging of confidence is itself exhilarating and must somehow be part of the subject of the film. Shall we try expressing the subject as one in which the works and the emotions and the entanglements of human beings are at every moment reduced to insignificance by the casual rounds of earth and sky? I think the film does indeed contain a metaphysical vision of the world; but I think one feels that one has never quite seen the scene of human existence—call it the arena between earth (or days) and heaven—quite realized this way on film before.

The particular mode of beauty of these images somehow invokes a formal radiance which strikes me as a realization of some sentences from Heidegger's *What Is Called Thinking?* (Harper Torchback, 1972).

> When we say "Being," it means "Being of beings." When we say "beings," it means "beings in respect of Being." . . . The duality is always a prior datum, for Parmenides as much as for Plato, Kant as much as for Nietzsche. . . . An interpretation decisive for Western thought is that given by Plato. . . . Plato means to say: beings and Being are in different places. Particular beings and Being are differently located. (p. 227)

> According to Plato, the idea constitutes the Being of a being. The idea is the face whereby a given something shows its form, looks at us, and thus appears, for instance, as this table. In this form, the thing looks at us. . . . Now Plato designates the relation of a given being to its idea as participation. (p. 222)

> The first service man can render is to give thought to the Being of beings. . . . The word [being] says: presence of what is present. (p. 235)

> The presence we described gathers itself in the continuance which causes a mountain, a sea, a house to endure and, by that duration, to lie before us among other things that are present. . . . The Greeks experience such duration as a luminous appearance in the sense of illumined, radiant self-manifestation. (p. 237)

(I do not wish to hide the knowledge that years ago Malick translated Heidegger's *The Essence of Reasons* for the Northwestern University Studies in Phenomenology and Existential Philosophy.) If Malick has indeed found a way to transpose such thoughts for our meditation, he can have done it only, it seems to me, by having discovered, or discovered how to acknowledge, a fundamental fact of film's photographic basis: that objects participate in the photographic presence of themselves; they participate in the re-creation of themselves on film; they are essential in the making of their appearances. Objects projected on a screen are inherently reflexive, they occur as self-referential, reflecting upon their physical origins. Their presence refers to their absence, their location in another place. Then if in relation to objects capable of such self-manifestation human beings are reduced in significance, or crushed by the fact of beauty left vacant, perhaps this is because in trying to take dominion over the world, or in aestheticizing it (temptations inherent in the making of film, or of any art), they are refusing their participation with it.

Beyond offering this instance—whether I am right or wrong in my experience of it—as an extreme illustration of the unpredictability of what we may have to count as an element of the medium of film to which significance is given in a particular film, I offer it as a case which suggests the unpredictability of the audience for what may be taken as the study of film. The poignance of this question of audience can be brought out by thinking of the accelerating professionalization of the study of film. To ask those inside the subject, attempting to make it academically or anyway intellectually respectable, to think about Heidegger is to ask them to become responsible for yet another set of views and routines that are inherently embattled within English-speaking intellectual culture and whose application to the experience of film is hard to prove. To ask those outside the subject, those being asked to lend it the respectability of their academies, to think about Heidegger in this context is to ask them in addition to grant film the status of a subject that invites and rewards philosophical speculation, on a par with the great arts. This is no small matter, for as writers as different as Robert Warshow and Walter Benjamin more or less put it, to accept film as an art will require a modification of the concept of art. And even if some among them grant that film is as brilliant and beautiful a subject as, say, jazz, what then? Jazz can indefinitely postpone the question of high art because its accomplishments exist in relation to music as a whole, some of which is definitively high. Whereas film has only itself for direct reference; distinctions between high and low, or between major and minor, if they are to be drawn, must be drawn within the body of film itself, with no issue postponable and none definitive until someone says otherwise. But who is to say that this status of uncertainties is less creative in principle than the status of academic certainties accorded the remaining arts whose names are great?

S.C.

Brookline, Massachusetts
May 1979

Bibliographical note. The second half of "Leopards in Connecticut" (*The Georgia Review,* Summer 1976) consists of a reading of Howard Hawks' *Bringing Up Baby;* its first half considers the legitimacy of introducing film into a university curriculum and expands on relations between the writings of Warshow and of Benjamin. "Pursuits of Happiness" (*New Literary History,* Summer 1979) consists of a reading of Preston Sturges' *The Lady Eve* that expands on ideas broached in discussing *Bringing Up Baby,* to the effect that certain Hollywood talkies of the 30's and 40's form a definite genre that invokes narrative features established in Shakespearean romance. "What Becomes of Things on Film?" (*Philosophy and Literature,* Fall 1978) relates something I call "the discovery of a natural subject of film" to certain masterpieces (e.g., Bergman's *Persona,* Bunuel's *Belle de Jour,* Hitchcock's *Vertigo,* Capra's *It's a Wonderful Life*) that employ a particular mode of juxtaposition between sequences that clearly are and others that are not clearly meant to be taken as of an objective reality. "On Makavejev On Bergman" (in *Film and Dreams: An Approach to Bergman,* a volume of essays from a conference held at Harvard in January 1978, edited by Vlada Petric, scheduled for publication in 1980) attempts to read Dusan Makavejev's *Sweet Movie* as a whole, and fragments of his *WR: Mysteries of the Organism,* by characterizing something like a new principle in the way he constructs those films, specifically in the way he uses documentary footage along with fictional material.

In conclusion, a note of thanks: to Gus Blaisdell and to Arnold Davidson for helpful comments on a draft of this new Foreword.

Preface

Memories of movies are strand over strand with memories of my life. During the quarter of a century (roughly from 1935 to 1960) in which going to the movies was a normal part of my week, it would no more have occurred to me to write a study of movies than to write my autobiography. Having completed the pages that follow, I feel that I have been composing a kind of metaphysical memoir—not the story of a period of my life but an account of the conditions it has satisfied.

A book thus philosophically motivated ought to account philosophically for the motive in writing it. What broke my natural relation to movies? What was that relation, that its loss seemed to demand repairing, or commemorating, by taking thought? It is not a sufficient answer to point to the emergence, as part of ordinary moviegoing in America, of the films of Bergman, Antonioni, Fellini, Godard, Resnais, Truffaut, *et al.*, because while they invited reflection they also (perhaps thereby) achieved a continuity with Hollywood movies—or, generally, with the history of movies—that Hollywood itself was losing. They were no longer foreign. Nor is it sufficient to answer that what was lost was a form of public entertainment, the need for which society and I had outgrown—as in the cases, say, of the circus and vaudeville. We have not outgrown the need for entertainment; some movies still provide it; it was never all, or the importance, of what movies provided, any more than it is all that novels or music provide. To account for the motive in writing this book may be the most accurate description of its motive.

The immediate history of its composition is easier to tell. Every teacher knows the excitement, and chaos, in learning about a subject by undertaking to teach it. In 1963 I chose to use the movie as the topic of a seminar in aesthetics. Its pedagogical advantages looked promising: everybody would have had memorable experiences of movies, conversation naturally developed around them, and the absence of an established canon of criticism would mean that we would be forced back upon a faithfulness to nothing but our experience and a wish to communicate it. The members of the seminar, many of them literate and gifted, enjoyed the idea. But it was a failure. Or rather, what was learned was important enough, but it came from our failures. Each week I assigned one or two students the responsibility of opening the discussion by reading a two- or three-page description—nothing but description—of the film we all had seen. It turned out that the descriptions were never quite accurate, not always because some gross turn in the plot was out of order or an event had been forgotten, but often because more was described than had been shown. (For example, "The car followed her to the hotel." But in viewing the film, we had not known until later that the structure was a hotel.) After that, I noticed that almost every summary statement of a movie, whether in newspaper "criticism" or in brochures for a projected series, contains one or more descriptive inaccuracies. Is that because summaries don't really matter? Or because it is unclear what one wants from them? Only about operas, certainly not about novels or stories or poems or plays, would we accept so casual and sometimes hilariously remote an account as we will about movies.

It occurs at the highest level. Consider Truffaut's description of part of *I Confess*:

As it happens, Father Michael was being blackmailed by Vilette over a love affair prior to his ordination as a priest and Keller had worn a cassock during the crime. These coincidences, together with the fact that Father Michael is unable to provide an alibi for the night of the crime, add up to a strong web of circumstantial evidence against him. [François Truffaut, *Hitchcock* (New York, 1969), p. 148.]

But Father Michael wasn't being blackmailed; the woman in the affair was. It *feels* as if he is, and not merely by Vilette; but that's the movie. And then, "unable to provide an alibi," taken in its usual sense, is false. Father Michael *refuses* to provide (what he at that stage thought would be) an alibi because it would implicate the woman. One reservation Hitchcock expresses to Truffaut about *I Confess* is that its essential premise of the inviolability of the confessional is not acceptable to a civilian audience. But the priest's early refusal to give an alibi, at no matter what danger to himself, works to prepare the believability of the premise.

Another failure in the seminar's work was no less pervasive, and far more disheartening. The willingness to forgo theory and criticism was too proud a vow, particularly in view of our continuing inability to discover categories we had confidence in, or to make comparisons (e.g., with the novel, plays, and painting) that really carried the weight we wished upon them. A frequent reaction to these dead ends was to start getting technical; words flowed about everything from low-angle shots to filters to timings and numbers of set-ups to deep focus and fast cutting, etc., etc. But all this in turn lost its sense. On the one hand, the amount and kind of technical information that could be regarded as relevant is more than any of us knew; on the other hand, the only technical matters we found ourselves invoking, so far as they were relevant to the *experience* of particular films, which was our only business, are in front of your eyes. You can see when a shot begins and ends and whether it's long, middle, or close; you know whether the camera is moving back or forth or sideways, whether a figure brings himself into the field of the camera or the camera turns to get him; you may not know how Hitchcock gets the stairwell to distort that particular way in *Vertigo,* but you can see that he got it. Then what is the reality behind the idea that there is always a technical something you don't know that would provide the key to the experience?

When the term was over, I started trying to work out bits of the questions the seminar had started in me. Over the next three or four years, the writing I was doing dealt mainly with problems in the philosophy of art, with the philosophical problem of other minds, and with the experience of two plays. Questions about movies kept coming to the surface, but on the whole I kept them aside. In an essay on *King Lear* (later published in a collection of mine entitled *Must We Mean What We Say?*) I managed to suppress them entirely; but months of immersion in the idea of theater—especially in ideas of an audience, of the actor, and of the theater's enclosed and total world—had had their effect, and as soon as that essay was done I found I wanted to extend its thoughts to the work of film.

Several intellectual discoveries had in the meantime better prepared me to say what I wanted. I came to read Rousseau's *Letter to d'Alembert* for the first time. The accuracies in what is often taken as Rousseau's paranoia helped me to overcome a certain level of distrust I had developed about movies and about my interest in them—as though I had, in thinking about movies, forgotten what there is to distrust in the uses of any art. More specifically, Rousseau's unobtrusive obsession with *seeing* (it is about all "spectacle")—with our going to the theater in order to be seen and not to be seen, with our use of tears there to excuse our blindness and coldness to the same situations in the world outside, with his vision that true spectacles in the good city will permit us to let ourselves be seen without shame—guided and confirmed my sense of the level at which viewing, in an audience and out, needs to be followed. At the same time, I began to study Heidegger's *Being and Time,* some of whose methods and concepts (especially his philosophical confidence in his native tongue, and his suspicion of it, and his concept of world, and his way of limiting knowing as our access to the world) were live for me. The final, or immediate, stimulus to consecutive writing came in early 1968 when I read some essays by André Bazin.

A word may be in order here about my title. When I learned of an essay of Heidegger's called "The Age of the World View," the mere words suggested to me, from my knowledge of *Being and Time,* a range of issues—that ours is an age in which our philosophical grasp of the world fails to reach beyond our taking and holding views of it, and we call these views metaphysics. I have half-deliberately avoided that essay; I have enough problems. I of course want the sense of *Weltanschauung* in my title, and though I felt it arise naturally in the way I was thinking about film, I was helped to it by my awareness of Heidegger's.

In May 1968 I read a version at the University of Illinois of what appears here as the first five chapters. In the following year I read similar versions, together with some new material, at the School of Letters in the University of Indiana and at Millersville State College in Lancaster, Pennsylvania.

Having got this far with the work, I had some words I could believe in to account for my experience of film, and I felt I should then proceed systematically; that I should somehow find a way to view and review a good number at least of American talkies, and then test the words against them. This proved to be impossible—not just practically, but because my thoughts would not form around any such procedure. I realized that I was seeing fewer movies than ever before and wanting to see fewer, and at the same time memories of old movies, and of the friends I had seen them with, kept on asserting themselves. Those facts underlay my desire to come to terms with movies, and I knew that no words of mine about film would be worth writing or reading unless they could first see that desire through. Therefore I am often referring to films I have seen only once, some as long as thirty years ago. In a few instances I have seen a film three times, but in no case enough times to feel I possess it the way it deserves and I would like: completely and wordlessly. (I have not hesitated to let the *Late Show* refresh my memory when it could, but I think I have in no case given a reading of a film that I have not seen in the flesh.) I mention this as a warning, should anyone require it, that this is not a history of any stretch of the movies; as an apology for the off memories that may crop up; and as a confession that a few faulty memories will not themselves shake my conviction in what I've said, since I am as interested in how a memory went wrong as in why the memories that are right occur when they do.

Time in which to bring this work to its present conclusion was given me by a fellowship in the Center for the Humanities at Wesleyan University, to which I am deeply grateful. It is a particular pleasure to thank the staff of the Center, especially Mrs. Tanya Senff and Mrs. Joan Farrell, for helping to make my year in residence there as efficient and as enjoyable as I could have hoped it to be. The director of the Center, Professor Victor Gourevitch, with a chemistry of tact known best to himself, managed both to see that the fellows of the Center were kept free for their own work and also to keep them mindful, in presiding at our Monday night lectures and Tuesday colloquia, that a community of scholars requires and deserves something more than the private enterprise of its members.

I am grateful to John Hollander and to Elisabeth Sifton for a number of suggestions about my manuscript, as well as to Terrence Malick and to my wife, Cathleen Cohen Cavell.

Much of what follows, preeminently but not solely about

painting, would not be mine to say apart from the writing and conversation of Michael Fried, and the looking and reading he has assigned me in the history of the arts and in the criticism of Clement Greenberg, among others. I have had occasion to acknowledge this before. I state it again here at the outset, because of course I keep finding new help from Fried's work, but also because it would be a poor repayment were he to be held responsible for my misguided or unthinking uses of it—above all for my obsession with wanting to put everything my own way. I would have written a little book about film if Michael Fried and I had never met. But it would not have been this one.

A book is written for two audiences: the one it may create, whose conversation it invites; and the one that has created it, whose conversation it invokes. Members of the latter may have been dead before the writer was born; if alive, they may be strangers, enemies, or friends he no longer has the right to name. Of the live company present to me as I wrote and whom I have otherwise not acknowledged, I single out Rogers Albritton, asking him to stand for the rest.

S.C.

Middletown, Connecticut
May 1971

The World Viewed

1

An Autobiography of Companions

When Tolstoy asked, "What is art?" his answer was to dismiss most of the great art of the past. There's the unflinchingness of genius for you. And why should one care about it? What reason is there to care about any radical criticism of one's culture —about, say, the fact that Plato and Rousseau wished to dismiss poetry and theater from their republics; or that Matthew Arnold thought poetry had lost its voice; or that Hegel and Marx thought philosophy had come to an end, or ought to; or that Wagner and Walt Whitman and Thoreau and Nietzsche thought that man and his society would have to be transformed before the thing they had it at heart to say could be understood? The trouble is, we are sometimes unsure whether we have survived these prophecies or whether our lives now are realizing their worst fears. My question, therefore, is not whether we ought to care about Tolstoy's answer, but whether we can avoid caring and, in particular, what explanation we give ourselves for his answer—when, that is, we find ourselves caring about it. Shall we say Tolstoy was wrong about art? Could we really believe that? Shall we say that he was crazy when he wrote his book about art? The book doesn't sound or feel like the work of a crazy man. An answer I used to give myself was: Tolstoy is asking himself not about the nature of art, but about the nature of the importance of art. It was when I came to see that these are not separate questions—that the answer to the question "What is the importance of art?" is grammatically related to, or is a way of answering, the question "What is art?"—that I came to an understanding of what Tolstoy was talking about, and came to comprehend further ranges in my caring about art. Tolstoy knew its saving importance; that is how he knew that whatever importance the rich are likely to attach to art, it is not the true importance of art; and why he cared that the poor (most people) attach no importance at all to it. I assume that what Tolstoy saw was there to be seen, and that it is more evident now than when he wrote, if less apparent. Then how can it not raise the question of the importance of art? Are we so sophisticated that the inaccessibility of art is of no concern to us? Or are we in possession of a theory that explains to our satisfaction why art need not be of importance?

Why are movies important? I take it for granted that in various obvious senses they are. That this *can* be taken for granted is the first fact I pose for consideration; it is, or was, a distinctive fact about movies. Music, painting, sculpture, poetry—as they are now sought by artists of major ambition, artists devoted to the making of objects meant as the live history of their art—are not *generally* important, except pretty much for the men and women devoted to creating them. For them, the arts are of *such* importance, and that importance raises such questions, that no one free of the questions is free to share their arts with them. These artists have virtually no audiences any longer, except in isolated or intermittent cases. The arts will differ in the extent of their isolation from audience and in the extent to which they suffer from this isolation. Painting seems to be in the most fortunate position at the moment, music in the least. Perhaps this indicates that there are now more ways of responding to paintings than there are of entering music. But rich and poor, those who care about no (other) art and those who live on the promise of art, those whose pride is education and those whose pride is power or practicality—all care about movies, await them, respond to them, remember them, talk about them, hate some of them, are grateful for some of them.

This first fact is paired with a second. The movie seems naturally to exist in a state in which its highest and its most ordinary instances attract the same audience (anyway until recently). Anyone ought to be able to rise to the occasion of recognition at the end of *City Lights,* to the eloquence of Garbo's moods, to the intelligence and manliness of Olivier's *Richard the Third,* to the power of justice in Henry Fonda's young Lincoln, to Carole Lombard's wit, to Emil Jannings' despair, to Marilyn Monroe's doomed magnetism, to Kim Stanley's sense of worthlessness, to the mutual pleasure and trust William Powell and Myrna Loy give one another, to Groucho's full and calm acceptance of Harpo's raging urgencies, to the heartbreaking hesitations at the center of an Astaire routine. And the highest sensibility must thrill at the knowledge with which Fonda interrupts the mythical question—"Say, what's your name, stranger?"—looking around straight into Walter Brennan's eyes, dropping it as he walks out, "Earp. Wyatt Earp"; and hate and fear Basil Rathbone's courtly villainies or Richard Widmark's psychotic killers or Lee Marvin's Liberty Valance, at once completely gratified and perfectly freed of guilt at their lucid and baroque defeats; and participate in the satisfaction of one of Kirk Douglas's or Burt Lancaster's rages. Merely to think of the way Bette Davis makes her entrance in *Jezebel* —bursting into view on a rearing horse, her elegant riding habit amplifying the dash with which she dismounts, then jamming the point of her whip back into the side folds of her skirt to free her boot for the step into the house where she knows she is awaited with dazzled disapproval—merely to think of the way, in *Now, Voyager,* her restoration to sanity is signaled by an opening shot on her sheer-stockinged ankles and legs, released from the thick, shapeless, dark cotton wrappings and health shoes into which her wicked mother had charmed her—these moments provide us with a fair semblance of ecstasy. (Anyone who thinks such responses are "camp" either is camping himself or else grew up in a different world from mine.)

But people who attend to serious music do not attend to light dinner music, say, or movie music. They may admire Cole Porter, Rodgers and Hart, Jerome Kern, the Beatles, jazz. But then everyone should admire inspired inventiveness, true sentiment, rocking joy, passionate honesty, and the turning of captivity and grief into radiant shouts and virtuoso murmurs of community. And people who read serious novels do not on the whole read potboilers (with the occasional exception of the detective story and science fiction, sociological curiosities of their own). There are, of course, in literature a few instances of very great artists who are at the same time popular. But my claim is that in the case of films, it is generally true that you do not really like the highest instances unless you also like typical ones. You don't even know what the highest are instances of unless you know the typical as well.

This necessary region of indiscriminateness creates three separable nightmares: (1) For the conscientious movie reviewer who feels, or whose editor assumes, that he must cover every opening, taking with him a little high hope and some handy cynicism, not knowing whether he is to report on another sign of the times or to summon words to praise a new ambition. (2) For the fastidious writer about film who takes an indiscriminate attention to movies as a manifestation of bad taste and of a corrupt industry and society, rather than as a datum in understanding the appetite for film. (3) For those trying to awaken both from empty indiscriminateness and from futile discrimination.

About (1): It was not the least of James Agee's talents to live with this nightmare graciously. He had no need for the seedy pleasure of feeling superior to drivel, or for the grudging admiration of those no better than oneself who happen to have got the breaks, or for the hatred and fear of (other) intellectuals who were just coming around to movies or talked inflated incomprehensibilities about them. His gift for finding and describing *something* to like, in no matter what yards of junk, adapted an old line of literary criticism, the "praise of beauties," [1] to the most unpromising territories. In Agee's hands, this gift established a significant fact about movies: that there is always something to find, often enough to justify a hundred minutes of speculative solitude.

The significance of this fact is brought out against the light of the *auteur* theory of film.[2] It was a clarifying shock to realize that films were directed, that some human being had undertaken to mean, or was at any rate responsible for, all the angles of a movie. I certainly felt rebuked for my backwardness in having grown to fatherhood without really knowing where movies came from, ready to admit that I must have had an idea that they sprang full grown from iron-gated sunglassed heads of studios. But then, apart from the great directors and a few eccentrics and specialists, the evidence of relation between a film and its director—after the titles—is often no more than that one can find *something* to attribute to the man. So I became interested again in my former backwardness. How could anyone not have known what the *auteur* theory forces us to know? Is it explanation enough to cite the money conspiracy of Hollywood production, and the build-up of a star system that overshadowed its makers? There may be many such explanations, but they will not answer the first question, which is how such a setup could so often have yielded movies worth possessing and questioning.

The *auteur* emphasis turns us away from an aesthetic proposition even more unnoticeable in its obviousness—that a movie comes from other movies. Each of the arts knows of this self-generation, however primitive our understanding remains about the relation between tradition and the individual talent.

But with movies the idea looks too good, or bad, to be true; movie directors haven't got an established history behind them to remind them that they exist, that a tradition is something in which individuals work out their individuality. An immediate block to the thought of movies having an internal history is that we know, or ought to know, their origin. There was a time in living memory when there were no movies at all, and the *first* one surely couldn't have come from others. Very well, I concede the first. But how are the other arts different? Whatever the original state of an art, a new work is born in civilization from the powers of the art itself. The obscurity about "the first" painting or piece of prose or movie is no more historical than conceptual. It may seem that a terrible literalization of aesthetic history took place in Hollywood, that the steps a tradition takes to continue itself were leveled and occupied by legions of precise slaves, with no leader and no memory but a bank. Still, you can't deny the monuments. One remembers a remark of Ingmar Bergman's, likening the making of movies to the construction of a medieval cathedral: a mass of craftsmen, each perfect at his work, together mounting an aspiration no man could achieve alone. But he was pretty clearly thinking of himself as the unknown master builder. Neither a romanticism of anonymity nor a romanticism of individuality is going to account for the power that movies have or have had for us.

About (2): Some people have now stopped worrying and started loving the unminding devotions of the eye and ear, claiming them as a natural reaction to the demise of the printed word. This claim has an ugly effect on certain professors of literature who believe their day either done or to have dawned with a new call to save the books from the barbarians. No doubt it is true that more people than ever do not read. In my experience it is also true that more people read, and read better. There are more people, from more places. And some among the people I know who like movies best are among the best readers I know. The question for me—and it prompts and pervades the occasions I have found to speak concretely about particular films—is why the standards of rigor and range that we have learned to take for granted (or criticize) when we give or are given readings of books are ignored or unavailable when we give or are given readings of movies. (I do not deny that there is a problem about the idea of "reading a movie." Is it greater, or other, than the problem about the idea of "reading a poem," when, of course, that is not the same as reciting the poem?)

About (3): A standing discovery of the *auteur* theory was of the need for a canon of movies to which any remarks about "the movie" should hold themselves answerable. Without this, the natural circle of theory and evidence will not inscribe the knowledge we want; for example, some generalization will be ruled out or in on the ground that some work or other counters or exemplifies it, even when we know nothing about why we give weight to that work. The danger is not so much that evidence will be lacking as that there will be evidence for everything and nothing, that theory will not warrant enough confidence to repudiate ill-gathered evidence to test what tests it. Organization by directors' *oeuvres* is a beginning, but it will include too much and too little; or else "organization" will only start meaning "arranged alphabetically by director," keeping dumb about the ranking in quality or centrality we assign a given work within an *oeuvre,* and about the relation of a given *oeuvre* to the medium that has made place for it.

I am not in a position to establish such a canon, hardly even the modest collection of talkies at my disposal and from which I begin. But since I am bent on going ahead anyway, I will take what bearings I have, trying at each point to meld the ways of thinking that have invited my conviction with the experiences of films that I have cared about.

It is the nature of these experiences to be lined with fragments of conversations and responses of friends I have gone to movies with. And with the times of sharing just afterwards—

running across lots as Indians, or in formation as biplanes, gradually giving way to sessions in which for hours we reconstructed the movie's score or dialogue or plot, or to the contentment in simply naming moments, with the pure unwanting for more than small syllables of joy or disgust or the creeps. I am merely amused or embarrassed or tender when I remember what I thought the first time I read a book I later followed to another depth; but I remain faithful to responses I first had to movies, even if I can no longer share them. The events associated with the experiences of books and music are only occasionally as important as the experience of the works themselves. The events associated with movies are those of companionship or lack of companionship: the audience of a book is essentially solitary, one soul at a time; the audience of music and theater is essentially larger than your immediate acquaintance—a gathering of the city; the crowd at a movie comprises various pools of companions, or scattered souls with someone missing. I don't care whether anyone quite knows the week of awe I spent at the age of twelve reading *Les Misérables*; there are always twelve-year-olds and there is always that book for them. But movies, unless they are masterpieces, are not there as they were. The hours—through the Laughton-Gable *Mutiny on the Bounty; The Crusades; Union Pacific; Dawn Patrol; Captain Blood; Algiers; Charlie Chan; Wuthering Heights; Stella Dallas; King's Row; Ball of Fire;* the Ronald Colman *Prisoner of Zenda; Random Harvest; Lost Horizon; Juarez; Dead End; The Last of the Mohicans; Broken Arrow; The General Died at Dawn; Mildred Pierce; The Phantom of the Opera; Strike Up the Band; Singin' in the Rain; The Cat People; Phantom Lady; Cry of the City; Murder, My Sweet; White Heat;* and a hundred others—were hours and days of awe; momentous, but only for the moment; unrecapturable fully except in memory and evocation; gone. If you see them now for the first time, you may be interested and moved, but you can't know what I know.

I have mentioned my increasing difficulty over the past several years to get myself to go to new movies. This has to do partly with an anxiousness in my response to new films I have seen (I don't at all mean I think they are bad), but equally with my anxiousness in what I feel to be new audiences for movies (not necessarily new people, but people with new reasons for being there), as though I cannot locate or remain together with my companions among them. I take this as something of more than clinical interest.

One could say that movie showings have begun for the first time to be habitually attended by an audience, I mean by people who arrive and depart at the same time, as at a play. When moviegoing was casual and we entered at no matter what point in the proceedings (during the news or short subject or somewhere in the feature—enjoying the recognition, later, of the return of the exact moment at which one entered, and from then on feeling free to decide when to leave, or whether to see the familiar part through again), we took our fantasies and companions and anonymity inside and left with them intact. Now that there is an audience, a claim is made upon my privacy; so it matters to me that our responses to the film are not really shared. At the same time that the mere fact of an audience makes this claim upon me, it feels as if the old casualness of moviegoing has been replaced by a casualness of movie-viewing, which I interpret as an inability to tolerate our own fantasies, let alone those of others—an attitude that equally I cannot share. I feel I am present at a cult whose members have nothing in common but their presence in the same place. Matters are otherwise—not necessarily pleasanter—if the film is already part of history and is itself something around which a transient cult has formed. I suppose that the old casualness harbored the value of illicitness that from the beginning was part of moviegoing. But the strictures of the new audience do not dispel illicitness or make it unnecessary; the audience is not a gathering of citizens for honest confession and acceptance of one another. The new need for the gathering is as mysterious as the old need for privacy; so the demand that I forgo privacy is as illicit as my requirement to preserve it.

The importance of memory goes beyond its housing of knowledge. It arises also in the *way* movies are remembered or misremembered. That will be a live topic in what follows, because my way of studying films has been mostly through remembering them, like dreams. Unlike dreams, there are other equally essential ways of getting at movies, like reading their scripts and learning their outer history and viewing them again and counting and timing their shots. I am going to press my way here, not just because I am not equipped for or provided with any other alternative, but because I wouldn't at this stage know what further documentation would be documentation for. My business is to think out the causes of my consciousness of films as it stands.

From this lack of scholarship I expect three kinds of advantages: first, that what I have to remember will be recalled by others; second, that since my remembering is itself a datum that wants accounting for, and since a book cannot reproduce, or quote, the images or scenes remembered, I will always be pushed to an account, however brief, of the object as a whole from which they stand out. This is a special advantage, because it is arguable that the only instruments that could provide data for a theory of film are the procedures of criticism. Third, in allowing the thinking to have its head, I should at least avoid those embarrassed bursts of theory that writing about film typically lets out; and at most I will have examples from which to ask why movies seem naturally to produce their metaphysical outcries, often supported by a mere conjunction of technical details together with a plot outline of roughly the consistency of opera programs. In the paucity of humane criticism dealing with whole films, and in the lack of fit between their technical description and a phenomenological account of them, movies have achieved the condition of music. At the moment, I remember three instances of what I mean by "humane criticism dealing with whole films" by which I have been instructed: James Kerans on *Grand Illusion*; William Hedges on *Children of Paradise*; Annette Michelson on *2001: A Space Odyssey*.[3] But it is generally true of the writing about film which has meant something to me that it has the power of the missing companion. Agee and Robert Warshow[4] and André Bazin manage that mode of conversation all the time; and I have found it in, among others, Manny Farber, Pauline Kael, Parker Tyler, Andrew Sarris.

The requirement for a *certain* indiscriminateness in the accepting of movies (I don't say you have to appreciate Singing Cowboy or Comedy Horror movies) has its analogues in the past of the established arts: anyone who is too selective about the classical composers whose music he likes doesn't really like music; whereas a distaste for various moments or figures in literature may be productive. But this requirement not merely is unlike the case of the other arts now, it is the negation of their very condition: for it can be said that anyone who cultivates broadly the current instances of music or painting or theater does not appreciate, and does not know, the serious instances of those arts as they now occur. This condition of modernist art has been described by Michael Fried[5] as one in which an art leaves no room, or holds no promise, for the minor artist: it is a situation in which the work of the major artist condemns the work of others to artistic nonexistence, and in which his own work is condemned to seriousness, to further radical success or to complete failure. This state of affairs is, in one light, sadder, certainly crueler, than the one Tolstoy described. For Tolstoy could allow himself to blame society and artists for their shortcomings, whereas if we seek to place blame, it will have to be upon the necessities of the separate arts themselves: upon music, for refusing tonality; upon sculpture, for no longer allowing a material to be sculpted; upon painting, for refusing not merely the presence of humanity in its content but evi-

dence of the human hand in its making. Or we will have to
blame reality for withdrawing itself from our powers. In another way, our state is happier than Tolstoy's. For while the
community of serious art is small, it is not exclusive—not the
way an elite is exclusive. It is esoteric, but the secret is open to
anyone. Art now exists in the condition of philosophy. If this is
cold, it is clarifying; for now blame can be squarely placed for
an art's *de facto* exclusiveness. The good city does not require
art to be made for everyone. Its responsibilities are to get out of
the way of the artist, so that he can determine whether our
loves and griefs can still be placed the way art has always
placed them. And its responsibilities to its citizens are to free
them so that each can determine for himself the relevance a serious art may have to his life, or not have. The socialist's *demand* for a future art is in the end no different from the capitalist's praise of the given: both want art to do, or prove, what can
only be done socially. This is not a compliment to art; it is
merely a back-handed tribute to its ancient power, and a
healthy fear of it.

It is often said, perhaps in response to the continuities I have
noted about films (between high and low audiences, and between their high and low instances), that film is *the* modern art,
the one to which modern man naturally responds. Beyond
what I have said already, there are two immediate reasons for
distrusting that idea: (1) It assumes that the other arts are *not*
capable of eliciting the old values of art. That *may* be true; but
it may also be that someone who claims it is true is not in a position to recognize the live article when he sees it. And it shows
a poor view of what is "natural," for if there is anything seriously to be called "the modern man," one fact about him is
that what is natural to him is not natural, that naturalness for
him has become a stupendous achievement. (2) If film is seriously to be thought of as an art at all, then it needs to be explained how it can have avoided the fate of modernism, which
in practice means how it can have maintained its continuities

of audiences and genres, how it can have been taken seriously without having assumed the burden of seriousness. For the blatant fact about film is that, if it is art, it is the one live traditional art, the one that can take its tradition for granted. Is that what calling it the modern art was supposed, more or less, to mean? In that sense, the idea of its modernity is either empty (suggesting merely that there is *some* connection between the art and its historical context), or false (suggesting that the traditional arts are no longer alive), or incoherent (suggesting that movies are a new and improved version of art, like a modern detergent or the modern kitchen). The modernist is incomprehensible apart from his questioning of specific traditions, the traditions that have produced him. The modernizer is merely blind to the power of tradition, mocking his chains.

The movie's ease within its assumptions and achievements— its conventions remaining convenient for so much of its life, remaining convincing and fertile without self-questioning—is central to its pleasure for us. We shall sometimes think of this as film's naïveté, but that is perhaps a naïve way of looking at the matter. It does not, in any case, explain film's absorption in its conventions, but simply redescribes it. The question remains, how has film been able to provide this pleasure? From another side, the more we learn (from the Hollywood memoirs of Ben Hecht, say) of the corruptions and stupidities in the industry that formed to produce those objects, the more we are likely to wonder how the films we care about can ever have been made. This is not a problem if the only films you care about are carefully chosen masterpieces: few regimes are so perfectly terrible and efficient that they prevent every drop of originality from leaking through their clutches. But if one's range of care is wider, then how is one to explain the effect of those ordinary instances, which seem just to have been made for the industry to make? What is the power of film that it could survive (even profit artistically from) so much neglect and ignorant contempt by those in power over it? What is film?

2

Sights and Sounds

The beginning of an answer is given by the two continuously intelligent, interesting, and to me useful theorists I have read on the subject. Erwin Panofsky puts it this way: "The medium of the movies is physical reality as such." [6] André Bazin emphasizes essentially this idea many times and many ways: at one point he says, "Cinema is committed to communicate only by way of what is real"; and then, "The cinema [is] of its essence a dramaturgy of Nature." [7] "Physical reality as such," taken literally, is not correct: that phrase better fits the specialized pleasures of *tableaux vivants,* or formal gardens, or Minimal Art. What Panofsky and Bazin have in mind is that the basis of the medium of movies is photographic, and that a photograph is *of* reality or nature. If to this we add that the medium is one in which the photographic image is projected and gathered on a screen, our question becomes: What happens to reality when it is projected and screened?

That it is reality that we have to deal with, or some mode of depicting it, finds surprising confirmation in the way movies are remembered, and misremembered. It is tempting to suppose that movies are hard to remember the way dreams are, and that is not a bad analogy. As with dreams, you do sometimes *find* yourself remembering moments in a film, and a procedure in *trying* to remember is to find your way back to a characteristic mood the thing has left you with. But, unlike dreams, other people can help you remember, indeed are often indispensable to the enterprise of remembering. Movies are hard to remember, the way the actual events of yesterday are. And yet, again like dreams, *certain* moments from films viewed decades ago will nag as vividly as moments of childhood. It is as if you had to remember what happened *before* you slept. Which suggests that film awakens as much as it enfolds you.

It may seem that this starting point—the projection of reality—begs the question of the medium of film, because movies, and writing about movies, have from their beginnings also recognized that film can depict the fantastic as readily as the natural.[8] What is true about that idea is not denied in speaking of movies as "communicating by way of what is real": the displacement of objects and persons from their natural sequences and locales is itself an acknowledgment of the physicality of their existence. It is as if, for all their insistence on the newness of the medium, the antirealist theorists could not shake the idea that it was essentially a form of painting, for it was painting which had visually repudiated—anyway, forgone—the representation of reality. This would have helped them neglect the differences between representation and projection. But an immediate fact about the medium of the photograph (still or in motion) is that it is not painting. (An immediate fact about the *history* of photography is that this was not at first obvious.)

What does this mean—not painting? A photograph does not present us with "likenesses" of things; it presents us, we want to say, with the things themselves. But wanting to say that may well make us ontologically restless. "Photographs present us with things themselves" sounds, and ought to sound, false or paradoxical. Obviously a photograph of an earthquake, or of Garbo, is not an earthquake happening (fortunately), or Garbo in the flesh (unfortunately). But this is not very informative. And, moreover, it is no less paradoxical or false to hold up a photograph of Garbo and say, "That is not Garbo," if all you mean is that the object you are holding up is not a human creature. Such troubles in notating so obvious a fact suggest that we do not know what a photograph is; we do not know how to place it ontologically. We might say that we don't know how to think of the *connection* between a photograph and what it is a photograph of. The image is not a likeness; it is not exactly a replica, or a relic, or a shadow, or an apparition either, though all of these natural candidates share a striking feature with photographs—an aura or history of magic surrounding them.

One might wonder that similar questions do not arise about recordings of sound. I mean, on the whole we would be hard put to find it false or paradoxical to say, listening to a record, "That's an English horn"; there is no trace of temptation to add (as it were, to oneself), "But I know it's really only a recording." Why? A child might be very puzzled by the remark, said in the presence of a phonograph, "That's an English horn," if something else had already been pointed out to him as an English horn. Similarly, he might be very puzzled by the remark, said of a photograph, "That's your grandmother." Very early, children are *no longer* puzzled by such remarks, luckily. But that doesn't mean we know why they were puzzled, or why they no longer are. And I am suggesting that we don't know either of these things about ourselves.

Is the difference between auditory and visual transcription a function of the fact that we are fully accustomed to hearing things that are invisible, not present to us, not present with us? We would be in trouble if we weren't so accustomed, because it is the nature of hearing that what is heard comes *from* someplace, whereas what you can see you can look *at*. It is why sounds are warnings, or calls; it is why our access to another world is normally through voices from it; and why a man can be spoken to by God and survive, but not if he sees God, in which case he is no longer in *this* world. Whereas we are not accustomed to seeing things that are invisible, or not present to us, not present with us; or we are not accustomed to acknowledging that we do (except for dreams). Yet this seems, ontologically, to be what is happening when we look at a photograph: we see things that are not present.

Someone will object: "That is playing with words. We're not seeing something not present; we are looking at something perfectly present, namely, a *photograph*." But that is affirming something I have not denied. On the contrary, I am precisely describing, or wishing to describe, what it means to say that there is this photograph here. It may be felt that I make too great a mystery of these objects. My feeling is rather that we have forgotten how mysterious these things are, and in general how *different* different things are from one another, as though we had forgotten how to value them. This is in fact something movies teach us.

Suppose one tried accounting for the familiarity of recordings by saying, "When I say, listening to a record, 'That's an English horn,' what I really mean is, 'That's the *sound* of an English horn'; moreover, when I am in the presence of an English horn playing, I still don't literally hear the horn, I hear the sound of the horn. So I don't worry about hearing a horn when the horn is not present, because *what* I hear is exactly the same (ontologically the same, and if my equipment is good enough, empirically the same) whether the thing is present or not." What this rigmarole calls attention to is that sounds can be perfectly copied, and that we have various interests in copying them. (For example, if they couldn't be copied, people would never learn to talk.) It is interesting that there is no comparable rigmarole about visual transcriptions. The problem is not that photographs are not visual copies of objects, or that objects can't be visually copied. The problem is that even if a photograph were a copy of an object, so to speak, it would not bear the relation to its object that a recording bears to the sound it copies. We said that the record reproduces its sound, but we cannot say that a photograph reproduces a sight (or a look, or an appearance). It can seem that language is missing a word at this place. Well, you can always invent a word. But one doesn't know what to pin the word *on* here. It isn't that there aren't sights to see, nor even that a sight has by definition to be especially *worth* seeing (hence could not be the sort of thing we are *always* seeing), whereas sounds are being thought of here, not unplausibly, as what we always hear. A sight *is* an object (usually a very large object, like the Grand Canyon or Versailles, although small southern children are frequently held, by the person in charge of them, to be sights) or an extraordinary happening, like the aurora borealis; and what you see, when you sight something, is an object—anyway, not the sight of an object. Nor will the epistemologist's "sense-data" or "surfaces" provide correct descriptions here. For we are not going to say that photographs provide us with the sense-data of the objects they contain, because if the sense-data of photographs were the same as the sense-data of the objects they contain, we couldn't tell a photograph of an object from the object itself. To say that a photograph is of the surfaces of objects suggests that it emphasizes texture. What is missing is not a word, but, so to speak, something in nature—the fact that objects don't *make* sights, or *have* sights. I feel like saying: Objects are too *close* to their sights to give them up for reproducing; in order to reproduce the sights they (as it were) make, you have to reproduce *them*—make a mold, or take an impression. Is that what a photograph does? We might, as Bazin does on occasion, try thinking of a photograph as a visual mold or a visual impression. My dissatisfaction with that idea is, I think, that physical molds and impressions and imprints have clear procedures for getting *rid* of their originals, whereas in a photograph, the original is still as present as it ever was. Not present as it once was to the camera; but that is only a mold-machine, not the mold itself.

Photographs are not *hand*-made; they are manufactured. And what is manufactured is an image of the world. The inescapable fact of mechanism or automatism in the making of these images is the feature Bazin points to as "[satisfying], once and for all and in its very essence, our obsession with realism." [9]

It is essential to get to the right depth of this fact of automatism. It is, for example, misleading to say, as Bazin does, that "photography has freed the plastic arts from their obsession with likeness," [10] for this makes it seem (and it does often look) as if photography and painting were in competition, or that painting had wanted something that photography broke in and satisfied. So far as photography satisfied a wish, it satisfied a wish not confined to painters, but the human wish, intensifying in the West since the Reformation, to escape subjectivity and metaphysical isolation—a wish for the power to reach this world, having for so long tried, at last hopelessly, to manifest fidelity to another. And painting was not "freed"—and not by photography—from its obsession with likeness. Painting, in Manet, was *forced* to forgo likeness exactly because of its own obsession with reality, because the illusions it had learned to create did not provide the conviction in reality, the connection with reality, that it craved.[11] One might even say that in withdrawing from likeness, painting freed photography to be invented.

And if what is meant is that photography freed painting from the idea that a painting had to be a picture (that is, *of* or *about* something else), that is also not true. Painting did not free itself, did not force itself to maintain itself apart, from *all* objective reference until long after the establishment of photography; and then not because it finally dawned on painters that paintings were not pictures, but because that was the way to maintain connection with (the history of) the art of painting, to maintain conviction in its powers to create paintings, meaningful objects in paint.

And are we sure that the final denial of objective reference amounts to a complete yielding of connection with reality—once, that is, we have given up the idea that "connection with reality" is to be understood as "provision of likeness"? We can be sure that the view of painting as dead without reality, and the view of painting as dead with it, are both in need of development in the views each takes of reality and of painting. We can say, painting and reality no longer *assure* one another.

It could be said further that what painting wanted, in wanting connection with reality, was a sense of *presentness*[12]—not exactly a conviction of the world's presence to us, but of our presence to it. At some point the unhinging of our consciousness from the world interposed our subjectivity between us and our presentness to the world. Then our subjectivity became what is present to us, individuality became isolation. The route to conviction in reality was through the acknowledgment of that endless presence of self. What is called expressionism is one possibility of representing this acknowledgment. But it would, I think, be truer to think of expressionism as a representation of our *response* to this new fact of our condition—our terror of ourselves in isolation—rather than as a representation of the world from within the condition of isolation itself. It would, to that extent, not be a new mastery of fate by creating selfhood against no matter what odds; it would be the sealing of the self's fate by theatricalizing it. Apart from the wish for selfhood (hence the always simultaneous granting of otherness as well), I do not understand the value of art. Apart from this wish and its achievement, art is exhibition.

To speak of our subjectivity as the route back to our conviction in reality is to speak of romanticism. Perhaps romanticism can be understood as the natural struggle between the representation and the acknowledgment of our subjectivity (between the acting out and the facing off of ourselves, as psychoanalysts would more or less say). Hence Kant, and Hegel; hence Blake secreting the world he believes in; hence Wordsworth competing with the history of poetry by writing out himself, writing himself back into the world. A century later Heidegger is investigating Being by investigating *Dasein* (because it is in *Dasein* that Being shows up best, namely as questionable), and Wittgenstein investigates the world ("the possibilities of phenomena") by investigating what we say, what we are inclined to say, what our pictures of phenomena are, in order to wrest the world from our possessions so that we may possess it again. Then the recent major painting which Fried describes as objects of *presentness* would be painting's latest effort to maintain its conviction in its own power to establish connection with reality—by permitting us presentness to ourselves, apart from which there is no hope for a world.

Photography overcame subjectivity in a way undreamed of by painting, a way that could not satisfy painting, one which does not so much defeat the act of painting as escape it altogether: by *automatism*, by removing the human agent from the task of reproduction.

One could accordingly say that photography was never in competition with painting. What happened was that at some point the quest for visual reality, or the "memory of the present" (as Baudelaire put it), split apart. To maintain conviction in our connection with reality, to maintain our presentness, painting accepts the recession of the world. Photography maintains the presentness of the world by accepting our absence from it. The reality in a photograph is present to me while I am not present to it; and a world I know, and see, but to which I am nevertheless not present (through no fault of my subjectivity), is a world past.

3

Photograph and Screen

Let us notice the specific sense in which photographs are of the world, of reality as a whole. You can always ask, pointing to an object in a photograph—a building, say—what lies behind it, totally obscured by it. This only accidentally makes sense when asked of an object in a painting. You can always ask, of an area photographed, what lies adjacent to that area, beyond the frame. This generally makes no sense asked of a painting. You can ask these questions of objects in photographs because they have answers in reality. The world of a painting is not continuous with the world of its frame; at its frame, a world finds its limits. We might say: A painting *is* a world; a photograph is *of* the world. What happens in a photograph is that *it* comes to an end. A photograph is cropped, not necessarily by a paper cutter or by masking but by the camera itself. The camera crops it by predetermining the amount of view it will accept; cutting, masking, enlarging, predetermine the amount after the fact. (Something like this phenomenon shows up in recent painting. In this respect, these paintings have found, at the extremest negation of the photographic, media that achieve the condition of photographs.) The camera, being finite, crops a portion from an indefinitely larger field; continuous portions of that field could be included in the photograph in fact taken; in principle, it could all be taken. Hence objects in photographs that run past the edge do not feel cut; they are aimed at, shot, stopped live. When a photograph is cropped, the rest of the world is cut *out*. The implied presence of the rest of the world, and its explicit rejection, are as essential in the experience of a photograph as what it explicitly presents. A camera is an opening in a box: that is the best emblem of the fact that a camera holding on an object is holding the rest of the world away. The camera has been praised for extending the senses; it may, as the world goes, deserve more praise for confining them, leaving room for thought.

The world of a moving picture is screened. The screen is not a support, not like a canvas; there is nothing to support, that way. It holds a projection, as light as light. A screen is a barrier. What does the silver screen screen? It screens me from the world it holds—that is, makes me invisible. And it screens that world from me—that is, screens its existence from me. That the projected world does not exist (now) is its only difference from reality. (There is no feature, or set of features, in which it differs. Existence is not a predicate.) Because it is the field of a photograph, the screen has no frame; that is to say, no border.

Its limits are not so much the edges of a given shape as they are the limitations, or capacity, of a container. The screen *is* a frame; the frame is the whole field of the screen—as a frame of film is the whole field of a photograph, like the frame of a loom or a house. In this sense, the screen-frame is a mold, or form.[13]

The fact that in a moving picture successive film frames are fit flush into the fixed screen frame results in a phenomenological frame that is indefinitely extendible and contractible, limited in the smallness of the object it can grasp only by the state of its technology, and in largeness only by the span of the world. Drawing the camera back, and panning it, are two ways of extending the frame; a close-up is of a part of the body, or of one object or small set of objects, supported by and reverberating the whole frame of nature. The altering frame is the image of perfect attention. Early in its history the cinema discovered the possibility of *calling* attention to persons and parts of persons and objects; but it is equally a possibility of the medium not to call attention to them but, rather, to let the world happen, to let its parts draw attention to themselves according to their natural weight. This possibility is less explored than its opposite. Dreyer, Flaherty, Vigo, Renoir, and Antonioni are masters of it.

4

Audience, Actor, and Star

The depth of the automatism of photography is to be read not alone in its mechanical production of an image of reality, but in its mechanical defeat of our presence to that reality. The audience in a theater can be defined as those to whom the actors are present while they are not present to the actors.[14] But movies allow the audience to be mechanically absent. The fact that

I am invisible and inaudible to the actors, and fixed in position, no longer needs accounting for; it is not part of a convention I have to comply with; the proceedings do not have to make good the fact that I do nothing in the face of tragedy, or that I laugh at the follies of others. In viewing a movie my helplessness is mechanically assured: I am present not at something happening, which I must confirm, but at something that has happened, which I absorb (like a memory). In this, movies resemble novels, a fact mirrored in the sound of narration itself, whose tense is the past.

It might be said: "But surely there is the obvious difference between a movie house and a theater that is not recorded by what has so far been said and that outweighs all this fiddle of differences. The obvious difference is that in a theater we are in the presence of an actor, in a movie house we are not. You have said that in both places the actor is in our presence and in neither are we in his, the difference lying in the mode of our absence. But there is also the plain fact that in a theater a real man is *there,* and in a movie no real man is there. That is obviously essential to the differences between our responses to a play and to a film." What that means must not be denied; but the fact remains to be understood. Bazin meets it head on by simply denying that "the screen is incapable of putting us 'in the presence of' the actor"; it, so to speak, relays his presence to us, as by mirrors.[15] Bazin's idea here really fits the facts of live television, in which the thing we are presented with is happening simultaneously with its presentation. But in live television, what is present to us while it is happening is not the world, but an event standing out from the world. Its point is not to reveal, but to cover (as with a gun), to keep something on view.

It is an incontestable fact that in a motion picture no live human being is up there. But a human *something* is, and something unlike anything else we know. We can stick to our plain description of that human something as "in our presence while we are not in his" (present *at* him, because looking at him, but not present *to* him) and still account for the difference between his live presence and his photographed presence to us. We need to consider what is present or, rather, since the topic is the human being, *who* is present.

One's first impulse may be to say that in a play the character is present, whereas in a film the actor is. That sounds phony or false: one wants to say that both are present in both. But there is more to it, ontologically more. Here I think of a fine passage of Panofsky's:

> Othello or Nora are definite, substantial figures created by the playwright. They can be played well or badly, and they can be "interpreted" in one way or another; but they most definitely exist, no matter who plays them or even whether they are played at all. The character in a film, however, lives and dies with the actor. It is not the entity "Othello" interpreted by Robeson or the entity "Nora" interpreted by Duse, it is the entity "Greta Garbo" incarnate in a figure called Anna Christie or the entity "Robert Montgomery" incarnate in a murderer who, for all we know or care to know, may forever remain anonymous but will never cease to haunt our memories.[16]

If the character lives and dies with the actor, that ought to mean that the actor lives and dies with the character. I think that is correct, but it needs clarification. Let us develop it slightly.

For the stage, an actor works himself into a role; for the screen, a performer takes the role onto himself. The stage actor explores his potentialities and the possibilities of his role simultaneously; in performance these meet at a point in spiritual space—the better the performance, the deeper the point. In this respect, a role in a play is like a position in a game, say, third base: various people can play it, but the great third baseman is a man who has accepted and trained his skills and instincts most perfectly and matches them most intimately with his discoveries of the possibilities and necessities of third base. The screen performer explores his role like an attic and takes stock of his physical and temperamental endowment; he lends his being to the role and accepts only what fits; the rest is nonexistent. On the stage there are two beings, and the being of the character assaults the being of the actor; the actor survives only by yielding. A screen performance requires not so much training as planning. Of course, both the actor and the performer require, or can make use of, experience. The actor's role is his subject for study, and there is no end to it. But the screen performer is essentially not an actor at all: he *is* the subject of study, and a study not his own. (That is what the content of a photograph is—its subject.) On a screen the study is projected; on a stage the actor is the projector. An exemplary stage performance is one which, for a time, most fully creates a character. After Paul Scofield's performance in *King Lear*, we know who King Lear is, we have seen him in flesh. An exemplary screen performance is one in which, at a time, a star is born. After *The Maltese Falcon* we know a new star, only distantly a person. "Bogart" *means* "the figure created in a given set of films." His presence in those films is who he is, not merely in the sense in which a photograph of an event is that event; but in the sense that if those films did not exist, Bogart would not exist, the name "Bogart" would not mean what it does. The figure it names is not only in our presence, we are in his, in the only sense we could ever be. That is all the "presence" he has.

But it is complicated. A full development of all this would require us to place such facts as these: Humphrey Bogart was a man, and he appeared in movies both before and after the ones that created "Bogart." Some of them did not create a new star (say, the stable groom in *Dark Victory*), some of them defined stars—anyway meteors—that may be incompatible with Bogart (e.g., Duke Mantee and Fred C. Dobbs) but that are related to that figure and may enter into our later experience of it. And Humphrey Bogart was both an accomplished actor and a vivid subject for a camera. Some people are, just as some people are both good pitchers and good hitters; but there are so few that it is surprising that the word "actor" keeps on being used in place of the more beautiful and more accurate word "star"; the stars are only to gaze at, after the fact, and their actions divine our projects. Finally, we must note the sense in which the creation of a (screen) performer is also the creation of a character—not the kind of character an author creates, but the kind that certain real people are: a type.

5

Types; Cycles as Genres

Around this point our attention turns from the physical medium of cinema in general to the specific forms or genres the medium has taken in the course of its history.

Both Panofsky and Bazin begin at the beginning, noting and approving that early movies adapt popular or folk arts and themes and performers and characters: farce, melodrama, circus, music hall, romance, etc. And both are gratifyingly contemptuous of intellectuals who could not come to terms with those facts of life. (Such intellectuals are the alter egos of the film promoters they so heartily despise. Roxy once advertised a movie as "Art, in every sense of the word"; his better half declaims, "This is not art, in any sense of the word.") Our question is, why did such forms and themes and characters lend themselves to film? Bazin, in what I have read of him, is silent on the subject, except to express gratitude to film for revivifying these ancient forms, and to justify in general the legitimacy of adaptation from one art to another. Arnold Hauser, if I understand him, suggests wrong answers, in a passage that includes the remark "Only a young art can be popular," [17] a remark that not only is in itself baffling (did Verdi and Dickens and Chaplin and Frank Loesser work in young arts?) but suggests that it was only natural for the movies to pick up the forms they did. It *was* natural—anyway it happened fast enough—but not because movies were destined to popularity (they were at first no more popular than other forms of entertainment). In any case, popular arts are likely to pick up the forms and themes of high art for their material—popular theater naturally *burlesques*. And it means next to nothing to say that movies are young, because we do not know what the normal life span of an art is supposed to be, nor what would count as a unit of measure. Panofsky raises the question of the appropriateness of these original forms, but his answer is misleading.

> The legitimate paths of evolution [for the film] were opened, not by running away from the folk art character of the primitive film but by developing it within the limits of its own possibilities. Those primordial archetypes of film productions on the folk art level—success or retribution, sentiment, sensation, pornography, and crude humor—could blossom forth into genuine history, tragedy and romance, crime and adventure, and comedy, as soon as it was realized that they could be transfigured—not by an artificial injection of literary values but by the exploitation of the unique and specific possibilities of the new medium.[18]

The instinct here is sound, but the region is full of traps. What are "the unique and specific possibilities of the new medium"? Panofsky defines them as dynamization of space and spatialization of time—that is, in a movie things move, and you can be moved instantaneously from anywhere to anywhere, and you can witness successively events happening at the same time. He speaks of these properties as "self-evident to the point of triviality" and, because of that, "easily forgotten or neglected."

One hardly disputes this, or its importance. But we still do not understand what makes these properties "the possibilities of the medium." I am not now asking how one would know that these are *the* unique and specific possibilities (though I will soon get back to that); I am asking what it means to call them possibilities at all.

Why, for example, didn't the medium begin and remain in the condition of home movies, one shot just physically tacked on to another, cut and edited simply according to subject? (Newsreels essentially did, and they are nevertheless valuable, enough so to have justified the invention of moving pictures.) The answer seems obvious: narrative movies emerged because someone "saw the possibilities" of the medium—cutting and editing and taking shots at different distances from the subject. But again, these are mere actualities of film mechanics: every home movie and newsreel contains them. We could say: To make them "possibilities of the medium" is to realize what will give them *significance*—for example, the narrative and physical rhythms of melodrama, farce, American comedy of the 1930s. It is not as if film-makers saw these possibilities and then looked for something to apply them to. It is truer to say that someone with the wish to make a movie saw that certain established forms would give point to certain properties of film.

This perhaps sounds like quibbling, but what it means is that the aesthetic possibilities of a medium are not givens. You can no more tell what will give significance to the unique and specific aesthetic possibilities of projecting photographic images by thinking about them or seeing some, than you can tell what will give significance to the possibilities of paint by thinking about paint or by looking some over. You have to think about painting, and paintings; you have to think about motion pictures. What does this "thinking about them" consist in? Whatever the useful criticism of an art consists in. (Painters before Jackson Pollock had dripped paint, even deliberately. Pollock made dripping into a medium of painting.) I feel like saying: The first successful movies—i.e., the first moving pictures accepted as motion pictures—were not applications of a medium that was defined by given possibilities, but the *creation of a medium* by their giving significance to specific possibilities. Only the art itself can discover its possibilities, and the discovery of a new possibility is the discovery of a new medium. A medium is something through which or by means of which something specific gets done or said in particular ways. It provides, one might say, particular ways to get through to someone, to make sense; in art, they are forms, like forms of speech. To discover ways of making sense is always a matter of the relation of an artist to his art, each discovering the other.

Panofsky uncharacteristically skips a step when he describes the early silent films as an "unknown language . . . forced upon a public not yet capable of reading it." [19] His notion is (with good reason, writing when he did) of a few industrialists forcing their productions upon an addicted multitude. But from the beginning the language was not "unknown"; it was known to its creators, those who found themselves speaking it; and in the beginning there was no "public" in question; there were just some curious people. There soon was a public, but that just proves how easy the thing was to know. If we are to say that there was an "unknown" something, it was less like a language than like a fact—in particular, the fact that something is intelligible. So while it may be true, as Panofsky says, that "for a Saxon peasant of around 800 it was not easy to understand the meaning of a picture showing a man as he pours water over the head of another man," this has nothing special to do with the problems of a moviegoer. The meaning of that act of pouring in certain communities is still not easy to understand; it was and is impossible to understand for anyone to whom the practice of baptism is unknown. Why did Panofsky suppose that comparable understanding is essential, or uniquely important, to the reading of movies? Apparently he needed an explanation for the persistence in movies of "fixed iconography"—"the well-remembered types of the Vamp and the Straight Girl . . . the Family Man, and the Villain," characters whose conduct was "predetermined accordingly"—an explanation for the persistence of an obviously primitive or folkloristic element in a rapidly developing medium. For he goes on, otherwise inexplicably, to say that "devices like these became gradually less necessary as the public grew accustomed to interpret the action by itself and were virtually abolished by the invention of the talking film." In fact such devices persist as long as there are still Westerns and gangster films and comedies and musicals and romances. *Which* specific iconography the Villain is given will alter with the times, but that his iconography remains specific (i.e., operates according to a "fixed attitude and attribute" principle[20]) seems undeniable: if Jack Palance in *Shane* is not a Villain, no honest home was ever in danger. Films have changed, but that is not because we don't need such explanations any longer; it is because we can't *accept* them.

These facts are accounted for by the actualities of the film medium itself: types are exactly what carry the forms movies have relied upon. These media created new types, or combinations and ironic reversals of types; but there they were, and stayed. Does this mean that movies can never create individuals, only types? What it means is that this is the movies' way of creating individuals: they create *individualities*. For what makes someone a type is not his similarity with other members of that type but his striking separateness from other people.

Until recently, types of black human beings were not created in film: black people were stereotypes—mammies, shiftless servants, loyal retainers, entertainers. We were not given, and were not in a position to be given, individualities that projected particular *ways* of inhabiting a social role; we recognized only the role. Occasionally the humanity behind the role would manifest itself; and the result was a revelation not of a human individuality, but of an entire realm of humanity becoming visible. When in *Gone With the Wind* Vivien Leigh, having counted on Butterfly McQueen's professed knowledge of midwifery, and finding her as ignorant as herself, slaps her in rage and terror, the moment can stun us with a question: What was the white girl assuming about blackness when she believed the casual claim of a black girl, younger and duller and more ignorant than herself, to know all about the mysteries of childbirth? The assumption, though apparently complimentary, is dehumanizing—with such creatures knowledge of the body comes from nowhere, and in general they are to be trusted absolutely or not at all, like lions in a cage, with whom you either do or do not know how to deal. After the slap, we are left with two young girls equally frightened in a humanly desperate situation, one limited by a distraction which expects and forgets that it is to be bullied, the other by an energetic resourcefulness which knows only how to bully. At the end of Michael Curtiz' *Breaking Point*, as the wounded John Garfield is carried from his boat to the dock, awaited by his wife and children and, just outside the circle, by the other woman in his life (Patricia Neal), the camera pulls away, holding on the still waiting child of his black partner, who only the unconscious Garfield knows has been killed. The poignance of the silent and unnoticed black child overwhelms the yarn we had been shown. Is he supposed to symbolize the fact of general human isolation and abandonment? Or the fact that every action has consequences for innocent bystanders? Or that children are the real sufferers from the entangled efforts of adults to straighten out their lives? The effect here is to rebuke Garfield for attaching so much importance to the loss of his arm, and generally to blot out attention to individual suffering by invoking a massive social evil about which this film has nothing to say.

The general difference between a film type and a stage type is that the individuality captured on film naturally takes precedence over the social role in which that individuality gets expressed. Because on film social role appears arbitrary or incidental, movies have an inherent tendency toward the democratic, or anyway the idea of human equality. (But because of film's equally natural attraction to crowds, it has opposite tendencies toward the fascistic or populistic.) This depends upon recognizing film types as inhabited by figures we have met or may well meet in other circumstances. The recognized recurrence of film performers will become a central idea as we proceed. At the moment I am emphasizing only that in the case of black performers there was until recently no other place for them to recur in, except just the role within which we have already met them. For example, we would not have expected to see them as parents or siblings. I cannot at the moment remember a black person in a film making an ordinary purchase—say of a newspaper, or a ticket to a movie or for a train, let alone writing a check. (*Pinky* and *A Raisin in the Sun* prove the rule: in the former, the making of a purchase is a climactic scene in the film; in the latter, it provides the whole subject and structure.)

One recalls the lists of stars of every magnitude who have provided the movie camera with human subjects—individuals capable of filling its need for individualities, whose individualities in turn, whose inflections of demeanor and disposition were given full play in its projection. They provided, and still provide, staples for impersonators: one gesture or syllable of mood, two strides, or a passing mannerism was enough to single them out from all other creatures. They realized the myth of singularity—that we can still be found, behind our disguises of bravado and cowardice, by someone, perhaps a god, capable of defeating our self-defeats. This was always more important than their distinction by beauty. Their singularity made them more like us—anyway, made their difference from us less a matter of metaphysics, to which we must accede, than a matter of responsibility, to which we must bend. But then that made them even more glamorous. That they should be able to stand upon their singularity! If one did that, one might be found, and called out, too soon, or at an inconvenient moment.

What was wrong with type-casting in films was not that it displaced some other, better principle of casting, but that factors irrelevant to film-making often influenced the particular figures chosen. Similarly, the familiar historical fact that there are movie cycles, taken by certain movie theorists as in itself a mark of unscrupulous commercialism, is a possibility internal to the medium; one could even say, it is the best emblem of the fact that a medium had been created. For a cycle is a genre (prison movies, Civil War movies, horror movies, etc.); and a genre is a medium.

As Hollywood developed, the original types ramified into individualities as various and subtle, as far-reaching in their capacities to inflect mood and release fantasy, as any set of characters who inhabited the great theaters of our world. We do not know them by such names as Pulcinella, Crispin, Harlequin, Pantaloon, the Doctor, the Captain, Columbine; we call them the Public Enemy, the Priest, James Cagney, Pat O'Brien, the Confederate Spy, the Army Scout, Randolph Scott, Gary Cooper, Gable, Paul Muni, the Reporter, the Sergeant, the Sheriff, the Deputy, the D.A., the Quack, the Shyster, the Other Woman, the Fallen Woman, the Moll, the Dance Hall Hostess. Hollywood was the theater in which they appeared, because the films of Hollywood constituted a world, with recurrent faces more familiar to me than the faces of the neighbors of all the places I have lived.

The great movie comedians—Chaplin, Keaton, W. C. Fields—form a set of types that could not have been adapted from any other medium. Its creation depended upon two conditions of the film medium mentioned earlier. These conditions seem to be necessities, not merely possibilities, so I will say that two necessities of the medium were discovered or expanded in the creation of these types. First, movie performers cannot project, but are projected. Second, photographs are of the world, in which human beings are not ontologically favored over the rest of nature, in which objects are not props but natural allies (or enemies) of the human character. The first necessity—projected visibility—permits the sublime comprehensibility of Chaplin's natural choreography; the second—ontological equality—permits his Proustian or Jamesian relationships with Murphy beds and flights of stairs and with vases on runners on tables on rollers: the heroism of momentary survival, Nietzsche's man as a tightrope across an abyss. These necessities permit not merely the locales of Keaton's extrications, but the philosophical mood of his countenance and the Olympic resourcefulness of his body; permit him to be perhaps the only constantly beautiful and continuously hilarious man ever seen, as though the ugliness in laughter should be redeemed. They permit Fields to mutter and suffer and curse obsessively, but heard and seen only by us; because his attributes are those of the gentleman (confident swagger and elegant manners, gloves, cane, outer heartiness), he can manifest continuously, with the remorselessness of nature, the psychic brutalities of bourgeois civilization.

6

Ideas of Origin

It is inevitable that in theorizing about film one at some point speculate about its origins, because despite its recentness, its origin remains obscure. The facts are well enough known about the invention and the inventors of the camera, and about improvements in fixing and then moving the image it captures. The problem is that the invention of the photographic picture is not the same thing as the creation of photography as a medium for making sense. The historical problem is like any other: a chronicle of the facts preceding the appearance of this technology does not explain why it happened when and as it did. Panofsky opens his study of film by remarking, "It was not an artistic urge that gave rise to the discovery and gradual perfection of a new technique; it was a technical invention that gave rise to the discovery and gradual perfection of a new art." We seem to understand this, but do we understand it? Panofsky assumes we know what it is that at any time has "given rise" to a "new art." He mentions an "artistic urge," but that is hardly a candidate to serve as an explanation; it would be about as useful as explaining the rise of modern science by appealing to "a scientific urge." There may be such urges, but they are themselves rather badly in need of explanation. Panofsky cites an artistic urge explicitly as the occasion for a new "technique." But the motion picture is not a new *technique,* any more than the airplane is. (What did we use to do that such a thing enables us to do better?) Yet some idea of flying, and an urge to do it, preceded the mechanical invention of the airplane. What is "given rise to" by such inventions as movable type or the microscope or the steam engine or the pianoforte?

It would be surprising if the history of the establishment of an artistic medium were less complex a problem for the historical understanding than (say) the rise of modern science. I take Bazin to be suggesting this when he reverses the apparent relation between the relevant technology and the idea of cinema, emphasizing that the idea preceded the technology, parts of it by centuries, and that parts of the technology preceded the invention of movies, some of it by centuries. So what has to be explained is not merely how the feat was technically accomplished but, for example, what stood in the way of its happening earlier. Surprisingly, Bazin, in the selection of essays I have read, does not include the contemporary condition of the related arts as a part of the ideological superstructure that elicited the new material basis of film. But it is certainly relevant that the burning issue during the latter half of the nineteenth century, in painting and in the novel and in the theater, was realism. And unless film captured possibilities opened up by the arts themselves, it is hard to imagine that its possibilities as an artistic medium would have shown up as, and as suddenly as, they did.

The idea of and wish for the world re-created in its own image was satisfied *at last* by cinema. Bazin calls this the myth of total cinema. But it had always been one of the myths of art; each of the arts had satisfied it in its own way. The mirror was in various hands held up to nature. In some ways it was more fully satisfied in theater. (Since theater is on the whole not now a major art for us, it on the whole no longer makes contact with its historical and psychological sources; so we are rarely gripped by the trauma we must once have suffered when the leader of the chorus stopped contributing to a narrative or song and turned to face the others, suffering incarnation.)

What is cinema's way of satisfying the myth? Automatically, we said. But what does that mean—mean mythically, as it were? It means satisfying it without *my* having to do anything, satisfying it *by* wishing. In a word, *magically*. I have found myself asking: How could film be art, since all the major arts arise in some way out of religion? Now I can answer: Because movies arise out of magic; from *below* the world.

The better a film, the more it makes contact with this source of its inspiration; it never wholly loses touch with the magic lantern behind it. This suggests why movies of the fantastic (*The Cabinet of Dr. Caligari, Blood of a Poet*) and filmed scenes of magic (say, materialization and dematerialization), while they have provided moods and devices, have never established themselves as cinematic media, however strongly this "possibility" is suggested by the physical medium of film: they are technically and psychologically trivial compared with the medium of magic itself. It is otherwise if the presented magic is itself made technically or physically interesting (*The Invisible Man, Dr. Jekyll and Mr. Hyde, Frankenstein, 2001: A Space Odyssey*), but then that becomes another way of confirming the physicality of our world. Science presents itself, in movies, as magic, which was indeed one source of science. In particular, projected science retains magic's mystery and forbiddenness. Science-fiction films exploit not merely certain obvious aspects of adventure, and of a physicality that special effects specialize in, but also the terrific mumbo-jumbo of hearsay science: "My God, the thing is impervious to the negative beta ray! We must reverse the atom recalcitration spatter, before it's too late!" The dialogue has the surface of those tinbox-and-lever contraptions that were sufficiently convincing in prime *Flash Gordon*. These films are carried by the immediacy of the fantasy that motivates them (say, destruction by lower or higher forms of life, as though the precariousness of human life is due to its biological stage of development); together with the myth of the one way and last chance in which the (external) danger can be averted. And certainly the beauty of forms and motions in Frankenstein's laboratory is essential to the success of *Frankenstein*; computers seem primitive in comparison. It always made more sense to steal from God than to try to outwit him.

How do movies reproduce the world magically? Not by literally presenting us with the world, but by permitting us to view it unseen. This is not a wish for power over creation (as Pygmalion's was), but a wish not to need power, not to have to bear its burdens. It is, in this sense, the reverse of the myth of Faust. And the wish for invisibility is old enough. Gods have profited from it, and Plato tells it in Book II of the *Republic* as the Myth of the Ring of Gyges. In viewing films, the sense of invisibility is an expression of modern privacy or anonymity. It is as though the world's projection explains our forms of unknownness and of our inability to know. The explanation is not so much that the world is passing us by, as that we are displaced from our natural habitation within it, placed at a distance from it. The screen overcomes our fixed distance; it makes displacement appear as our natural condition.[21]

What do we wish to view in this way? What specific forms discover this fundamental condition of the medium of film?

7

Baudelaire and the Myths of Film

This wish, and these forms, can be glimpsed in a famous but puzzling text of the nineteenth century: Baudelaire's *The Painter of Modern Life*. I call it puzzling, because Baudelaire, in so many ways the prophet of the modern, has seemed to me merely perverse or superficial in this most ambitious of his theoretical statements about art. His perversity and superficiality were fated partly by his lung-bursting inflation of Delacroix, partly by his comparative casualness about what his friends Courbet and Manet were accomplishing. Baudelaire called for a realization of the other half of art whose first half is "the eternal and unchangeable." The half he wanted he named "modernity," that which is "ephemeral, fugitive, contingent upon the occasion," the "description of contemporary life," and in particular the "nature of beauty in the present time." And he says: "The pleasure we derive from the depiction of the present arises not only from the beauty in which it can be attired, but also from its essential quality of being the present." [22] But the quality of presentness is exactly what Courbet and Manet themselves craved, and in establishing it as it could be established in painting, they were establishing modernist painting.[23]

What did that have to do with Dandies and Cosmetics and Uniforms and the other paraphernalia of Baudelaire's universe? That these were forms of contemporary happiness, and for that reason our adornments, would prove nothing about their possibilities for serious art. (But then Baudelaire is a progenitor not only of modernists but also of their parodies, the modernizers.) Nothing less than everything is new in a new period—not merely attirements, but physiques and postures and gaits, and nudity itself. Courbet's and Manet's nudes are as different from their ancestors as a Dandy is from a Magus. Baudelaire knew this, he insisted upon it; so why did he succumb to the idea that these natural and historical and phenomenological transformations were something artists should *make* happen? And why did his response to this apparent lack in art take the forms it did? In particular, why was he (and it is the poet Baudelaire in question) willing to forgo serious art in favor of modest draftsmanship, and why did his attention find that special set of iconographical items he proposed?

Out of his despair of happiness, out of his disgust with its official made-up substitutes, and out of his knowledge of his isolation and estrangement from the present and the foreignness of the past (and, I believe, in his experiments with hashish), he found the wish for photography, in particular for motion pictures—the wish for that specific simultaneity of presence and absence which only the cinema will satisfy.

One might wonder why actual photographs did not satisfy the wish. He says why, or shows why, in the *Salon* he wrote in the same year he wrote *The Painter of Modern Life*.[24] Photographs did not look like photographs to him; they looked like *imitation paintings,* which is more or less what they were and what they may have remained. Photography, as its name records, was being praised as "the royal road to drawing." [25] Hindsight reveals that photography would soon stop imitating paintings and invent itself. But hindsight is of its essence blind to the past, a way of looking away from the present. Similarly, an overview is of its essence a losing substitute for perspective. An overview will tell you, for example, that the invention of photography influenced painting, whereas the reverse is nearer the truth: from that height you couldn't tell a painting from a photograph. Of course, photography *eventually* affected (some) painting, but only when painting had already affected itself and was good and ready.

Read as an anticipation of film, Baudelaire's little book seems to me, in dozens of its terms, insights, and turns of phrase, to take on the power it must have had for him. Let me simply recall the titles of his chapters, pondering them against our knowledge of cinema: Fashion, The Man of the World, Crowds, The Child, War-Sketches, Pomps and Ceremonies, The Military Man, The Dandy, Cosmetics, Women and Courtesans, Carriages. Here are stores of cinematic obsession, and they are more convincingly so the more one appreciates the meaning they have for Baudelaire and the particular way they occur in movies.

Take what he says about Carriages: "Whatever the posture into which it may be thrown, whatever the gait at which it may be travelling, a carriage, like a ship, is lent by its movement a mysterious and complex grace which it is very difficult to note down in shorthand." [26] Difficult? It is impossible to imagine its being seen on paper; but it is the very grain of moving pictures. Baudelaire's carriages carry the weight of all those conveyances and machines whose movements are so lovingly studied in the film—not, as it is typically put, because "we like to see things move," but because their characteristic movements have that "mysterious and complex grace" divined by Baudelaire. Film returns to us and extends our first fascination with objects, with their inner and fixed lives; and it studies what is done in and with them, which Baudelaire also mentions. What is done in and with one of these contrivances, where they are placed and why—this is something with a drama of its own, its unique logic of beginning, middle, and end; and they create the kind of creature who may use them. These are forms that effect cinematic possibilities. When Baudelaire speaks of "the pleasure that the artistic eye obtains . . . from the series of geometrical figures that the object in question . . . successively and rapidly creates in space," he is not describing anything a draftsman showed him; he is having a prophetic hallucination.

In praising Cosmetics, he refers not merely to make-up, but also to fashion generally and beyond that to the artifices necessary to civilized life as a whole: its streets, parks, buildings, furnishings, commodities—the secretions and scaffoldings of our forms of life. For Baudelaire they take on the value of specific *settings*—which is their indispensable value in film, where sets must be in reality, whether genuine or counterfeit. They have to have *all* of the surfaces and sides of reality, for a film takes place wholly behind the scenes. Baudelaire's vision is confirmed in his insistence that "to appreciate fashions . . . one must not regard them as lifeless objects. . . . They must be seen as vitalized and vivified by the lively woman who wore them. Only thus can one understand their spirit and meaning." [27] He is not simply saying that clothes being worn take on a life of their own. He is responding to the fact that they simultaneously conceal and reveal the body.

In paintings and in the theater, clothes reveal a person's character and his station, also his body and its attitudes. The clothes *are* the body, as the expression is the face. In movies, clothes conceal; hence they conceal something separate from them; the something is therefore empirically there to be unconcealed. A woman in a movie is *dressed* (as she is, when she is, in reality), hence potentially undressed. Earlier, Baudelaire says that "a woman and her garb [are] an indivisible whole," but the passage strikes one as uncharacteristically pious. (He begins: "What poet would dare, in depicting the delight caused by a beauteous apparition, to distinguish between the woman and her garb?") A nude is a fine enough thing in itself, and no reason is required to explain nakedness; we were born that way, and besides, "the human body is the best picture of the human soul." But to be undressed is something else, and it does require a reason; in seeing a film of a desirable woman we are looking for a reason. When to this we join our ontological status—invisibility—it is inevitable that we should expect to find a reason, to be around when a reason and an occasion present themselves, no matter how consistently our expectancy is frustrated. The ontological conditions of the motion picture reveal it as inherently pornographic (though not of course inveterately so). The million times in which a shot ended the instant the zipper completed the course down the back of a dress, or in which the lady stepped behind a shower door *exactly* as her robe fell, or in which a piece of clothing fell into the view of a paralyzed camera—these were not sudden enticements or pornographic asides; they were satisfactions, however partial, of an inescapable demand. All the Hays Offices in the world could not prevent that; they could merely enforce the interruptions. A woman and her garb are a divisible whole.

While I was completing this book, the system of audience classification of films was introduced in this country, and with it a new sense of censorship escaped. An immediate result was to make nude scenes mandatory in adult films, like blood. I have no judgment about this. Nor am I prepared to guess whether and how open sexuality will work upon serious film. Genitalia seem to be as difficult either to follow around or to ignore as the microphone was in early talkies. Will we learn really to take them for granted? And would that mean looking them over at every opportunity in no matter what company and alongside no matter what others? In my experience the new half-freedom unhinges the camera; it either becomes fixated or skittish-lyrical. The interruption occurs at a more painful point. For me, the sexuality in *Belle de Jour* works well, because it extends Buñuel's knowledge of its crude beauty and privacy; it works well in *Women in Love*, because the film is serious in its details and unembarrassedly stylish, and set in the past, and because nudity recurs enough to keep your attitude from wobbling, and because the occasions for getting undressed are righter than usual—it's pleasant to find it remembered that such things sometimes take normal people by surprise; it works well in the mild *Prime of Miss Jean Brodie*, in which a self-possessed young girl dressing from scratch turns out to yield an unpredictably tender and eventful plash of motions.

Straight pornography is not a problem: a drug is not a food. I find it said by more than one liberal that the moral question about pornography is its invasion of the last corner of privacy. From the point of view of the performers, this is ludicrous— like saying that the moral problem about child labor is that the kids worked in poor light. From the point of view of the audience, it is bullying; pornography is more likely to be privacy's last proof. The members of an audience at a pornographic film are more respectful of one another's needfulness; and though each is penetrated with the knowledge the others must be having, no one supposes that this lessens his privacy. And even if you attend a pornographic film telling yourself you merely want to know what it's like, you ought to be impressed by the absolute attention, the common awe, when all holds are unbarred. An artist must envy that power. That such an experience, however accurate and appropriate there, is for many people confined to the occasion of viewing a pornographic film, deprived of what it analogues in serious art or in actual sex, is an indictment of society's invasion and enforcement of privacy.

8

The Military Man and the Woman

In a different category are the three major types of character Baudelaire selects: the Dandy, the Woman, and the Military Man. These, as Baudelaire describes them, are not merely further items in cinema's daily sustenance; they have been movies' presiding geniuses.

The military man represents man in uniform, which is to say, men doing the work of the world, in consort, each exercising the virtues of his position or failing them; each bearing the marks of his condition. This figure asserts the myth of community, the idea that society is man's natural state. There are many films—there are genres of film—with nothing but men in them, or with just one or two peripheral women.

Now listen to what Baudelaire says about Woman:

> The Being who for most men is the source of the most vivid and also (let it be said to the shame of the sensual pleasures of philosophy) the most lasting delights; the Being towards whom, or for whose benefit, all the efforts of most men are directed; that Being who is as terrible and incommunicable as God (but with this difference, that the Infinite does not communicate because it would blind and overwhelm the Finite, whereas the Being of whom we speak is perhaps incomprehensible only because she has nothing to communicate;) . . . for whom, but especially *through whom*, artists and poets create their finest jewels; the source of the most enervating pleasures and the most fruitful griefs . . . a ray of light, a look, an invitation to happiness, sometimes a watchword. . . .[28]

And so on. One remembers how much of the history of film is a history of the firmament of individual women established there. Individual men, even the greatest, with few exceptions are fads or conveniences by comparison. Remarkable directors have existed solely to examine the same woman over and over through film. A woman has become the whole excuse and sole justification for the making and preserving of countless films: in many of Garbo's films, or Dietrich's, next to nothing may be memorable, or even tolerable, but these women themselves. The miracle is that they are enough. You can make a set of satisfying films in which Bette Davis is supported (if that is the word) by George Brent; but reverse the qualities and the thing would be impossible. The distribution of emphasis between a man and a woman in a film is like its distribution in a *pas de deux*. The most durable male star cannot survive a cipher as his object, and if one is for some reason repelled by a given woman, no man can rescue the film. I don't much like Fred MacMurray, but I can easily tolerate him for the pleasure of the good films he is in and for the women around him (e.g., Barbara Stanwyck). But even Tyrone Power will have trouble getting me back to see a film with Alice Faye in it.

If it is true that the movies' way of asserting community is typically through male comradeship (rather than, as in novels and the theater, through families); and that women are anti-community (because they interfere with comradeship); and that neither the woman outside (i.e., sexuality) nor the movie wife (i.e., frigidity) are reproductive, except accidentally, which further interferes with community; then we had better stop drawing the morals of movies too hastily.

Is it true in movies that virtue is always rewarded and vice vanquished? The woman outside may not get the man (in a sense), so she suffers for her acceptance of sexuality. Civilization exacts its discontents from us all. But her recognition of sexuality permits her intelligence and depth and independence. At those prices, what is virtue rewarded with, and who wants marriage? (The question achieves its highest range and assessment in *Children of Paradise*.) When the man goes home to his wife, his life is over (*Intermezzo*; *Now, Voyager*; *The Man in the Gray Flannel Suit*), or the woman outside suffers a death or withdrawal in time for the man's incorporation of her into his marriage (*Under Two Flags*; *Destry Rides Again*; *High Noon*; in *A Stolen Life* the good and bad mothers-lovers are literally twins, and nothing so perfectly declares the permanence of the stolen identity as the good sister's overt confession and outward sloughing of it), or the man's identity is doubled so that it is half of him who withdraws or is killed by the other half (*The Corsican Brothers*; *The Prisoner of Zenda*; *The Man in the Iron Mask*; *Shane*; *The Man Who Shot Liberty Valance*). As though marriage itself is as illicit as sexuality outside. In *The Lady Eve* this is managed comically—the man thinks (so to speak) that they aren't married. In *The Great Lie* it is handled with full hysteria—the man only thinks his wife is his child's mother, and in a couple of senses she is. In *The Postman Always Rings Twice* and *Double Indemnity*, the woman seduces her seducer and sanctions the killing of her husband, which both of them understand as his test of love; then the lovers die because they have killed, but also, since they have removed the husband in order to be together, because they transgress the deeper law against combining sex and marriage.[29] In a thousand other instances the marriage must not be seen, and the walk into the sunset is into a dying star: they live happily ever after—as long as they keep walking. In two prominent instances in which the marriage is established from the beginning and is worth having at the end, the drama turning upon getting it back together (*Philadelphia Story*; *Woman of the Year*), it is the man whose feeling is constant and predominant; where the woman works the reconciliation (*The Awful Truth*), she is made to use wiles and finally requires the aid of a door *ex machina*.

Bergman's *Smiles of a Summer Night* is close enough to the surface of this tradition for its brilliance to remember and

confirm that old resourcefulness. (*Lesson in Love,* an earlier
comedy with the same leads, reads at once as a study of high
Hollywood comedies of the thirties and forties and as a set of
sketches for the later masterpiece.) Here the woman also effects
the reconciliation, and through a calculated set of arrangements. But her efforts are not wiles. She gives the weekend
party because she is asked for help by her former lover, and she
gives him more than he asked, or knew he was asking, in con-
triving for him to discover the truth of his desires. When at the
end she has joined together the young lovers and sent them
packing, and she "puts his love into her pocket," one is not suspicious of her drama but perplexed that she finds him worthy
of it. The passiveness of her man is neither contemptible nor
stimulating to the woman, but a fact within her acceptance of
him. The film's faithfulness to itself justifies the self-confident
wittiness of its references to *A Midsummer Night's Dream* (the
young lovers communicate through a chink in the wall—the
bed moved from one room into another; the girl passes out
from spells and the confusion of adults in conflict, and then
finds her true love in the young ass she first sees upon awak-
ening; as they flee, her scarf floats from the carriage, with the
idea of her virgin's blood on it, dead to her old husband). Always excepting *Rules of the Game,* it is about as close as we've
got to another *Marriage of Figaro.* Alas.

A believable family has seemed as hard to get on film as a
believable intellectual or university classroom (difficulties no
doubt magnified by the backgrounds of the people who used to
make movies). The best families I think of were in *Pride and
Prejudice, How Green Was My Valley, The Little Foxes, Meet
Me in St. Louis, I Remember Mama, To Kill a Mockingbird,
Splendor in the Grass*—all of which are set in the elegiac past,
and which either have extraordinary child actors, or a couple
of performances so electric they seem to unify the relationships
of everyone around them (Olivier and Greer Garson), or one of

those exceptional casts who play together throughout (many of my acquaintances will not believe that Warren Beatty, Natalie Wood, Pat Hingle, and Zohra Lampert are as good, in particular as good together, as to my eye they are).

Critics of the movie's traditions of sexual or intellectual or political simplicities and evasions seem to have an idea that what is lacking is verbal or visual explicitness. No one will deny that inexplicitness can be abused, but so can explicitness. An avoided subject is not confronted by calling it names.

The Children's Hour (1962) is evidently proud of its new freedom to mention explicitly the homosexual attachment which had to be cast into heterosexuality for its earlier version as *These Three* (1936). I find the pride misplaced; the earlier version is psychologically deeper and more adult. I do not suppose that William Wyler lost his talent in the quarter-century between the two versions; the performances of Audrey Hepburn and Shirley MacLaine are expert and touching, and do not individually suffer in comparison with those of Merle Oberon and Miriam Hopkins; and Fay Bainter actually makes something out of the role of the gullible guilt-intoxicated old woman. But these talents are stifled by a structure that depends upon halfhearted explicitness to guarantee sincerity and depth of feeling.

The homosexuality in the relation between the two women, at least their genuineness and exclusiveness of feeling, is much plainer in the first movie version, in which we meet the women as roommates in a girl's college, about to graduate into the unwelcoming and depressed world of male competition to which educated women are still abandoned. Their strategy is to avoid entering it, to reproduce their world of women by starting their own school for girls. Every move in the drama is powered by a woman: it is an aunt of the dominant friend who leaves the property that makes it possible to start the school; the other's aunt trips off its destruction, providing an occasion for the

quick student of insinuation and bitchery (this role set up Bon-
ita Granville for her imminent use as Hollywood's idea of the
fascist child) to practice upon her constricted matriarch, both
of them emitting the venom of their favored family, infertile in
everything but manipulation and its consequences. This world
of women depends upon a pact to expel desire and fruitfulness.
Heterosexuality is as direct a threat to it as homosexuality.
What is monstrous to it is not merely overt perversion, but desire itself. It was a valid insight that produced the male's entrance (Joel McCrea) through the rafters of the decaying house
(now the niece's) enveloped in beekeeper's clothing. He
frightens the young arrivals, both because of the eeriness of
his appearance and the unexpectedness of his place of invasion, but surely also because he presents maleness as the source
of stings, and as impervious to their repulsions. To introduce
homosexuality in such an environment merely shows it as a
deeper strategy to avoid the intrusive company of males. That
may be part of some theory of homosexuality; but these events
cannot confirm it, they can merely purvey it, and with no idea,
implicit or explicit, about why such a choice should ever be
made.

An external, peeping treatment of the subject shows in the
later version's mechanical dramaturgy of the suicide. The dominant friend has a close-up premonition, upon which she runs
back to the house to prevent her vision of her friend's self-de-
struction. But where did she get this vision? From her wish?
And where did her friend get it? Must she kill herself because
she cannot live with the knowledge that she is homosexual?
That destroys our sense of the moving confession of love she
has just given. Is it because she has brought destruction upon
her friends? But she has not, unless they will it.

The two versions meet at a piece of business that the later
preserves almost intact—the point at which, in the interview
between man and woman that sends the man away, a hand of
one covers the mouth of the other to stop a question. This is

the point at which the films declare themselves as studies of explicitness. In *These Three*, it is a moment of courtesy and tenderness; the man touches the woman's mouth to stop her from the explicit question that would mean her distrust of him. It was to be a simple question of fact: Did you succumb to the vulgarest of temptations and betray me with my best friend? It is more humiliating to ask than to answer; but he answers. The hand over her mouth leaves her asking herself what has brought her to this question. When she answers that, she can accommodate her love. In *The Children's Hour*, the point is lost. It is the woman who stops the man's question. But it is no longer a question of external fact; it is not, did you or did you not? but, do you return her love or do you not? That may be painful, but it is not humiliating to ask or answer, and he has a right to know, and reason to want to. The friendship of the three, his caring about both of the women, gives him the right; and his reason is his, as it were, feminine intuition of the question. (James Garner, affable enough in his way, is not capable of that knowledge. Imagine the young Joel McCrea in the later version and you see more easily its wrongness.) Her stopping the question is therefore an evasion, and her explicit denial of it is a further falseness. At the end, we read her isolation not as ostracism but as the sealing of a secret victory: she was loved, someone died for love of her, and she returns the love, but now it will never need to show; vulnerability is bypassed.

If you understand homosexuality as an avoidance of consequential love or as the theft of love, you have yet to distinguish it from the avoidance and thefts in heterosexual, or parental, or any other love. The unhappy ending of *The Children's Hour* stops at what the surviving woman wishes to be accepted as the truth: the society of women and the world of men and the views of children have wronged her and are miserable things compared with her purity. The happy ending provided in *These Three* is right: it shows that happy endings require trust and a faithfulness to one's desire which overcomes what faithfulness must always overcome—the meanness and maliciousness of opinion.

A film like *Mr. Smith Goes to Washington* is not explicit about the causes of political corruption; it suggests, populistically, that they are matters of personal greed or other private sins and that they are curable by the individual or mass goodness of the little people. Still, the image of its abrupt close marks out the region which will have to be explored for details of a further significance. On the floor of the Senate, Jean Arthur kneels beside Mr. Smith's prostrate, rejected form, supporting his head in the ambiguous birth-death posture of a Pietà. The corrupted senator (Claude Rains) flies to their side, his life of respectable conspiracy broken into by the scene, to confirm to the gathered world the truth of the swooned man. One of the senator's hands points down to the couple, the other is raised up in oratorical dedication, like Liberty's ambiguous upraised, threatening arm. Whom does the truth kill? Who is in a position to speak it, or to hear it, or to act upon it if he knows he has heard?

If inexplicitness in sexual matters invites the itch of suggestiveness, explicitness cuts feeling from an attachment to anything beyond itself. If you are William Blake, you might find visual equivalents of "The head Sublime, the heart Pathos, the genitals Beauty, the hands and feet Proportion" (you will of course want to include "The eyes of fire, the nostrils of air, the mouth of water, the beard of earth"). But if you're merely D. H. Lawrence and you're sickened, rightly, at the world's furtiveness about certain words and deeds, then you may write *Lady Chatterley's Lover* and try to exorcize the bad magic of certain words and deeds with a magic of repetition and literalness. Admirable enough. But it leaves the importance of the subject incomprehensible, the metaphysical facts of sexuality, as in his *Women in Love*, in which moon and water and meadows and beasts and snow peaks are not symbolic evasions but tracings of that universe of feeling in which each of us finds or loses the space of our desire. From the fact that the birds and the bees become insufficient it doesn't follow that all we ever need are the ABC's. What you need is the tact in each case to be specific enough. (Pornography, so far at least, combines the absolutely explicit with the completely unspecific.)

9

The Dandy

Who is the Dandy? Baudelaire is insistent enough in his descriptions:

> Dandyism is an institution as strange and obscure as the duel. . . . Dandyism, an institution above laws, has laws to which all its representatives . . . are subject. . . . [The] dandy does not make love his special aim. . . . [He is] free from the need to follow any profession. . . . For the true dandy . . . [personal appearance and material elegance] are . . . symbols of the aristocratic superiority of his personality. . . . What then is this ruling passion . . . ? It is, above all, a burning need to acquire originality, within the apparent bounds of convention. . . . It is the delight in causing astonishment, and the proud satisfaction of never oneself being astonished. . . . The characteristic beauty of the dandy consists, above all, in his air of reserve, which in turn arises from his unshakeable resolve not to feel any emotion. It might be likened to a hidden fire whose presence can be guessed at; a fire that could blaze up, but does not wish to do so.[30]

We still feel the power of this myth, of this figure still staking himself upon a passive potency. (My life is my art, said Oscar

Wilde. That's two ways in one of forgoing immortality. One ought to get something for that.) Our most brilliant representatives of the type are the Western hero and Bogart; but we include the smaller and more jaded detectives and private eyes of the past generation; and the type is reiterated in the elegant nonprofessional solver of mysteries (Warren William comes to mind, though William Powell is the transcendent figure here), a branch inspired by Sherlock Holmes ("the delight in causing astonishment" indeed) and exhausted in James Bond's greasy taste for the refined.[31] Such heroes are not outside society because they have been pushed out, or because society holds them, by its own force, above its head; they have stayed out. There is therefore about them the suspicion that their freedom is never more than fantasy, like Huckleberry Finn's—that while their profession is risks, their selves are never chanced. The latest avatar, self-proclaimed and claiming to be the last, appears as Peter Fonda in *Easy Rider*. The equation of the motorcycle with the horse is worked into the ground (the specific iconography that puts the type on a motorcycle comes from Brando in *The Wild Ones*), and when Peter Fonda is caught in a full-length stroll, or standing with his legs locked, or relinquishing to us a small smile, his perfect manifestation of Henry Fonda brings an entire history deep into the present; and the mood of the film is strong enough to hold it.

The feature of the "hidden fire" is essential. Our conviction in the strength of the hero depends upon our conviction in the strength and purity of character he has formed to keep his fires banked. Otherwise he is merely physically indomitable, and no man is; in that case, his success over evil would be arbitrary, an aesthetic and moral cheat. He does not *know* he will succeed; what he knows is himself, his readiness. The private hero must be a hero of privacy.

The Villain of the piece may either be a lout or a swell—generally, some combination of the two. In each, the hero faces one of his doubles and comes to his kind of terms with it. In the first case he kills brutishness, false masculinity (*Stagecoach, My Darling Clementine, Hombre*); in the second he kills vanity, false dandyism (*Destry Rides Again, Shane, The Appaloosa*). The Villain of *The Maltese Falcon* is the woman, another range of the dandy's double, and she is both brutish (hence a fake man) and so wholly caught up in appearances that she can't tell a dandy from a brute. But one's love must not wait for justification by its object, and Bogart-Spade loves her. He tells her when it has all come out, in some of the best dialogue ever set to film, that she is "going over" for what she has done, that he is sending her over for the way she is. But in finishing her he does not finish his love for her, and this makes him true to type (his feeling is not dead, but banked); and because that shows the depth of his strength, he is the greatest instance of the type.

There will be moments in which the hero's emotion blazes up, showing that what is happening takes place over fire. This is the meaning of Bogart's familiar mannerisms (the lips caught back, the distracted tug at the ear lobe). The Bogart character also has a fixed attribute that indicates its depth—the occasion usually found for him, when he is alone, to laugh at himself, as if at all types and their confinement, putting him and them in perspective. The moment in *The Maltese Falcon* occurs after his first interview with the Fat Man, at the end of which Bogart had affected a petulant rage of impatience. In *The Big Sleep* it happens just before he puts on the queer act for the broad in the rare-books front. In *To Have and Have Not* it occurs in response to the "You know how to whistle, don't you?" lines.

In *The Man Who Shot Liberty Valance*, the John Wayne character knows that when he kills the brute (and Lee Marvin's brute is also a false dandy, with his silver-handled whip) he is killing half of himself. He has to do it because he knows that the James Stewart character is incapable of preserving himself either from the brute or from true or false dandies; and he must survive, because he is the only real man around who has left room for the woman in himself (Wayne calls him "tenderfoot," and he is frequently shown in an apron and with books of law); hence only he is capable of preserving civilization, marrying privacy with society. So Wayne breaks not only society's law but his own, murdering in secret in order to establish justice. This is the best that can be done so long as men go on believing that the force of force is greater than the power of justice, and that justice comes from nowhere. *Liberty Valance* is the fullest expression of the knowledge of the cost of civilization to be found in this genre of film, and therefore it is the greatest instance of it. (The valence of liberty: the power with which one man's freedom combines with, or shuns, the freedom of another.) In so fully opening the legend of the West, it ends it. Shane's beauty is of a different valence. What Shane knows, as he rides back out of the valley, is only that *he* is not made for civilization, which he finally learned, as we did, when after his climactic duel he twirled his brilliant pistol (the whole screen looming it) back into its holster. His satisfaction pins him to his fate; he recognizes that he cannot forgo his mark of mastery, his taste for distinction, the privilege in his autonomy.

The man who shoots Liberty Valance in that act also kills the identity of the tenderfoot, because the secret transforms the tenderfoot into "the man who shot Liberty Valance." This transfer of identity establishes the limits of the identities: power may prevent chaos, but it is impotent to establish the order of community; powerlessness may attract destruction, but accepting the limitation of one's individual power can attract higher power to one's aid. And a stern moral is drawn: justice, to be done, must be seen to be done; but justice, to be established, must not be seen to be established. No single man can establish it, only men together, each granting the other a certain right over his own autonomy. Were there still a place beyond our lives from which Athena could appear, the just city could be seen to be established, all could recognize the justice of justice. Such are the traumatic births of law in the new world. In the old world, at once less new and less primitive, the homologous trauma lay in the deaths of kings, not in the establishment but in the replacement of legitimacy.[32]

If we accept the inner relation of the bad and the good man —that both are outside the law, the one because he's strong enough to get away with it, the other because he's strong enough to impose his own code upon himself and have it respected, hence that each denies the other's existence and is fated to try to rid his outer realm of the other—then it cannot be true that the satisfaction of powerful Westerns consists merely in viewing again and again the triumph of good over evil. If that were all, the arbitrariness of victory would have only the anxious pleasure in watching a game of chance. The anxiety in the Western is a deeper one, watching the play of fate. The victory is *almost* arbitrary, and the hair's-breadth lets in the question: What is the fate that chooses the stronger to defend the good? Evil is always victorious in the short run, why not forever? Why is it the fate of good in an evil world *ever* to attract strength in its behalf, and strengthen it? Because God is a mighty fortress? So is a mighty fortress; and it is very hard to tell one from another. And in the all but complete absence of public virtue, and the all but invincible power of the empty demagogue and the empty mass filling one another's spirits, how much do we depend upon a point at which the desire for good appears fairer than the taste of rancor and the smell of power? Plato asked it first, and while he undertook to prove that justice brings happiness to the just, he did not claim that justice would in fact prevail; he predicted the opposite. The question is not, Why should I be moral?—to which the answer may be that you are too cowardly for much of anything else. The question is whether the fate of goodness will be to lose its power to attract, whether all men and women will despair of happiness.

Every American city has someone in it who remembers when part of it was still land. In the world of the Western there is only land, dotted here and there with shelters and now and then with a dash of fronts that men there call a city. The gorgeous, suspended skies achieved in the works of, say, John Ford, are as vacant as the land. When the Indians are gone, they will take with them whatever gods inhabited those places, leaving the beautiful names we do not understand (Iroquois, Shenandoah, Mississippi, Cheyenne) in place of those places we will not understand. So our slaughtered beauty mocks us, and gods become legends.

10

End of the Myths

I assume it is sufficiently obvious that these ways of giving significance to the possibilities of film—the media of movies exemplified by familiar Hollywood cycles and plots that justify the projection of types—are drawing to an end. And this means, in our terms so far, that they no longer naturally establish conviction in our presentness to the world. Why this has happened is another story, as complex as the comparable events in other arts. To say that the "conventions have become exhausted" is no explanation; if that means anything, it merely restates the historical fact.

Within the last decade film has been moving into the modernist environment inhabited for generations by the other major arts, within which each art has had to fight for its survival, to justify its existence in its own way. Of course, many films are still made within traditional genres—detective movies, romances, war films, etc. But there is no longer the same continuity between these movies and the films we take seriously, or between the audiences awaiting each. (The sociological-economic division between the remaining movie palaces and the small art houses is not an accurate guide to the division between the commodity and the serious work.) The continued production of traditional movies provides evidence at once for their completion as media of seriousness and for an examination of what we mean by "cinematic" and by "exploration of the possibilities of the medium itself."

Traditional movies move with the times; they can no more look like their ancestors than the sets and gaits and clothes appearing in them can feel like those of an earlier era. They will be dressed up, with fancier cutting and dreamier color and extremer angles and more explicit dialogue. It is this dressing up which is sometimes taken as an investigation of new possibilities of the cinematic medium. But what is new in these products? It is hardly news that the camera can move, even rapidly; that it can subtend varying directions and distances from its subject; that a story can be told by abrupt editing from scene to scene. One takes mechanical extensions of these known quantities as explorations of the cinematic to the extent that one accepts these quantities as constituting the significance of "cinematic." But these extensions bear roughly the relation to the history of cinema that late-nineteenth-century chromaticism bears to the history of music. After Wagner, composers had any lengths of chromatic alteration and modulation at their disposal, only practically no one knew to what point these new "possibilities" should be employed, what forms would provide coherence for "altered" tones that were no longer alterations *of* anything. Everything was altered. Alteration *became* everything—but only after a few strokes of genius permitted new sources of organization, new dimensions of equivalence and subordination, to manifest themselves (Mahler, Schönberg, Debussy).

One might say that *certain* possibilities, particular directions within the medium, came to an end. There are physical limits upon how fast a camera can move or a scene change, how far a lens can blur and still depict human actions and events to the aided eye. (To get past these limits an obvious solution would be to forgo the depiction of human actions and events, a solution not unheard of elsewhere in the arts, but this line is not my present concern.) Why are directors led to push possibilities (or why are they pushed by them) to their limits? An answer to this question would be part of an investigation of modernism.

One answer is that mere extensions of known quantities were an effort on the part of film-makers to retain interest in movies —their interest in making them and their public's interest in viewing them. But interest is not enough to keep an art alive, any more than an interest in children is enough to motivate the care they require. (In art, as elsewhere, one has to get beyond the fear of boredom.) It requires belief, relation to one's past, conviction that one's words and conduct express oneself, that they say what one means, and that what one means is enough to say.

To speak of the mechanical intensification of the known quantities of filming is to speak of a familiar direction of artistic—of religious, of human—desperation: the recourse to rhetoric as a cover for the absence of conviction rather than as a mode for its release. In the case of movies specifically this suggests, in terms so far developed, that conviction in the movies' originating myths and geniuses—in the public world of men, the private company of woman, the secret isolation of the dandy—has been lost, or baffled.

We no longer grant, or take it for granted, that men doing the work of the world together are working for the world's good, or that if they are working for the world's harm they can be stopped. These beliefs flowered last in our films about the imminence and the experience of the Second World War, then began withering in its aftermath—in the knowledge, and refusal of knowledge, that while we had rescued our European allies, we could not preserve them; that our enemies have prospered; that we are obsessed with the ally who prospered and prepared to enter any pact so long as it is against him; that the stain of atomic blood will not wash and that its fallout is nauseating us beyond medicine, aging us very rapidly. It is the knowledge, and refusal to know, that we are ceding to Stalin and Hitler the permanent victories of the war (if one of them lost the old world battle, he shares the spoils of the present war of the worlds), letting them dictate what shall be meant by communism and socialism and totalitarianism, in particular that they are to be equated. We lash ourselves to these ideas with burning coils of containment, massive retaliation, moon races, yellow perils, red conspiracies, in order that in the spasms of our fixed fury we do ourselves no injury, in order not to see the injury we have done, and do. So the mind tears itself apart trying to pull free.

We no longer grant, or take it for granted, that stylish dumb women are as interesting as stylish intelligent ones; we don't even think they look alike. At least, it is not obvious to me that Madeleine Carroll and Anita Louise and Hedy Lamarr were, as it were, objectively less beautiful or vivid than Carole Lombard and the young Rosalind Russell and Katharine Hepburn and Audrey Hepburn; but these latter convey an intelligence that animates their presence. Our complexity of response to Marilyn Monroe turns upon her body and its paces, but equally upon the compassion that was lost and confusing within it and upon a capacity for wit and laughter one could give one's soul to elicit and satisfy. One recalls further that the leading women of the Bogart character—Mary Astor, Ingrid Bergman, Lauren Bacall—while two of them have been among the most desirable public women of our time, are each possessed of an intelligence that gives them an independence from men, hence makes them worth winning, worth yielding independence for.

My impression is that the French leading ladies—e.g., Dan-ielle Darrieux, Michele Morgan, Edwige Feuillere, Arletty—do not have to pretend that their favors were won rather than con-ferred for their own reasons. (It helps if the culture allows the male to be younger than she.) Garbo and Dietrich sometimes seem to be suppressing a running giggle at their lover's igno-rance of that fact. It is utterly appropriate that Melvyn Doug-las wins Ninotchka when he makes an ass of himself, providing her with the occasion for that world-historical laugh. The myth is familiar—about the Princess unable to laugh, whose father the King promised half his kingdom . . . ; she was given to a youth who could do nothing right and who passed outside her window carrying his donkey on his back. The idea is picked up in *Smiles of a Summer Night*. Everybody must have some fa-vorite examples of actors and actresses whose careers failed to do them justice. I think of Frances Farmer, Ann Dvorak, Ann Sheridan, Jane Greer. Whatever the personal and public rea-sons for this, my private theory is that they weren't given con-texts in which their intelligence could operate freely, so they are likely to be seen as cynical, or hysterical.

Just as we no longer take it for granted that a demonstrative woman is capable of intimacy, we no longer grant that a super-ficially cold one probably is. We know that the Hitchcock her-oine—Grace Kelly, Kim Novak, Tippi Hedren—is supposed to excite a promise of passion by the very coldness of her surface. But these women also have in common a certain denseness that lends the additional promise of vulgarity, thus heightening the perverseness of the lust they invite. A nice registering of this occurs in the inferior *To Catch a Thief*, in which the girl (Grace Kelly) catches the thief (Cary Grant) by lifting her necklace at him, exciting his obsession for jewels (she herself having already been caught by excitement at his obsession), upon which the camera lifts up to a display of fireworks outside the window. One's first response is a laugh at the laughability of the movie cliché; but then one realizes that Hitchcock too is grinning, that he has converted this conventional movie dodge into a specific display of this girl's imagination. We are not here asked once more by a film to accept the symbol for the deed; here the conventional symbol exposes a conventional imagination of the deed. The stricture of her imagination is reassuring, it pulls the teeth of the vampire; because this woman, unlike the Laurentian castrator, can be won by satisfying her crudity, and that is child's play compared with commanding the attention of a free woman. She does not want to incorporate her man but to be absorbed into his fantasy. It is a common enough parody of the sharing of fantasy required in the marriage of true minds.

A terrible psychic price will be paid for this reassurance. *Marnie* continues Hitchcock's examination of our world of stolen love, a world whose central figures are thieves of love; and he reactivates his long obsession with the phony psychological explanations we give ourselves to ward off knowledge. *Psycho* is some ultimate version of this obsession; the brutal rationality of the "psychiatrist" at the end, tying up the loose ends of our lives, exhibits one form in which our capacity for feeling, our modulation of instinct, is no longer elicited by human centers of love and hate, but immediately by the theories we give ourselves of love and hate. Knowledge has not replaced love as our address to the world, but knowledge has replaced the world as the object of our passion. So science turns back into magic, theory becomes incantation, and intellectual caution produces psychic promiscuity.

In *The Birds* a new dialectical step is taken. Explanation is stifled, the universe now sees to it that the consequences of our actions hunt us to a conclusion. Now when love is teased nature is not amused, but aroused. The townspeople in the café scene get the idea that the girl is connected to the brimming birds, but they are looking for some high scientifico-magical explanation of her power over them. The birds, however, are merely doing what comes naturally—when, to be sure, instinct has gone a bit funny, as in our nature it has. In principle it is no more strange than a neighborhood of tomcats assembling in due season around a particular house. (You may for a while think that first bird which gives the girl a peck as she approaches in the rowboat is an outrider of the mother's minions. But that is not necessary in order to keep other girls—for example, Suzanne Pleshette—away from her shore; and pretty soon the mother's power is out of the running, followed by the dust and smoke of her departing truck.) I cannot otherwise read that image of Tippi Hedren during the final, largely invisible attack on the house, slowly writhing and slightly lifting back into the corner of the sofa, her arms stretched back. She is framed alone; we enter this picture of her at those gripping knees. The rut of virginity, its brain burning, is now claimed by the cycle of nature. But too late. When she then—the rest of the family in exhausted sleep—is aroused by the soft frenetic rustling and silent whistling in the upstairs room and responds to its call, as it has responded to hers, and goes to be rutted by all the birds of heaven, she is beyond satisfaction by a human male. No single creature can penetrate this Leda. The sky itself must empty into her lap if ecstasy is not to be denied.

Time changes. During the Second World War, at the end of *Notorious*, a Hitchcock hero rescued another sickened lady from a dangerous house, supporting her dazed body on the long walk to his car. But that lady will stand again on her own feet, facing her lover. From a woman enacted by Ingrid Bergman we can hardly withhold the power of love: she may be disloyal to her feelings (out of loyalty to her country, and to spite her lover), but she is not forgetful of them or detached from them. The new lady will not be recovered; she has flown into her own imagination; she and her man will never be equal to one another; they move in different elements. If all modern love is perverse, because now tangential to the circling of society, then the promise of love depends upon the acceptance of perversity, and that in turn requires the strength to share privacy, to cohabit in one element, unsponsored by society. This fancy lady's private element is unsharable; no man is a bird of her feather. We believe this without explanation, shown what has happened to nature in our culture. Here Hitchcock earns his title from Greek comedy.

So he can be relied upon to let terror take a measure of sexuality. It's a valid idea. In horror movies, sexuality is not suggested but directly coded onto, or synchronized with, the knives and teeth as they penetrate. Here is an obvious reason not to be quick about equating films with dreams. Most dreams are boring narratives (like most tales of neurotic or physical symptoms), their skimpy surface out of all proportion with their riddle interest and their effect on the dreamer. To speak of film adventures or glamours or comedies as dreams is a dream of dreams: it doesn't capture the wish behind the dream, but merely the wish to have interesting dreams. But horror films specifically do infuse boring narratives with the skin-shrinking haunts of dreams.

We no longer grant, or take it for granted, that a man who expresses no feeling has fires banked within him; or, if we do grant him depth, we are likely not to endow him with a commitment to his own originality, but to suppose him banking destructive feeling. Antonioni's leading men come to mind, and most of Bergman's and Godard's. Within the Hollywood tradition, Yul Brynner and James Coburn and Sean Connery and Michael Caine measure the distance we have come, along the line of silent strength, from Gary Cooper and Henry Fonda and James Stewart and Bogart and even Alan Ladd. The rebirth of unexpressed masculine depth required the rebound of culture that created the new possibility of the cool; the young Montgomery Clift and Marlon Brando are early instances of it; James Dean and Paul Newman and Steve McQueen count on it; its latest original was Belmondo. Conviction in their depth depends upon their being young, upon the natural accuracy of their physical movements (like athletes between plays), suggesting unknown regions of physical articulateness and endurance. In this figure, the body is not unhinged from the mind, as in the brute; it is the expression of selfhood, of the ability to originate one's actions. (Spinoza spoke of wisdom as aptness of the body. Yeats called it bodily decrepitude, but that was his problem.) The vanity in the young man's careless slouch has perhaps not been sufficiently appreciated; but it should also be recognized that this is not the vanity of personal appearance or fashion, but the vanity of personal freedom: of distinctness, not of distinction. It is the democratic equivalent of the dandy. Its guiding myth is the myth of youth itself, that life has not yet begun irretrievably, that the time is still for preparation, and that when the time comes to declare oneself, one will be recognized. When society requires greater uniformity, consensus crowding out the claims of consent, then the strategy of individuality and distinctness is to become identifiable within uniform—not by it, adopting its identity, but despite it, accepting no privilege or privation accruing from it.

11

The Medium and Media of Film

If defining "the medium of an art" is to help us to understand what has in fact been achieved and accepted within the various physical bases of an art, and if the physical basis of movies, being irreducibly photographic, necessitates or makes possible the meaningful use of human reality and of nature as such, then the genres and types and individualities that have constituted the media of movies are fixed in that specific collection of human beings with which movies have been made—in their utterly specific rhythms of voice and gesture and posture, and in those particular streets and carriages and chambers against and within which those specific beings had their being. They are now gone or old. When they and their particular locales are gone, Hollywood is ended. Its ending is the end of its media, of those arrangements whose significance was unquestioned, conviction in which was immediate. What, then, are the media of movies? What possibilities are now to be explored?

Traditional movies can still be made that are satisfying to view: ones with new wrinkles to old formats (e.g., a black man and woman working a straight forties romance, as in *For Love of Ivy*; a black city-slicker detective impounding the admiration of a southern sheriff in a fifties murder mystery, as in *In the Heat of the Night*; a personally impeccable and cosmically successful black doctor confronting a liberal family with its values in a thirties problem picture, as in *Guess Who's Coming to Dinner*—obviously a lucrative vein has been struck here); or ones with more convincing and luxurious props (as in the James Bond series, which dresses up Saturday serials with more baroque violence, more expensive sex, better make-believe technology, and, in the case of *From Russia with Love*, four complete climaxes for the conclusion—a satisfactory bargain); or, at the highest level of taste and craftsmanship, well-made adventures or struggles in completely realized exotic settings, where the commonest actions require and justify new forms of human motion and give room to an actor of traditional grandeur (as in Kurosawa's historical films with Toshiro Mifune, or in Arthur Penn's choreographing of Anne Bancroft and Patty Duke in *The Miracle Worker*). Brando is still capable of bringing off this last possibility almost unaided by direction (as in *Sayonara*, in which he achieves the subtlest portrait known to me of a certain sort of genteel southerner, with a sweet and stubborn affectionateness unapproached by northern and western men in search of women). Laurence Olivier, say in *Sparta-cus* or in *Bunny Lake Is Missing*, is not, because while his ac-complishment as an actor outstrips Brando's, it is not called upon; and as a natural subject of film he is weaker. George C. Scott is an intermediate case in this select company, managing to make room for his gifts, as actor and as subject, in spaces so different as *The Hustler* and *Dr. Strangelove*.

When a film deliberately avoids cinematic traditions in an effort to modernize its looks, it is likely to run up against a problem quite unforeseen in what we had experienced of film's possibilities. I hope I am not alone in simply being unable to recall the names or faces or presences of so many of the men and women who have come to people American movies over the past five or ten years. (This indistinctness has sometimes made the movies they are in feel like what I used to think of as foreign films.) Featurelessness is perhaps an inaccurate idea; the fact is that many of them look alike to me, or each resem-bles one of those upsetting composite drawings of, say, the Presidents of the United States or one of those face-shapes that run through various hair styles on a barber-shop chart. It is as if an up-to-date string of Goldwyn Girls had each been given lines to assume in addition to their poses and then named and sent off to various regions of the studio lot. Baudelaire's per-ception of union between a woman and her cosmetics is here realized with perfect literality: the new actresses tend to *be* cosmetics, or prosthetics; the adornment that was the whole point of the old chorus line has moved from its position as live landscape into the soul of the action. They are as like one an-other as the rooms they live in, the beds they use, the converti-bles they drive, the cities they pass through, the airplanes that take them there. Samuel Fuller manages to thrive on this indis-tinctness of his people, not letting it deny their humanity. He does it by single-minded insistence on forgoing the characteri-zation, plot complexity, and symbolism on which movies used to depend, preserving only the blocks of crude emotion that all humans share—base levels of sentimentality, magazine hopes, eyes-open sex—and working an inventiveness with treachery and violence that lends a kind of originality to these inarticulate, mass lives. This single-minded intention discovers a way of achieving old-fashioned movies.

Of course, there are exceptions. Lana Turner missed the fate of indistinctness because she was one of its originals. (It is a dangerous and prophetic moment, in *The Bad and the Beautiful,* when she interrupts Kirk Douglas's gaudy night with the "starlet": the two women are all but indistinguishable except in age and spatial location.) Natalie Wood and Tuesday Weld miss it because the nervous awkwardness of their voices and bodies is out of register with the evenness of their looks. Offbeat temperaments still appear, like Zohra Lampert, but, like Joan Loring in the 1940s, say, they do not get enough parts. Anthony Perkins, for all his good looks and good acting, was headed for this indistinctness until Hitchcock discovered a natural meaning for it in the split, or theft of personality; psychological vampirism. Perkins' later parts, in *Pretty Poison* and in *The Champagne Murders,* trade on this: the power of his role depends upon his *not* being what his role in *Psycho* showed him to be. This rapid dialectic, from innocence to guilt and forward ironically to innocence, is a perspicuous instance of the kind of history I have hypothesized as the natural result of a star's successive incarnations. (The outlaw past underlying the Bogart character is only the purest instance of a familiar route: the interpenetration of lawman and outlaw winds through figures as various or distant as James Cagney and Lloyd Nolan and Howard Duff. Their histories become part of what the movies they are in are about. So an account of the paths of stars across their various films must form part of the internal history of the world of cinema.)

The interchangeability of the new performers—and of course, not merely of their faces and trappings, but of their demeanor and posture and cadences, and the way they inhabit

their trappings—is a perfect negation of that condition of movies I described as one in which an individuality is the subject of
film. These figures no more lend themselves to such study than
they do to imitation. To impersonate one is to impersonate all;
their personalities are already impersonations. This, further,
negates or literalizes the condition I characterized as the ontological equality of objects and human subjects in photographs;
for these figures are no longer the human part of nature.[33]

What needs accounting for is simultaneously that the tradition is still available to current successful films, and also that
serious works are in the process of questioning their relation to
the tradition, that they are moving into the modernist predicament in which an art has lost its natural relation to its history,
in which an artist, exactly because he is devoted to making an
object that will bear the same weight of experience that such
objects have always borne which constitute the history of his
art, is compelled to find unheard-of structures that define
themselves and their history against one another. (Without this
constancy of human experience, history would not develop
meaningfully, would not have its ironies and losses and narrow
escapes. That is, there would be no human history but merely
another species of natural evolution—a condition we may yet
arrive at. And the history of an art is a human history.) When
in such a state an art explores its medium, it is exploring the
conditions of its existence; it is asking exactly whether, and
under what conditions, it can survive.

What conditions of movie-making are to be explored? What
"possibilities" of the medium of movies are now given significance?

The material basis of the media of movies (as paint on a flat,
delimited support is the material basis of the media of painting[34]) is, in the terms which have so far made their appearance,
a succession of automatic world projections. "Succession" includes the various degrees of motion in moving pictures: the

motion depicted; the current of successive frames in depicting it; the juxtapositions of cutting. "Automatic" emphasizes the mechanical fact of photography, in particular the absence of the human hand in forming these objects and the absence of its creatures in their screening. "World" covers the ontological facts of photography and its subjects. "Projection" points to the phenomenological facts of viewing, and to the continuity of the camera's motion as it ingests the world.

The categories of succession and projection include the ones most emphasized in what I have heard and read about the aesthetics of film. In particular, they include what many take to be the basic question of the subject, namely, whether it is the possibility of cutting from one view to another (one sense of succession) or the possibility of continuous projection of an altering view (altered by depth of focus or by moving the camera) which is the essence of the cinematic. I have not made myself trace the experience and the philosophy which led, say, Eisenstein to opt for montage and Bazin for continuity; nor have I collected enough instances of the one and of the other to know my mind on the topic. My excuse for speaking in ignorance of this question is that I have a hypothesis about it, namely, that it is not *a* question. I should be in a better position to say what that hypothesis comes to after developing the categories of world and automatism.

It is not to be expected that a given discovery shows the significance of an isolated possibility of the art, or that a given possibility yields up some single significance. For whatever is meant by a medium's "possibilities," each is what it is only in view of the others. This is why the general answer to the common question, "In what ways do movies differ from novels or from theater?" ought to be: "In every way." It is why the idea that a movie should be "cinematic" is either as bad or as special as the idea that a poem should be poetic, or as empty.

12

The World as Mortal: Absolute Age and Youth

Two recent developments in movie-making seem to me to acknowledge the *a priori* condition that its medium is photographic and its subject reality. The first development has to do with the fact we recently looked at, that the particular human beings whose characteristics helped to fix the media of movies are now old or gone. (Their children are now in films, constituting the latest class with hereditary privilege. Like all second generations, with their subjection to merciless acceptability, most of them look and feel alike; they share the same past, or lack of past, somewhere within the even heat of West Los Angeles.) However unclear the issue of the artistic age of the movie, its absolute age is acknowledged in the use of these familiar faces explicitly as familiar ancients. Buster Keaton's appearance in *Sunset Boulevard* is an early instance that comes to mind; Andy Devine in *Liberty Valance* is another; Bette Davis in *The Star* is another. These films are appropriate vehicles for carrying this effect of aging, because they are *about* returning, about making a comeback, or going back to beginnings; we are meant to remember their stars as having been there, or somewhere in the same territory, when they and we were young. For many viewers of *Sunset Boulevard*, Buster Keaton and Stroheim bear greater initial responsibility for this effect than Gloria Swanson, whom they will not have seen young. But when we watch her watching her young films, the juxtaposition of the phases of her appearance cuts the knowledge into us, of the movie's aging and ours, with every frame.

The nostalgia of old photographs is the perception that mortality is at some point to be stopped in its tracks. The figures in them seem so vulnerable, so unknowing of what we know about them, of the knowledge in store for them. We could know this about ourselves, if we could turn the force of nostalgia toward an anticipation of the fact that every moment is always stopped from every other. In the very vulnerability of that embarrassed laugh, in the tilt of the hat, in the way the foot is turned, in the dust that lies on the shoe or in its hopeful shine, in the crook of the arm where the baby nods, the knowledge of mortality has room to live, even jauntily. There is no better place for the knowledge. The roundness of clocks is convenient, but it naturally misleads us about something clocks tell, because its hands repossess their old positions every day and every night. The reels on a projector, like the bulbs of an hourglass, repeat something else: that as the past fills up, the future thins; and that the end, already there against the axle, when the time comes for its running, seems to pick up speed.

In *Liberty Valance,* John Wayne is not seen old, and Stewart's performance of the present (i.e., as the old figure coming back) is felt as play-acting because it contrasts with his youth in *this* film (an old device of film, as of theater) rather than with the free accumulation of memories of him from film worlds of an earlier time. In *Ride the High Country*, the pathos of the aging cowboys (Randolph Scott and Joel McCrea) depends upon their being enacted by aging men whom we can remember as young cowboys. This is obvious, but the film is overrated, I believe, because it taps this particular source of feeling.

The occurrence of aging actors declares a condition that was naturally registered in the fact of recurrence itself: that movies depend upon the appearance in them of living men and women, mortals. The individuality of stars was defined by their self-identity through repeated incarnations. It is not only the waves of European directors over the past decade and a half who have wanted the depth of reference and range of inflection the use of a stock company of subjects brings to an individual work. Hollywood was an enormous stock company, America's only successful one, its State Theater. Though at first it seemed the reverse, those recurring figures in the films of Bergman, Godard, Resnais, Antonioni, Fellini, were part of what made them acceptable as movies, not merely as foreign films. And they were able to count on the power of recurrence after Hollywood, to achieve it, had to declare it by the assertion of age— that is, by nostalgia. (Hollywood, like America, finally pays for its invasions.) In *Beat the Devil* (1954), John Huston self-consciously exploited the knowledge that Bogart adventures could no longer inspire their old conviction. But in that film, instead of facing the loss (as he does in *The Treasure of the Sierra Madre*) and the nostalgia it releases (as he does in *The African Queen*), he pretends that nothing of value has passed. I find it about as funny as a mustache on the *Mona Lisa*.

The quality of distinctness assured through recurrence was equally obvious in the supporting players of Hollywood's stock company. Not to remember the name of a traditional Hollywood bit player is possible, if hardly excusable; not to remember their faces and temperaments is unthinkable. But the fact is that I cannot call back the faces of critical minor leads in several of the best recent neo-Hollywood films—*In the Heat of the Night, The Detective, Petulia, Pretty Poison, Bullitt*. In itself this may not be surprising. These figures just haven't been in enough films to have become memorable. But there is more to it. My feeling is that they *could* not become memorable. I have no sense of the range of role or temperament they may occupy, and these isolated films have been insufficient to establish that sort of resonance for them. But without that, there is no world before us. Neo-Hollywood is not a world.

One of the remarkable achievements of *Bonnie and Clyde* is its establishment of at least three supporting players, enough to survey a whole and specific world. A failure of *The Graduate* is the failure of its supporting players to accept and fill and specify the types they project. So their characters are thin and imposed—stereotypes. There is no reason for them to be as mean as they appear to be. Anne Bancroft, because the most accomplished and powerful of the actors involved, is caught in the most elaborated arbitrariness: for example, if her seduction of the graduate is the pure bad faith she enacts, why in her meetings with him is she so explicit in her wishes and humiliating in her unseducibility? And if she is really alcoholic or in painful sexual need, why is she so deliberate and indifferent in the event? Certainly one can make up explanations for any of these conjunctions, but they would be quite arbitrary in their application—not because we don't know enough about her character, but because we aren't convinced that we have been given *a* character to respond to. It may be that what we are meant to be given is a series of projections from the graduate's point of view. This is clearly going on in the well-realized passage radiating his new experience of his body, shown in punning cuts between the hotel room and his parents' house and the swimming pool: the progress of his first habitual exploration of one woman, the way his body has become marked and charted with the knowledge of hers, enclosing him within a new skin of mood and gesture and odor and boredom and bristle which he may feel at his neck as he lies in bed at home, in his mouth as he takes to smoking in his room, in his shoulders and groin and legs as he floats on the Abercrombie and Fitch rubber raft, in his hands and nose and teeth as he drinks beer from a punched can. But the primacy of his private life, which wants to be the subject of the film, is also denied by the film, as firmly as by his parents. The hotel sequence that leads up to the floating punning passage is a set piece of lobby-to-bedroom farce, depending for its effect upon the known quantities and rhythms of suspicious hotel clerks, lugubrious hotel receptions, the unfamiliar geography and properties of expense-account rooms, and upon a known source of audience response, its morbid appreciation of its own prejudice and tawdriness. Here the film's talented director takes revenge on all sides responsible for his success—on his audience, with whom he identifies and whom he despises; and on his hero, with whom he identifies and whom he patronizes.

But miracles are likely to be costly, and Mike Nichols' and Dustin Hoffman's graduate is a miraculous appearance of the myth of youth itself, soliciting an investment of feeling in every inflection of the young man's behavior out of all proportion to any feeling of his own. The investment is fully justified in the final act, beginning with his declaration to his parents that he is going to marry the girl and his drive to Berkeley to inform her of her future. From here to the end, the film finds ways to acknowledge indebtedness to, and thereby invoke the power of, several huge moments in the history of films about young love. Sustaining himself in flight—speeding when he can, running when he can't, and in between gliding on new currents of psychic resourcefulness—Hoffman takes upon himself the Belmondo figure created in *Breathless* and lightened in *That Man from Rio*: a real modern hero, equal to his demand for happiness; knowing that a woman may be more trouble than any public knowledge of her could rationally justify, and able to take the trouble; assailing daughters without fathers, or with defeated fathers. These women need to be won without anyone to award them. They have to award themselves—and not when their tests have been passed, since these tests of love cannot be passed. We are not swans, not showers of gold, neither real beasts nor real princes, and mountains of glassy courtesies will roll us back. We win only by overcoming the woman's power of testing altogether, by showing her that her destructiveness has not destroyed us, that her worth is no longer in need of proof; that her treasure, which she more and more fears may have been lost, is merely hidden, as befits grown women, and that I know this because I seek it and will not be lost.

The closing image of the young pair, at the back of the municipal bus, the spotless and prepared bride together with her exhausted and disheveled and victorious lover, calls upon *the* great movie image of leave-taking in wedding: Vigo's bride in *L'Atalante*, standing alone on the distant night-deck of her husband's craft—the boat, the shore, the water, the sky infiltrating one another, mixing their stars, suspending the lone figure still in her wedding gown, drifting into the unknown territory of marriage. Is that garb of white magic inappropriate to the black barge of work? A place of work may take on its blessing; and what garb is appropriate to the unknown, if not the garb of unknownness? We know they do not know what they are headed for, that the bus will stop somewhere; but we do not know that they will not survive together.

So far as we can grant that they might, the film reinstates the myth of modern marriage, which is the modern myth of romance. In classical comedy the stage at the end is littered with marriages, tangled pairs have at last been sorted out, age accepts its place, youth takes its own, and families are present to celebrate the continuance of their order. At some point, perhaps when the world went to war, society stopped believing in its ability to provide that continuity. It needed to know what modern romance asserted, that one couple can make it alone, unsponsored. The great movie genres of this idea are thirties comedies and musicals. In the big city, survival cannot wait upon security; it requires wit, invention, good spirits, the capacity to entertain, and the grace to retain oneself, since these are no longer to be had for the hiring. They were not foolish virgins who yielded to Cary Grant and Fred Astaire. What the community needed to know, in reduced circumstances, was not merely that its legitimacy is being acknowledged, but that it is worth acknowledging. In particular, that it still allows those meant for one another to find one another, and that they can accomplish happiness within the law. In practice this now means: it has allowed people who have found one another to be meant for one another.

The myth has died a thousand deaths, but each is equivocal. In *Holiday Inn* Astaire loses the girl to Bing Crosby; but that is perhaps because this girl requires comfort before all and is willing to go into exile to pay for it (i.e., into the Connecticut countryside with a crooner, subjected to "White Christmas" for the rest of her days). In *Damsel in Distress* Astaire wins, ludicrously, Joan Fontaine, but that just shows that not all girls can dance to this piper. In *Sabrina* Audrey Hepburn is won by the older, reliable brother, and *that* is felt as magic; but he is Humphrey Bogart, the cards were stacked. So it was not unthinkable that the myth should flare up again. I am reminded that the graduate is introduced to us as an athlete, in particular as a track man. If Lévi-Strauss is right to relate a mythic question about walking to the fact of being human, a reminder that we are earthlings (an insight recaptured by Thoreau, who recognized walking as a gait natural only to man), then perhaps a man for whom running (or dancing) is natural has a claim to our spirituality. Whether or not there is a man in the moon, and whether or not there is life, or we put life, on the moon, it is analytically true that men do not inhabit the moon.

13

The World as a Whole: Color

A second major property of film which can serve to declare its recording of a total world is color. It is usual merely to use color as a new form of packaging, one which my occasional market research on the subject has convinced me is profitable. This was not the sole or simple point of its use in *Gone With the Wind*, whose success, theatrical as well as financial, depended upon its appearance as a luxury item. What more convenient way to retail the old myth of the Old South? Glamour is the *content* of that myth. But this is merely the best cinematic instance of those romancings of history that have always tapped the popular purse: Technicolor was the natural visual equivalent of the Scott-descended prose such matters require when they take the form of books.

I think of two films of the 1930s that really defined or declared color as such, used it to explore that possibility of film: *The Wizard of Oz* is the obvious case, exploiting such devices as magic ruby slippers, a yellow brick road, Emerald City, white snow on a summer meadow, the horse of a different color, and the broad device of framing the color with those black and white scenes in Kansas. "Exploiting" these devices is not merely a matter of painting props to match some names: it required definitive performances from three of the best comics of the period (Bert Lahr, Jack Haley, Ray Bolger), inhabiting what are to my mind the best fantasy costumes ever created; further strokes of wit or luck in casting, obviously including Billie Burke and Margaret Hamilton as the good and the wicked witches; and one of the most continuously inventive scores and lyrics in movie musicals. The other example is the Errol Flynn *Robin Hood*, whose sets and locales and fights I still recall as I recall the shiny color illustrations in lost childhood books, sometimes protected by gauzy sheets that themselves seemed veils of magic, readying as they momentarily delayed the revelation of characters in the flesh. These films discovered that color can serve to unify the projected world in another way than by direct reliance upon, or implication toward, the spatial-temporal consistency of the real world. The world so unified is obviously not the real past world of photography, but a consistent region of make-believe, so it is essential to their rightness that these films are children's tales. Olivier's *Henry the Fifth* works this possibility to its greatest elegance.

The Cabinet of Dr. Caligari serves another manner of creating an artificially unified environment. But it competes with reality by *opposing* it—as its subjects do, as Germany did—with images that compose a conventional expression of madness, not by filtering reality through a normal stage of fantasy. Its feeling of constriction, of imagination confined to the shapes of theater, is a function of its existence in black and white, a point to which I return.

Recent films in color, when that fact about them goes beyond the necessity of luxury or amusement and becomes a declared condition of a medium, also allow color to create a world. But the world created is neither a world just past nor a world of make-believe. It is a world of an immediate future.

Among the works of serious directors, *Red Desert* is almost as explicit as the unfortunate *Fahrenheit 451* in its premonition that the world we inhabit is already the world of the future. And two of the better among recent neo-Hollywood productions achieve their power through this quality of futurity. The world of *Petulia*, in its settings among the outsized machines of advanced medical physics, might as well already be placed within the earth, clearly a natural future if the pollution of history becomes total. An environment become wholly interior is confirmed in the motel with the drive-in front desk and the rooms which open directly off the garage ramps. Here architecture bespeaks one clarified future, namely the possibility of absolute privacy—just at the moment that experience is ceasing any longer to be one's own. (The movie's stylistic consistency justifies a possibility familiar from experimental films: the periodic projection of a blood slide as a frame-filling abstraction in motion.) The world of *Bullitt* is not different from ours (but then, the future need not look much different from the present); yet the simplifications and opacities of the lives it presents are what ours may fully become when the subtlety and sensibility that human relationships require are no longer negotiable. The action does not take place against an independent world, as gangster and police movies take place against the normal life of a city, or Westerns beyond outposts of civilization; it forms a complete and abstract world. The effect of imminence is again accented by a concentration on the technology of hospital procedures, by the animation of the sounds and effects of the weapons in play, and further, for me, by the extraterrestrial quality lent by the telephoto lens to the cadenza of the car chase. That quality is complex, but it depends in the first instance on the accuracy of perception which realizes the hills of San Francisco as the ultimate site for the ancient motif of a car chase through a city. The narrative mode is not "Once upon a time . . ." but "What if one day . . ."

Hitchcock is the master of this effect, the perception of a familiar locale as a natural setting for a hitherto unrelated individual task or predicament: the tennis match in *Strangers on a Train*, the cymbal crash in *The Man Who Knew Too Much*, the crop-dusting plane in *North by Northwest*. These incidents work first within the ordinary lines of motion and suspense, but their further power depends upon the inflection they give to a familiar environment, above all to a sense that they are as natural to the place as the conventional events we might expect there. The environment is as innocent, and guilty, as a bystander. The effect is as of a revelation of the familiar. *Of course* the Great Plains is a region in which men are unprotected from the sky. *Of course* the rhythm of a tennis match is one of repeated crisis internal to the concepts of "double fault," "advantage," "break point," "set point." Only in boxing is it equally open to one participant to try to hurry the conclusion of the match, but there the violence is out under the lights; in tennis it is filtered by the sun and the whites and the decorous distances and the civilized and lucid sounds, of the ball strumming the racket, the referee's flat calls, the intimate audience. And what is revealed is the radical contingency of convention—as though society's web of expectancies may at any moment be torn, as though to span the abyss of the unexpected (that is to say, the future) were society's only point, and its work about to come undone unless the efforts of one or two ordinary souls are successful.

Two satisfying modern works are apparent exceptions to this notion that the declaration of color establishes a world of futurity. Godard's *Alphaville*—in my experience as underrated a film as most of the rest of Godard is overrated (with the exception of his masterpiece, *Breathless*)—turns on the premise that the cities we now inhabit are the future; yet that film is in black and white. And *Rosemary's Baby*, which is in color, is firmly rooted in the immediate past. But in *Alphaville* the black and white are made to function like colors. Visually this is accomplished by confining the interiors largely to bright metallic and glass and plaster expanses or passageways, and the exteriors to scenes at night; dramatically it has to do with Godard's presentation of character—in particular with his ability, or disability, in de-psychologizing or un-theatricalizing the characters, a point that I alluded to in mentioning *Dr. Caligari* and that I again postpone for the moment. *Rosemary's Baby*, on the other hand, goes back to an old insistence upon individual psychology and uses color to establish a world of private fantasy. The point of this color, however, is not so much to unify a world as to juxtapose opposing moods and to symbolize mutually exclusive environments.

The great example of this combination of fantasy and color symbolism is Hitchcock's *Vertigo*. The film establishes the moment of moving from one color space into another as one of moving from one world into another. In *Rosemary's Baby* this is accomplished by showing the modernizing of one apartment in the Dakota building, then moving between its open chic and a darker elegance. An instance in *Vertigo* is James Stewart's opening of a storage-room door—the whole car-stalking passage leading up to this moment shot in soft washed-out light— into a florist shop alive with bright flowers, predominantly red. The moment is almost comic in its display of assured virtuosity. I can't help sensing an allusion in *Rosemary's Baby* to the use of red and green traffic lights in *Vertigo* when Polanski almost crudely signals the elevator's descent into the underworld of the Dakota by holding on its livid down-light. (Blue cigarette smoke drifting from a room in which Rosemary's husband and the hell creature are overheard in conversation is also reminiscent of the smoke and dust Hitchcock likes to raise as signals of evil.)

I speak of "establishing a world of private fantasy" in these films. More specifically, each is *about* the power of fantasy, and in particular about its power to survive every inroad of science and civility intact, and to direct the destiny of its subject with, finally, his active cooperation.

Vertigo seems at first to be about a man's impotence in the face of, or faced with the task of sustaining, his desire; perhaps, on second thought, about the precariousness of human verticality altogether. But it turns out to be about the specific power of a man's fantasy to cause him not merely to forgo reality— that consequence is as widespread as the sea—but to gear every instant of his energy toward a private alteration of reality. Each of these ways of handling fantasy has its psychotic leanings, but neither of them need tip over.

It is a poor idea of fantasy which takes it to be a world apart from reality, a world clearly showing its unreality. Fantasy is precisely what reality can be confused with. It is through fantasy that our conviction of the worth of reality is established; to forgo our fantasies would be to forgo our touch with the world. And does someone claim to know the specific balance sanity must sustain between the elaborating demands of self and world, some neat way of keeping soul and body together? What was Freud's advice? To retrieve stifled fantasy so that its annihilating power can command the self's self-esteem, the admiration of men, and the love of women—to insist upon a world with room in it for fruitful work and love. Merely that. And analyses of ideology are bound to be external when they fail to honor—I do not say share—the ineradicable weave of fantasy within ideology. Marx thought it was separable and called it Utopianism, not seeing his own. What has happened to us is that after politics retrieved the fantasy of brotherhood orphaned in God's abandonment, the realities of politics so brutalized and specialized their charge that the orphan withdrew on its own; and now fantasy and politics each try to devour the other. Here are two directions of nihilism. Such phenomena are sometimes politely referred to as "the failure of our institutions."

Vertigo is just a movie, but no other movie I know so purely conveys the sealing of a mind within a scorching fantasy. James Stewart is not much of an antihero, but the totality of his longing—and the terrorizing defacement of his object's identity which his longing comes to require—mimics that convulsion of consciousness which transcends idolatry in favor of the fantastic reality of God, that point past imagination at which happiness and truth coalesce. (Not happiness and *virtue,* as Kant childishly thought. *That* conjunction takes place on earth or nowhere.) The modern Pygmalion reverses his exemplar's handling of his desire, and turns his woman to stone. The casting of Kim Novak in this role seems to me inspired, and gives her her most memorable role. The featurelessness of her presence and nonexistence of her acting allow full play to one's perversity; the lax voluptuousness of her smooth body—which Hitchcock insists upon as upon no other of his heroines, in the scene in which she is wrapped in a sheet, after her leap into San Francisco Bay—declaims perfect pliancy. At the least, Hitchcock trades on an idea that even Freud could not stomach— that the fantasy of a transcendent God is not, is perhaps the central experience which is not, original in childhood, but is the product of adults, of creatures whose knowledge is of childhood past.

This is the region within which I read Hitchcock's preoccupation with nuns and churches, a zone he loves to explore, in which superstition, expectancy, explanation, and obsession cross one another. To understand his effect, one needs to know the source of the rightness in his settings, not merely their irony and wittiness: Kim Novak's final fall from the tower being tripped off by the sudden fluttering of a nun, Stewart's world snapping at the high point of a church, from which, at the end of aspiration, he will reverse the direction of his vertigo and plunge to his love. The Hitchcock heroine is, as it were, a defrocked nun; so that just as she stands, one already sees more of her than normal. When to a nun's habit Hitchcock adds high heels (as in *The Lady Vanishes*), we have an overt acknowledgment of voyeurism, which is not merely one of his special subjects (explicit in *Rear Window* and *Psycho*) but a dominant mood of his narration as a whole (most blatant in the films with Tippi Hedren, in which we spy full length on her inner life). Voyeurism is a retracted edge of fantasy; its requirement of privacy shows its perversity. Modern advertising is its offspring; but its condition as publicity conceals its perversity. Narrative voyeurism is Hitchcock's way of declaring the medium of film, a condition of which is that its subjects are viewed from an invisible state.

Rosemary's Baby looks as if it might be about the fantasy of success, about its spiritual dangers and its costs, its typical acquiescence to power; about the temptingness of temptation and therewith about the power of the past to join hands with the future behind the back of the present. Offering one's child as a bribe to fortune is a common enough gamble for power, and makes Rosemary into the charmed pawn of the game, complete with the good wizard (in earlier films he would be a benevolent doctor) who knows, and can thereby dispel, the spells of the bad wizard (in earlier films, a mad scientist or a vampire who looks like a mad scientist). But in this film the white magic is overcome; and then we try to see the story both from Rosemary's point of view and from just outside, as though there were a radical ambiguity between the events as

they may be and her consistent interpretation of them. This
would be good enough, but Polanski goes further. What Rosemary comes to think may be happening, is happening. But the
cause of hell's power is not her husband's pact with it. Her own
succumbing to the fantasy of motherhood produces her world.
This fantasy presumably reached its height with the birth of
Christianity: natural fatherhood essentially external to the fact
of birth, pregnancy the condition of mystery, any woman may
be singled out among women to carry God within her—as if to
justify, or deny, her sense of violation. The girl's name is Rosemary. (The great modern telling of this fantasy is Kleist's *The
Marquise of O.* . . .) When Rosemary picks up the old *Time*
magazine with the question "Is God Dead?" smeared on its
cover, this suggests to her not merely a possible explanation of
what her husband and his new acquaintances are doing to her.
It is an annunciation of what she has until then obscurely felt
called upon to do. In the absence of God, it is up to her to
create God. And what is thus created, in isolation, is not God.
(The appearance of that issue of *Time* in itself mimics this dialectic. Nietzsche predicts in *The Joyful Wisdom* that the news of
God's death will take a century to reach our ears. The century
is now about finished, and the news has reached our ears. Only
it has come *as* news, i.e., as gossip, and in that form the knowledge Nietzsche speaks of cannot come to us at all, is further
from us than ever. For his intelligence was about *us,* that we
have killed God, and not to know that is no longer an absence
of information but the absence of conscience, of so much as
the possibility of self-knowledge.) Rosemary's is the original
sin of mothers, to regard what they give birth to as their *own*—
it is *Rosemary's* baby—rather than as a separate creature with
whose individual well-being they are, for a season, charged and
for which they are always answerable. That is all Kant meant
when he insisted, to liberal dismay, that the responsibility due
to children is logically indifferent to mother love and, for that

matter, to mother resentment. It sounds as if he thought children needn't be cared for, whereas his point was that they must be cared for whether you like them or not, and that caring for them is not automatically satisfied by liking them, nor indeed by anything less than helps them grow. This is what Rosemary knows, drawn at the end by the need of the child, too late, after she had already sacrificed it. For it is only from within a fantasy of possession that the child could (logically) have been *given*. The husband was in no position to give it; he could merely help arrange for Rosemary to confuse herself about whether she had in fact given herself to the Devil or only dreamed she had—as if that was the difference that mattered. A husband may fear, and need, his impotence; but only his wife can confirm it. Rosemary does not allow her husband to penetrate her dreams, allow him to be her devil, and give him his due. So children can go straight to the devil. (Some say the Devil may have already taken power over the world without our knowledge. He may have, but it is not beyond our knowledge. For the Devil deals in pacts and bargains, and we must call him up; God's medium is the covenant, or promise, and he calls us, and comes upon us, unbidden. He is no gentleman, and no gentleman's gentleman. Merely to speak of power and penetration avoids the issue, which is to know who it is one is prepared to satisfy.)

I have recorded my experience of the work of color in serious films as a de-psychologizing or un-theatricalizing of their subjects. My hypothesis is that, correctly understood, this would account for the feel of futurity in them (when, that is, the point is not the coloration of make-believe or the color symbolism of private fantasy). What is the connection?

Black and white was the natural medium of visual drama. This is painting's underlying legacy to photography: value contrast in painterly modeling is a means by which depicted gesture and posture takes on individual (as opposed to hieratic or symbolic) significance and in so doing becomes humanly dramatic. When this happens, theatricalism and realism are not, as we are now likely to suppose, opposed; rather, the acceptance of theatricalism is then a condition of our accepting a work as the depiction of human reality.[35] One impulse of photography, as immediate as its impulse to extend the visible, is to theatricalize its subjects. The photographer's command, "Watch the birdie!" is essentially a stage direction. One may object that the command is given not to achieve the unnaturalness of theater but precisely to give the impression of the natural, that is to say, the *candid;* and that the point of the direction is nothing more than to distract the subject's eyes from fronting on the camera lens. But this misses the point, for the question is exactly why the impression of naturalness is conveyed by an essentially theatrical technique. And why, or when, the candid is missed if the subject turns his eye into the eye of the camera.

The inherent drama of black and white film further clarifies what it is about film that invited the outline clarity of types and justified those decades of melodramas, comedies, machines and scenes of exploration, motions of adventure and chase. In accepting these works as movies we accepted what they depicted as reality. Of course it *was* reality, but reality—whether of land or city—dramatized. I do not say that our acceptance of film created the acceptance of this reality. On the contrary, I suppose that the ease with which we accepted film reality came from our having already taken reality dramatically. The movie merely confirmed what the nineteenth century completed.

In my early adolescence, about 1940, I was told by a man whose responses I cared about that he did not like movies to be in color because that made them unrealistic. Already a philosopher, I denied what I felt to be the validity of his remark and refuted it by pointing out that the real world is not in black and white, explaining further that his idea was only the result of having grown accustomed to the look of black and white films; I went on to prophesy that all films would eventually be made in color. I now have an explanation of the truth of his idea, of my sense then of its truth. It is not merely that film colors were not accurate transcriptions of natural colors, nor that the stories shot in color were explicitly unrealistic. It was that film color masked the black and white axis of brilliance, and the drama of characters and contexts supported by it, along which our comprehensibility of personality and event were secured. Movies in color seemed unrealistic because they were undramatic.

When princes and kings were thrown from the stage, what happened was not that the theater emptied but that it came to encompass social intercourse as a whole; you could not tell the stage from the house. If religion, as it left heaven, became drama, then drama, as it left art, became politics; and politics, no longer confined to one realm, pervaded society and the self; it became religion. And since heaven was conquered, and Reason turned its attention to each social detail and personal relation, not just globally (as in Hegel's interpretation of the French Revolution), but intimately (exemplified by Bentham's oakum-picking of English law and by William Morris's projected design for every article of use and of decoration), no realm of mystery was to be left to men's necessities, or any arbitrariness to their decisions. ("Design" is a pretty concept for this stage of mind, straddling the ideas of enjoyment and total calculation.) But mysteries in practice scarcely vanished; they merely disappeared, shoved deeper into wastes of the mind and into more decorously veiled environments of cities, left to spread. If knowledge and practice were more and more united to produce the décors and *mises en scène* of cultures, they were as far as ever from meeting at the conditions of social life. But since these conditions were now theoretically subject to question, one's failure to change society presented itself as impotence. The need for theoretical explanation of social behavior accordingly became unlimited. Everything was changing, but nothing can be changed; so everything, including those facts, stands in need of interpretation. And because society, though revealed to Reason, remained cold and unyielding, and because the abyss between earth and heaven deepened as it narrowed (since there *is* no reason and no place for which the good city is to be postponed); and because God was reabsorbed and became an eye and a roar in the wings of the mind —our total explanation of our condition, to be convincing, had to be dramatic.

When, to Hegel's comment that historical events occur twice, Marx added the tag, "the first time as tragedy, the second time as farce," he was expressing both the genius that set him apart from his age and the genius that placed him inside it. The ideas of "class conflict" and "classlessness," while not necessarily theatrical, are inherently liable, or phenomenologically vulnerable, to theatrical employment. At the moment Marx was calling for the end of philosophy's interpretation of reality in favor of a start toward changing reality, theory and practice were already joined (in service of isolated opportunities for expansion or social experiment); and philosophy was already becoming the possession of men at large (as a more impenetrable set of justifications for one's deadly sins). When everyman becomes his own philosopher, he simultaneously becomes his own sophist. The sophist remains philosophy's most intimate enemy, only now he does not take his form within a separate profession, but pervades every profession of reason. So philosophy, and serious writing generally, no longer knows to whom to direct its voice, no longer quite believes that a message in a bottle will find its way to another shore. Then it stands on darkening straits, casting unsystematic lines, in hopes of attracting to the surface some darting wish for sense. I am without the authority to excuse myself either for, or from, that position.

Part of the meaning of "Victorian" is the insane and independent *energy* of reason; part of it is the moralization of morality—as if to justify, after faith in faith, faith in the appalling consequences of the reign of reason, e.g., in the calculated ruin of generations and continents. Society and the perception of society move past drama into melodrama. Movies begin as Victorian theater. Nietzsche's calling for an attainment beyond good and evil is a prophecy against this melodrama of progress. If Machiavelli first described the theatricalization of politics—the Prince and the paupers, the General and the general, the man and the woman, the black and the white, the young and the old, depending for their position, their very social existence, upon their externalized (Empson calls it pastoral) views of one another—then Marx first planned the recovery from this mortal slapstick: whatever the fate of "class consciousness" in a theory of revolution, its significance stands as a permanent goal of social epistemology, scarcely a very satisfactory department of knowledge as nations go. For its claims are that history alone has excavated what we recognize as social position, that our place in society has become unknown to us, that knowledge of the self is acquired only together with knowledge of the self's society, of its stand in society—as though what is "unconscious" in an adult is not merely his psychic past but his social present, equally painful and difficult to recognize—and that just as having a self requires taking a stand upon the self, so having a social place means assuming that place.

In this condition, self-consciousness, for the foreseeable future, will start, and mostly continue, as embarrassment. For the discovery of modern society, whether in Machiavelli, in Rousseau, or in Marx, is the discovery of modern individuality, whether as isolated, as homeless, or as dispossessed. But we are as capable of knowing our individuality, or accepting the individuality of another, as we are of becoming Christ for one another. If it makes sense to speak of the Greeks as having discovered the self, or of the eighteenth and nineteenth centuries as having discovered childhood, then we can say that our recent accomplishment has been the discovery of adolescence, the point at which one's life is to be chosen and one gives oneself a name, and that our task is to discover the existence of community. Revolution, which begins the nineteenth century, is society's self-dramatization; as romanticism, which continues it, is the self's self-dramatization. But then drama was still a form of acknowledgment.

When dramatic explanations cease to be our natural mode of understanding one another's behavior—whether because we tell ourselves that human behavior is inexplicable, or that only salvation (now political) will save us, or that the human personality must be sought more deeply than dramatic religions or sociologies or psychologies or histories or ideologies are prepared for—black and white ceases to be the mode in which our lives are convincingly portrayed. But since until yesterday dramatic modeling was the mode in which the human appeared, and its tensions and resolutions were those in terms of which our human understanding of humanity was completely satisfied, its surcease must seem to us the vanishing of the human as such. Painting and sculpture found ways to cede human portrayal in favor of the unappeasable human wish for presentness and beauty—by, for example, finding ways to make paintings without value contrast among their hues. But movies cannot cede human figuration or reference (though they can fragment it, or can animate something else). Movies in color cede our recently natural (dramatic) grasp of those figures, not by denying so much as by neutralizing our connection with the world so filmed. But since it is after all our world that is presented to us, and since those figures presented to us do after all resemble us, but since nevertheless they are no longer psychically present to us, we read them as de-psychologized, which, for us, means untheatricalized. And from there it is only logical to project them as inhabiting the future, a mutation away from the past we know (as we know it).

Because I evidently require such clouds of history in order to adumbrate my conviction about these topics, let me at least avoid the appearance of thinking I have established more than is here. I have described certain uses of color in film—as packaging, as unifying the worlds of make-believe and of fantasy, and as projecting a future. I have not claimed that these are all its uses. In the passage in *Contempt* during which Brigitte Bardot turns her bright body in bed as part of a questioning of her lover, she is flooded in changing centerfold or calendar hues. Godard perceives here not merely our taste for mild pornography, but that our tastes and convictions in love have become pornographized, which above all means publicized, externalized—letting society tell us what to love, and needing it to tell us whether we do. Nor have I said that futurity can be projected only through color. In Bergman's harsh black and white mysteries, the future began a long time ago; it is already old. The melodrama consists not in watching to see whether death will be victorious, but whether we will arrive to ourselves in time to remove its sting. Nor have I said that all directors must be involved in futurity. The greatest will probably resist it, for the future has replaced the past as the object of timely elegy.

An innovator will have his own manner of projecting the future. Antonioni gets it, beginning with *L'Avventura*, with his spacing of film time, in particular by his fermata over single shots, which enclose an air of *presentiment*. This is an autograph emotion of surrealist painting;[36] and one is reminded of iconographic or thematic features of Antonioni's films that show him to be the inheritor of surrealism from painting. There is his obsession with the façades of uninhabited, new buildings (the town development in *L'Avventura*, before the appearance of the crowd of brute-men, is a transcription of Chirico); they are not haunted, we know nothing is present inside them, they have no past. There is his juxtaposition of old and new (Rome in particular was always a natural setting for that experience) —sometimes directly, say, in the alignment of a cathedral with new structures; sometimes obliquely, as in a yacht or helicopter posed against a bare island. In his settings, he no longer requires an antique bust in the center of an abandoned plaza, since he makes his people, humanity as a whole, seem archaic —whether searching for old feeling by drifting through a vacant golf course as through a dream park, or trying to sustain new feeling, enclosed (in one of his best passages) in the romance of a night drive through rain, the abstracted windshield wipers and the mechanical intermittence of passing light on the wet windows measuring the anxiety and the abstraction of the inhabitants from their capacity to feel. Absence is obviously a root topic in Antonioni, as it was in surrealism. In both it is registered by the sheen or finish of the frames, which, along with the clean, deep lines of perspective, perfects the avoidance of human clutter or arbitrariness; nothing is behind this space. In the Monica Vitti trilogy, there is the absence of not merely feeling, but of so much as the effort to explain that absence. Male impotence is no longer a personal problem, an ego-alien castration anxiety, but merely a portion of the new human landscape. When love is altogether over, unable even to stir a fantasy of future redemption, then we have forgone the futurity of our future. In the final shot of *L'Avventura* the woman puts her hand on the man's shoulder not because she forgives his betrayal, or even his inability to offer tears and beg forgiveness, but because she accepts that there is nothing to forgive, to forgo, no new place to be won on the other side of this moment. There is no man different from any other, or she will seek none. Her faithfulness is to accept their juxtaposition in a world of uneventful adventure (one event is as adventurous or routine as another, one absence or presence as significant or unimportant as another, change as unthinkable as permanence, the many as the one) and to move into that world with him.

For Godard's characters (after *Breathless*) there is no longer any problem of ending or change. They *are* somewhere else, already in a future. Godard establishes this not by altering the psychology of his characters, nor through their responses to their own inability to respond, but by depersonalizing them from the start. The neutralization of drama by means of color, or the creation of worlds of make-believe or of fantasy, is not merely useless for his effort but antithetical to it. He has no vision of another world his people may inhabit, his people are without fantasy (hence pastless and futureless, hence present-less), and the sort of depersonalization he requires depends both upon our responding to these characters as persons and upon our continuously failing to read their motions within the stresses of ordinary human emotion and motivation. Some critics, I believe, take Godard to have established in some such way a cinematic equivalent to Brecht's call for a new theater, in which the actor forces and maintains a distance between himself and his role, and between stage and audience, thereby preventing a sentimental reabsorption of the intelligence art secretes. But while I do not deny in this idea the possibility of a major discovery for the movie, I do not find that on the whole Godard has achieved it in the films of his I have seen. For a film director does not begin with a medium in which actor and character have conventionally or momentarily coalesced, nor with a conventional or passing denial of the distance between the stage and a coherent audience. "Actor" and "audience" lack clear application to film. So one reads the distance from and between his characters as one does in reality, as the inability to feel; and we attribute our distance from the filmed events, because of their force upon us, to Godard's position toward them. And because the events of the films do not themselves justify or clarify his position, it remains arbitrary. That alone would deprive him of a Brechtian justification.

It is sometimes claimed that the demand for a "position" from an artist is an archaic demand, a holdover from a romantic or moralistic view of art. Why can't the artist *simply* provide us with pleasure or merely show us the ways things are? But Godard's works do not on the whole provide me with pleasure,

and they give a sense of the ways things are only from the position of one who cannot see his responsibility in those ways—
first of all his responsibility in approaching an audience on his
topics. Works that do provide me with pleasure or a knowledge
of the ways things are equally provide me with a sense of the
artist's position toward this revelation—a position, say, of complete conviction, of compassion, of delight or ironic amusement, of longing or scorn or rage or loss. The fact is, an artist,
because a human being, does have a position and does have his
reasons for calling his events to our attention. What entitles
him to our attention is precisely his responsibility to this condition. It used to be that apprenticeship and mastery in a discipline could take care of individual responsibility. But when an
art demands that its disciple call its existence into question and
then affirm it, his responsibility is also in question.

In art—as now in politics, as formerly in religion, as in personal relations—finding the right to speak the truth is as
difficult as finding the truth. One could say that the *right* to
speak, in these arenas, is gone. Where the silence of attention is
not maintained by force, it is gathered through personal standing. When three stand on the same ground, there is a community.

Evidently Godard's admirers read his withdrawal of feeling
as a combination of knowingness and objectivity toward the
corruption of the world. But objectivity is a spiritual achievement, and apart from it knowingness is only a sentiment. In
that case, accepting Godard's work is simply sharing that sentiment.

The Belmondo figure in *Breathless* has achieved objectivity
by winning his subjectivity: when he refuses the girl's rejection
of his love, saying "There is no unhappy love," his position has
the power to turn that apparently empirical claim into a definition of his world. His last words to her ("You are a coward")
are accordingly not an accusation but, backed by his achievement, an observation. After that, Godard seems to have re-

garded such achievement as impossible or unnecessary for his characters or for his art. Yet without it, his claims to serious criticism of the world are empty. If you believe that people speak slogans to one another, or that women are turned by bourgeois society into marketable objects, or that human pleasures are now figments and products of advertising accounts and that these are directions of dehumanization—then what is the value of pouring further slogans into that world (e.g., "People speak in slogans" or "Women have become objects" or "Bourgeois society is dehumanizing" or "Love is impossible")? And how do you distinguish the world's dehumanizing of its inhabitants from your depersonalizing of them? How do you know whether your asserted impossibility of love is anything more than an expression of your distaste for its tasks? Without such knowledge, your disapproval of the world's pleasures, such as they are, is not criticism (the negation of advertisement) but censoriousness (negative advertising).

I do not wish to deny Godard's inventiveness, and no one can ignore his facility. But the forms of culture he wishes to hold in contempt are no less inventive and facile. Take two examples of his inventiveness compromised. Godard has found a way to stage an eyes-on interview with his subjects (in particular, with Anna Karina). But he has not done this by justifying a subject's acceptance of the camera—that is, by establishing a character capable in a given context of accepting her own self-awareness, knowing the effect she has on others (as, say, in Manet's *Olympia*)—but by taking a subject with no character, from whose person he has removed personhood, a subject incapable of accepting or rejecting anything. That is the condition of prostitution, and of advertisement. And Godard has created it, not captured it. These interviews might be read as screen tests, which is a potentially neat declaration of the medium, but success here would depend upon justifying the woman's submission to such a test and one's right to apply it. In fact, the interviews seem to me to veer, in their effect, toward my experience of those real-life testimonials more and more frequent in television commercials whose subjects are anonymous in everything but name.

Or take Godard's use of the sound of philosophy, in those longish dialogues his women elicit from actual philosophers. It is a good perception that recognized this sound for the cinema, that found that in an environment of nonsense and insinuation and cynicism the sound of sense still falls sweetly upon the human ear. But Godard hasn't seen it through, because he does not care whether what the philosopher says is valid or not— that is, he listens to it the way his girls do, or the way a bourgeois audience does, somewhere within embarrassment, envy, contempt, and titillation. And while his talent and wit lead him to remark that philosophy is now stimulated by pretty girls, either he fails to recognize the humor and sadness of this, or else he sees nothing further. From Plato on, sexual attractiveness has been an open motive to philosophy, as if to acknowledge the intimacy and mutuality of one soul's investigation of another. And if sexuality is the dialogue's conclusion, this need not mean that its point was seduction; it can acknowledge that the only successful conclusion of such investigation is mutual satisfaction, and that what remains between the participants is not a thing left unsaid. Where philosophy is foreplay, that at least refuses intellectuality as a *substitute* for sexuality (a more hilarious sense of "platonic"). The love that philosophy can teach is the power to accept intimacy without taking it personally. Its opposite is vanity, which takes every attention personally and none intimately. (Naturally, these states are commonly mistaken for one another.) Godard's girls walk away intact from these confrontations. Is this supposed to show that they are unseducible? So are prostitutes. Anyway, they are seduced—by slogans, advertisements, and illicitness.

Philosophy ought either to be a nobler seduction, or else its acceptance of separateness ought to be acknowledged as its power, its capacity to forgo further proof of love. Godard avoids the choice, most distinctly in *La Chinoise,* where the color suggests make-believe and so provides the out that the whole thing is child's play. In the long train dialogue at the end, the philosopher speaks with genuine intelligence about issues close to socialist grownups of intelligence. But since we have been shown that the girl before him is an unloving and dangerous nitwit, we have to conclude either (1) that the man cannot tell this, or (2) that he doesn't care because he wants her and is willing to pay out intimacy and intelligence to get what he wants, tickling her fancy that she has a mind and is capable of serious action, or (3) that this is the fate of intelligence in the capitalist world, or the fate of old intelligence upon the new young, or (4) that men and women have lost all ear for the differences between words (and deeds) of love, lust, instruction, valor, meanness, hope, or play. That all this is common in our world (and if you like, commonly deserved) is not news, and to spread its commonness is not art. Some people once thought that women do not have souls. Some thought that a group of people has its own soul. We no longer say such things. But just whom, or what group, does each of us treat as though it had a soul?

14

Automatism

I have spoken of film as satisfying the wish for the magical reproduction of the world by enabling us to view it unseen. What we wish to see in this way is the world itself—that is to say, everything. Nothing less than that is what modern philosophy has told us (whether for Kant's reasons, or for Locke's, or Hume's) is metaphysically beyond our reach or (as Hegel or Marx or Kierkegaard or Nietzsche might rather put it) beyond our reach metaphysically.

To say that we wish to view the world itself is to say that we are wishing for the condition of viewing as such. That is our way of establishing our connection with the world: through viewing it, or having views of it. Our condition has become one in which our natural mode of perception is to view, feeling unseen. We do not so much look at the world as look *out at* it, from behind the self. It is our fantasies, now all but completely thwarted and out of hand, which are unseen and must be kept unseen. As if we could no longer hope that anyone might share them—at just the moment that they are pouring into the streets, less private than ever. So we are less than ever in a position to marry them to the world.

Viewing a movie makes this condition automatic, takes the responsibility for it out of our hands. Hence movies seem more natural than reality. Not because they are escapes into fantasy, but because they are reliefs from private fantasy and its responsibilities; from the fact that the world is *already* drawn by fantasy. And not because they are dreams, but because they permit the self to be wakened, so that we may stop withdrawing our longings further inside ourselves. Movies convince us of the world's reality in the only way we have to be convinced, without learning to bring the world closer to the heart's desire (which in practice now means learning to stop altering it illegitimately, against itself): by taking views of it.

I said also that what enables moving pictures to satisfy the wish to view the world is the automatism of photography. I have not claimed that film which is not used photographically, to reproduce the world, cannot be used for the purpose of art. I remark only that film which is not used photographically, in the sense intended, is not being used in its power of automatism. *Reproducing the world is the only thing film does automatically.* I do not say that art cannot be made without this power, merely that movies cannot so be made. Of course we may have to forgo this power; it may lose its power for us. That just means that the movie will have lost its power. For what has made the movie a candidate for art is its natural relation to its traditions of automatism. The lapse of conviction in its traditional uses of its automatism forces it into modernism; its potentiality for acknowledging that lapse in ways that will redeem its power makes modernism an option for it.

One might explain the movie's natural relation to its traditions of automatism by saying that a given movie can naturally tap the source of the movie medium as such. And the medium is profounder than any of its instances. This sounds like other ideas one comes across currently. But the idea of a medium of art is stifled if one does not recognize that this was always true, that the power of a given sonnet or rondo or portrait was its power to stand for the form it took and thence to invoke the power of poetry or music or painting as such. Modernism signifies not that the powers of the arts are exhausted, but on the contrary that it has become the immediate task of the artist to achieve in his art the muse of the art itself—to declare, from itself, the art as a whole for which it speaks, to become a present of that art. One might say that the task is no longer to produce another instance of an art but a new medium within it. (Here is the relevance of series in modern painting and sculpture, and of cycles in movies, and of the quest for a "sound" in jazz and rock.) It follows that in such a predicament, media are not given *a priori*. The failure to establish a medium is a new depth, an absoluteness, of artistic failure.

It is in thinking of the power of an art as such that I think again about a hesitation I have sometimes felt toward regarding the movie as an art at all, its effects being too powerful or immediate to count as the effects of art. It may be that this hesitation arises when one is out of touch with some object which drops us into the power of its established art. Or it may come from the feeling that movies achieve this power too easily. But if this is more than a grudge against fortune (how hard must an artist work? and for what?), what does it signify? In paying my respects to James Agee, I noted that in any film, however unpromising, some moment of interest, even beauty, is likely to appear. That is what the camera, left to itself, is like: the objects it manufactures have for us the same natural interest, or fascination, or boredom, or nothing, or poignance, or terror, as the world itself. This needn't mean that we are unable to tell the good from the bad. So the question recurs: If we treat the movie in any of its occurrences as art, then how can we explain that, throughout a period in the remaining arts in which artists folded themselves double and risked absolute failure in their devotions, movie-makers were able to tap the source of their art so innocently? Which is to ask again how the movie for so long could have remained traditional. (For so long? For a mere sixty years? No, for *these* sixty years.)

I characterized the task of the modern artist as one of creating not a new instance of his art but a new medium in it. One might think of this as the task of establishing a new automatism. The use of the word seems to me right for both the broad genres or forms in which an art organizes itself (e.g., the fugue, the dance forms, blues) and those local events or *topoi* around which a genre precipitates itself (e.g., modulations, inversions, cadences). In calling such things automatisms, I do not mean that they automatically ensure artistic success or depth, but that in mastering a tradition one masters a range of automatisms upon which the tradition maintains itself, and in deploying them one's work is assured of a place in that tradition.

To pose the category of automatism accurately, I must go further into a region of modernist painting I have responded to and develop it there first. This will for the moment neutralize the presence of the physical mechanisms of camera and projector. These mechanisms produce the physical or material basis of the medium of film, which I am articulating as successions of automatic world projections. What gives significance to features of this physical basis are artistic discoveries of form and genre and type and technique, which I have begun calling automatisms.[37]

It may seem perverse of me, since I am intent upon keeping these levels of artistic fact separate, to use the concept of automatism—anyway, the term automatic—also in the description of film's physical basis. I do not take the perverseness here to be of my making. In part it has to do with the identity of the art of film itself—the fact that its medium just does have this manufacturing mechanism at its basis. In part it has to do with the fate of modernist art generally—that its awareness and responsibility for the physical basis of its art compel it at once to assert and deny the control of its art by that basis. This is also why, although I am trying to free the idea of a medium from its confinement in referring to the physical bases of various arts, I go on using the same word to name those bases as well as to characterize modes of achievement within the arts. Why not just stick to terms like "form," or, as Northrop Frye uses it, "genre"?[38] But confusion here is caused by precisely the fact that this concept is justified in both places. And it will not be dispelled by redefining or substituting some labels. It could also be said that modernist art is itself an investigation of this confusion, or of the complexities of this fact.

The complexities are at once historical and ontological. When in a philosophical frame of mind one says that the medium of an art is the physical basis of that art (e.g., that the medium of painting is paint, and the medium of writing is words, and the medium of music is sound), one may be either suppressing or assuming a knowledge of the history of forms in which these so-called media have been used to make objects of art; or one may be expressing a recognition that the established genres within the arts are "merely" "conventional," that they cannot be taken for granted any longer, that each of them places demands which constrict as well as release a subject. In Lessing's *Laocoön*, the search for the limits of individual arts takes place over an assumption that the different arts are different genres, as it were, of a total something called the Arts. But then, painting and poetry had something obvious in common: each narrated or pictured events. Lessing's point is that each must be faithful to its own way, dictated by the nature of its medium, of doing the common thing. What modernist painting proves is that we do not know *a priori* what painting has to do or be faithful to in order to remain painting. So there is no way, or ways, in which it does something differently from the way poetry does it. Its mode of existence is different. In insisting on its specific mode of existence, a modernist art seems to break down the concept of genre altogether: what a painter or poet or composer has to achieve in his painting or poetry or music is not a landscape or sonnet or fugue, but the idea of his art as such.

A description of the styles and genres of classical music would be a description of the media of classical music. In a modernist art, to which the concepts of style and genre lack clear application, the concept of a medium loses touch with ideas of manner and ordonnance, and seems to separate out for denotation the physical materials of the art as such. But what is the medium of painting or poetry or music as such? One of two responses seems forced upon us, and neither is an answer to the question. A first response will be: The medium of music as such is sound as such; the medium of painting is paint as such, etc. Such responses seem to mean that all sound is music, all areas of color are paintings. But this says nothing about the nature of music or painting; it is a claim about someone's—or humankind's—experience of the world, e.g., that nature, or a passage of time or space, is for certain creatures a medium of expression. (Something like this claim is what art itself, in romanticism, undertakes to maintain after religion has apparently abandoned the idea. To forgo art in favor of the natural, or contingent, is therefore not likely to be a favor either to nature or to art.) A second response will be: Nothing is *the* medium of, say, painting as such. A medium of painting is whatever way or ways paint is managed so as to create objects we accept as paintings. Only an art can define its media. A modernist art, investigating its own physical basis, searching out its own conditions of existence, rediscovers the fact that its existence as an art is not physically assured. It gracefully accepts our condemnation to meaning—that for separate creatures of sense and soul, for earthlings, meaning is a matter of expression; and that expressionlessness is not a reprieve from meaning, but a particular mode of it; and that the arrival of an understanding is a question of acknowledgment.

My impulse to speak of an artistic medium as an "automatism" is, I judge, due first to the sense that when such a medium is discovered, it generates new instances: not merely makes them possible, but calls for them, as if to attest that what has been discovered is indeed something more than a single work could convey. Second, the notion of automatism codes the experience of the work of art as "happening of itself." In a tradition, the great figure knows best how to activate its automatisms, and how best to entice the muse to do most of the work. In a modernist situation there is no such help: your work is all your own, there is no longer a natural relation between your work and its results, you are *looking* for what works (happens of itself). Only after the fact will the muse come to bless your work, or not. The automatisms of a tradition are given to the traditional artist, prior to any instance he adds to it; the master explores and extends them. The modernist artist has to explore the fact of automatism itself, as if investigating what it is at any time that has provided a given work of art with the power of its art as such. A third impulse in calling the creation of a medium the creation of an automatism is to register the sense that the point of this effort is to free me not merely from my confinement in automatisms that I can no longer acknowledge as mine (this was the point of the explicit efforts at automatic painting and writing early in the century), but to free the object from me, to give new ground for its *autonomy*.

15

Excursus: Some Modernist Painting

In a very useful and interesting monograph entitled *Dada, Surrealism and Their Heritage*, William Rubin relates the epochal paintings of Jackson Pollock to the idea of automatism: "What Pollock took from Surrealism was an idea—automatism—rather than a manner." [39] But what was the idea? The surrealists looked for automatisms which would create images; Pollock looked for an automatism with which to create paintings. The ideas are as different as the manners. Using automatism to create paintings is what painters have always done. In order that any new automatism he found might create paintings, he had newly to consider what constitutes a painting (*what* it was painters have always done, that is, made) and, in particular, to discover what would give any automatism of his the significance of painting.

The third feature I distinguished in the concept of automatism—its claim for the autonomy of the art object—indicates why it is inapt to think of Pollock's major work as "action painting." The "action" in question was a discovery of Pollock's that precisely *evaded* the traditional actions of painters, which he had found no longer made paintings, and it would have absolutely no artistic relevance unless it produced entities we accepted as paintings. (Calling a Pollock an action painting for the reason that the painter moved in new ways in painting it is about as useful as calling a treaty a piece of paper for the reason that it is written on paper. Though its being written on paper is certainly a significant fact about it.)

Then what was his discovery? The all-over line? What makes that a discovery, or an automatism? Its being a way of laying on paint quickly, with repeated gestures? But repetitive gestures and the search for quickness in application are in themselves not news. And again, it would have been no discovery at all had not *his* all-over line (applied *that* way, by trailing, in black and white, on that format, with that reticence of [other] color . . .) been accepted as painting. The question ought therefore to be: Since it makes paintings, what does his all-over line discover?

One fact of painting it discovered is as primitive as any: not exactly that a painting is flat, but that its flatness, together with its being of a limited extent, means that it is *totally there*, wholly open to you, absolutely in front of your senses, of your eyes, as no other form of art is. Total thereness is not what aestheticians used to mean, whatever they meant, by calling half of the arts spatial, distinguishing them from those which are temporal; for total thereness can be taken as a denial of (physical) spatiality, of what three-dimensional creatures who normally walk or sit or turn mean by spatiality. What is in three-dimensional space is not *all* there to the eyes, in the sense revealed.

What does it mean to say that a painter discovers, by painting, something true of all paintings, something that everybody has always known is true of paintings generally? Is it a case of something hidden in unconsciousness becoming conscious? It is like something hidden in consciousness declaring itself. The mode is revelation. I follow Michael Fried in speaking of this fact of modernist painting as an *acknowledging* of its conditions. Any painting might teach you what is true of all painting. A modernist painting teaches you this *by* acknowledgment—which means that responding to it must itself have the form of accepting it as a painting, or rejecting it. In ordinary cases of acknowledging something, I can acknowledge only what I know to be true of *me*, whereas this painting is supposed to be speaking for all painting, painting as such. Yes; that is where the art comes in. And there have always been some men who have been able to acknowledge something that other men accept as true also of them, or that they have to deny.

Painting, being art, is revelation; it is revelation because it is acknowledgment; being acknowledgment, it is knowledge, of itself and of its world. Modernism did not invent this situation; it merely lives upon nothing else. In reasserting that acknowledgment is the home of knowledge, it recalls what the remainder of culture is at pains to forget. To speak now of modernism as the activity of an avant-garde is as empty as it is in thinking about modern politics or war, and as comforting: it implies a conflict between a coherent culture and a declared and massed enemy; when in fact the case is more like an effort, along blocked paths and hysterical turnings, to hang on to a thread that leads from a lost center to a world lost.[40]

There may be any number of ways of acknowledging the condition of painting as total thereness—which is perhaps to say that there are any number of ways in which that condition can present itself, many different significances it may develop. For example, a painting may acknowledge its frontedness, or its finitude, or its specific thereness—that is, its presentness; and your accepting it will accordingly mean acknowledging *your* frontedness, or directionality, or verticality toward its world, or any world—or your presentness, in its aspect of absolute hereness and of nowness. Or a painting may declare that a painting, like nature, is of more than one color, and that its colors occur simultaneously. That would not be a simultaneity of events but of the reaches of a world.

Various of these "possibilities" of painting, these historical unfoldings, seem to me declared in the post-Pollock paintings I have responded to—especially those of Morris Louis, Kenneth Noland, Jules Olitski, Frank Stella. The quality or condition I wish to emphasize here comes out of my speaking of total thereness as an event of the wholly open, and of the declaration of simultaneity. The quality I have in mind might be expressed as openness achieved through instantaneousness—which is a way of characterizing the *candid.* The candid has a reverse feature as well: that it must occur independently of me or any audience, that it must be complete without me, in that sense *closed* to me. This is why candidness in acting was achieved by the actor's complete concentration within the character, absolutely denying any control of my awareness upon him. When theatrical conventions lost their naturalness and became matters of mutual complicity between actor and audience, then serious drama had to deny my control openly—by removing, say, any "character" for the actor to disappear into (Beckett), or by explicitly wedging the mutual consciousness of actor and audience between the actor and his character (Brecht).

This openness and closedness do not describe particular forms within paintings, but conditions of painting as a form of art. Their declaration seems to me most palpable in the work of Louis—because one has, especially in the Unfurled series, the frankness that leaves individual colors not merely separate but separated; and also because one sees how little may be required in order to make the object complete, to close it. Not that the *amount* of work is the issue—for we no longer need to be told that great masters can afford to finish a work without giving it a finish. Rather, these paintings acknowledge that no matter how much work goes into the making of a work, at some point the work must be *done,* given over, the object declared separate from its maker, autonomous; that he has seen it, that it is good. ("Finish" becomes a way of avoiding that renunciation and judgment.) That is, they acknowledge not merely what paintings are, but what the painting of them is. In altering the traditional actions by which paintings were painted, and nevertheless yielding paintings, these artists acknowledge two primitive features of paintings: first, the responsibility for making them is more significant than the manner in which they are made—in particular, they can (may even have to) be made without *painting* (opaquing an expanse by working paint all over it); second, the painting of them must get over and done with, come to a form, be brought into the open and to a close.

The failure to close with a work, win or lose, is the point of Kierkegaard's criticism of certain writers as "premise-authors," helpless to draw conclusions. Not that conclusions should always be drawn like morals, but writing requires the moral stamina to conclude, to achieve resolution, in the self and of the self's work. I was led to speak near the beginning of this essay of perfectly abstract painting as achieving a condition of photographs by their use of (the "possibility" of) cropping, which I characterized as "predetermining the amount after the fact." If one thinks of this in the context of traditional painting, cropping seems a superficial feature of the making of a painting, something distinctly after the fact, like mounting it or choosing a frame. But the nature of these new paintings gives significance to the fact of framing; they create a way of acknowledging finality as a specific spiritual step. With these paintings, the exactness of the cropping is essential to the *entire* achievement.

Again, the recession of manner (in the face, as it were, of the presentness of the painting itself) suggests why the concept of style has no clear application to these modernist works.[41] It is not merely that these artists' hands are clean, but that the "manner in which they paint" refers merely to the *technical* procedures they use, and there is no established connection between those procedures and the responses they yield. Nothing comes between the idea and its realization (between intuition and its expression, as Croce puts it—and, as Clement Greenberg found, what he says is patently correct for these artists).[42]

The singular candidness in Louis's Unfurleds has to do with the vast expanse of canvas he has, in candor, left white; not with the sheer fact that it is blank but with the effect upon that blankness of the side falls of colors, which bring the vastness to uncanny incandescence. In achieving these works without the trace of hands or wrists or arms, without muscle—the idea realizing itself—an automatism of canvas and paint (by means of those echoed rills, spanning those corners, in that scale . . .) is set in motion, admitting an overpowering beauty. I do not wish to exaggerate: only *Sigma* strikes me as of overpowering beauty among the Unfurleds I have seen, though all are beautiful. One automatism may not be so deep or fertile as another, the vein may give out or not be worth working, and sometimes a transition from one automatism to another is in its way a larger moment than a transition from one to another instance of a single automatism. (I think here of Louis's *High*, in which the veils are parted, as if toward the lower corners, but from which the force of the Veils series is removed and the force of the Unfurleds cannot be predicted.) But to speak of an automatism which admits a sometimes overpowering beauty is a way of characterizing nature.

The works of Pollock, Louis, Noland, and Olitski achieve in unforeseen paths an old wish of romanticism—to imitate not the *look* of nature, but its conditions, the possibilities of knowing nature at all and of locating ourselves in a world. For an old romanticist, these conditions would have presented themselves as nature's power of destruction or healing, or its fertility. For the work of the modernists I have in mind, the conditions present themselves as nature's autonomy, self-sufficiency, laws unto themselves. ("Not *how* the world is, but *that* it is, is the Mystical." [43])

This is not a return *to* nature but the return *of* it, as of the repressed. It is the release of nature from our private holds. No doubt such art will not repeal the enclosure acts, but it seeks to annul our spiritual-biological-political accommodations and attachments to enclosure. It reasserts that however we may choose to parcel or not to parcel nature among ourselves, nature is held—we are held by it—only in common. Its declaration of my absence and of nature's survival of me puts me in mind of origins, and shows me that I am astray. It faces me, draws my limits, and discovers my scale; it fronts me, with whatever wall at my back, and gives me horizon and gravity. It reasserts that, in whatever locale I find myself, I am to locate myself. It speaks of terror, but suggests elation—for the shaking of sentiment never got us home, nor the shiver of the picturesque. The faith of this romanticism, overcoming the old, is that we can still be moved to move, that we are free, if we will, to step upon our transport, that nature's absence—or its presence merely to sentiment or mood—is only the history of our turnings from it, in distraction or denial, through history or industry, with words or works. Hegel rose without arising, harped upon movement without readying us to take steps; that is why Marx and Kierkegaard, with opposite hopes, turned him over.

It is not as though we any longer trust or ought so fondly to trust our representations that the absence of them must mean to us the absence of the things represented. Art in the absence of representation could then declare that those earlier approaches to nature had indeed been the making of representations—not merely *of* the world, but *to* it, as appeals or protests. Why should there be fewer causes of painting the world than there are reasons for wording it: to appeal, protest, state, claim, assert, judge, comment, notice, witness, accuse, praise, interrogate, pledge, remember, behold . . . ? But at some point in the last century, such appeals and protests were found to be made on behalf of nobody, to nothing. At such a juncture, art, if it is to survive, ends.

It is a sad use of a few philosophical terms which discovers that pictures were never really objective on the ground that they were never perfect replicas of reality. But every semester somebody seems to make this discovery. It is as sensible to say that nature can never really be represented because paintings (or photographs) never fully resemble it, as to say that people can never be represented because their representatives are other people. In both cases faithfulness is required, and objectivity: then the questions are what you are being faithful to, or failing to be faithful to; and on behalf of whom, and to what it is, you appeal and protest; and why and when an objective representation, a likeness, fails to capture your interest in an object or an issue. Perhaps what we must be faithful to is our knowledge that distance from nature is no longer represented by perspective, which places us in relation to it, places nature before or away from us, and falsifies our knowledge that we are lost to nature, are absent from it, cannot face it. Then, upon such unpromising ground, an art that reveals without representation may give us perspective. For example, it may show us that a painting must be viewed alone, from the one place one occupies at any time—an acknowledgment not directly that one must view things for oneself, but that one must take them one at a time.

This is the meaning of the new fact of series, or the fact that a new medium establishes and is established by a series. Each instance of the medium is an absolute realization of it; each totally eclipses the others. For all our claims of "inevitability" in the working out of old masterpieces, we know that, say, a given fugue might have worked out differently, not merely in the sense that other fugues might have been written on the subject, but that *this* one might be more or less otherwise than it is, that there might be alternate versions. Then to call one version "inevitable" would be to praise it. But with a Pollock all-over line painting, or a Louis stripe, or a Noland chevron, or a Stella Zform, *any* change (of an angle, a shift of color or a color's width, or its distance from another color) would simply create a new instance, an absolutely new painting. If one speaks of a given instance as inevitable, that is no longer a term of praise, but a statement of its existence. These are works every one of whose properties is essential to them. This is the definition of a Leibnizian monad. Like a monad, like the world there is, the only fact about these paintings that does not follow analytically from a complete idea of them is that they exist in space and time. Existence in this world, like the existence of the world itself, is the only contingent fact about them. They are themselves, I feel like saying, contingencies, realizations.

Nothing but our acceptance of an instance determines whether its series is worth realizing, or how far it is worth going on generating its instances; when we find that a series is exhausted, it is absolutely past, over. As instances, they declare the evanescence of existence in space and time. (Literal or material objects do not declare evanescence, however transitory they or their arrangement may be. Metaphysically a pyramid is as evanescent as wrappings are, or as a flash of neon.) I think it is sometimes felt, by those angered or suspicious of such paintings, that no object the actual making of which is so unimportant could conceivably bear the major importance we have attached to works of art. It is true that their existence as instances is carried on their face; labor is not in them; they look as if they might as well have been made instantaneously, and that their use should take no longer. But the fact about an instance, when it happens, is that it poses a permanent beauty, if we are capable of it. That *this* simultaneity should proffer beauty is a declaration about beauty: that it is no more temporary than the world is; that there is no physical assurance of its permanence; that it is momentary only the way time is, a regime of moments; and that no moment is to dictate its significance to us, if we are to claim autonomy, to become free.

Acceptance of such objects achieves the absolute acceptance

of the moment, by defeating the sway of the momentous. It is an ambition worthy of the highest art. Nothing is of greater moment than the knowledge that the choice of one moment excludes another, that no moment makes up for another, that the significance of one moment is the cost of what it forgoes. That is refinement. Beauty and significance, except in youth, are born of loss. But otherwise everything is lost. The last knowledge will be to allow even that knowledge of loss to vanish, to see whether the world regains. The idea of infinite possibility is the pain, and the balm, of adolescence. The only return on becoming adult, the only justice in forgoing that world of possibility, is the reception of actuality—the pain and balm in the truth of the only world: that it exists, and I in it.

In its absolute difference and absolute connection with others, each instance of a series maintains the haecceity (the sheer that-ness) of a material object, without the need of its substance. Perhaps this quality is something minimal art wants to convey. But modernist paintings acknowledge it, so that I must respond to it, if I am to know it, by acknowledging my own haecceity, that my existence is inescapable from my presentness. In response to minimal art I am deployed, dematerialized, unidentifiable; the moment is not grounded, but etherealized; the momentous is not defeated, but landscaped. In response to modernist painting, I am concentrated, finitized, incarnate.

Because these abstractions retain the power of art, after the failure of representations to depict our conviction and connectedness with the world, they have overcome the representativeness which came between our reality and our art; overcame it by abstraction, abstracting us from the recognitions and engagements and complicities and privileged appeals and protests which distracted us from one another and from the world we have constructed. Attracted from distraction by abstraction. Not catching our attention yet again, but forming it again. Giving us again the capacity for appeal and for protest, for contemplation and for knowledge and praise, by drawing us back from private and empty assertion. These works exist as abstracts of intimacy—declaring our common capacity and need for presentness, for clear separateness and singleness and connection, for horizons and uprightness and frontedness, for the simultaneity of a world, for openness and resolution. They represent existence without assertion; authority without authorization; truth without claim, which you can walk in. It is out of such a vision that Thoreau in *Walden* ("The Pond in Winter") speaks of nature as silent.

Is the power of representation otherwise irretrievable? Is there no way to declare again the content of nature, not merely its conditions; to speak again from one's plight into the heart of a known community of which one is a known member, not merely speak of the terms on which any human existence is given? "Who knows what the human body would expand and flow out to under a more genial heaven?" "Who knows what sort of life would result if we had attained to purity?" [44]

16

Exhibition and Self-Reference

Movies from their beginning avoided (I do not say answered) modernism's perplexities of consciousness, its absolute condemnation to seriousness. Media based upon successions of automatic world projections do not, for example, have to establish presentness to and of the world: the world is there. They do not have to deny or confront their audiences: they are screened. And they do not have to defeat or declare the artist's presence: the object was always out of his hands.

Setting pictures to motion mechanically overcame what I

earlier called the inherent theatricality of the (still) photograph. The development of fast film allowed the subjects of photographs to be caught unawares, beyond our or their control. But they are nevertheless *caught;* the camera holds the last lanyard of control we would forgo. Freed from the painter's formalisms of composition, photography rebounds to the draftsman's formalisms of caricature. Artistry here must come to terms with this condition, exploit this new assertion of theatrical depth, explore the condition of capture itself—in order to discover what will register as candor and what instantaneousness can reveal of character and of the relation of character to its locale.

Why and when do we take an eyes-on pose to signify candor? In photographs of animals it tends to deprive them of their innerness, to anthropomorphize them. Is that because we project upon them a human capacity for recognizing the camera, a human prospect of self-consciousness? It also seems to me that photographs tend to anthropomorphize nature itself. Those primitives are not wrong to be terrorized upon seeing photographs of themselves. We are told that they fear their souls have been captured—and we laugh, pleased with that respect for our power. But it may be that they see their bodies being given a foreign animation. Is that wrong? —We are too used to what happens to us.

In motion, the photographic subject is released again. Or the viewer is released, in the face of a presenting of the past, from the links of nostalgia. But then another region of theatricality overtakes the image: the presenting of the past world becomes a presentation of it. Instead of being caught in a pose, the subject is cast in a type. The maker of films has then to find media within which types can project the world's presentness.

Film takes our very distance and powerlessness over the world as the condition of the world's natural appearance. It promises the exhibition of the world in itself. This is its promise of candor: that what it reveals is entirely what is revealed to it, that nothing revealed by the world in its presence is lost.

Am I saying that everything revealed by film is true? Then why, say, does Steichen take a thousand various pictures of the same cup and saucer? Perhaps he will not assume that we know beforehand how few or many revelations the truth will take, or how any may be made. Call truth infinite; certainly there is no reason to suppose the number of facts to be limited, and all are compatible (compossible). It is also a fact that the world has to be told not to dictate what we are to say about it, or when we have something to say, or from what angle and in what light and for how long. Descartes finds the possibility of error in the will's freedom to overreach our position; freedom is the price, and sets the task, of knowledge. A few years later, Milton found the possibility of error to be the price, and to set the task, of freedom. By the end of the next century, Kant's problem was not to check the will within God's ordinance, but to keep nature from swamping it. Hegel wished to ride it on the back of history. Romantics still shift between paralysis and omnipotence.

The paintings and sculpture I was citing seek to refuse knowledge that is not a mode of acknowledgment. Their achievement of certainty (through the candor of their total presentness, leaving no room for will), together with silence (through the naturalness of their beauty, leaving no need for will), works out an environment in which conscience is stirred. Someone who senses himself rebuked by modernism's custody of seriousness may say, as if expressing a new freedom of the arts, that now *anything* can be exhibited and so tried as art. But that is just the problem, that perhaps *all* you can do with your work and works is to exhibit them, that all hope for acknowledgment by and of the self is to be forgone, and all authority in one's intention, all belief in one's beliefs—stares of amusement or boredom replacing all acceptance and real rejection. People who claim to like this condition will be amused by the plight of the Hunger Artist or at any rate will feel that he rather exaggerates it.

Like religion, art had to learn to defeat theater, to close the remove of our vision from its object, to stand the self within the self again so that it may bear again the world's gaze.[45] If modernism's quest for presentness arises with the growing autonomy of art (from religious and political and class service; from altars and halls and walls), then that quest is set by the increasing nakedness of exhibition as the condition for viewing a work of art. The object itself must account for the viewer's presenting of himself to it and for the artist's authorization of his right to such attendance.

At such a point, someone may ask why I groan over the obvious. What more explanation need there be, in accounting for the caring for art, than that art provides pleasure and entertainment and amusement and recreation? I can share such impatience, and I do not wish to quarrel with it. But I groan the more. Not just because such an explanation further attenuates art, but because it further denatures pleasure and entertainment and amusement and recreation. For in the meanness of the beliefs we hold and in our disgust with the work we do, how can we imagine that our capacities during after-hours have remained intact, that we needn't question what pleases and amuses and entertains us? Or ask why it is that nothing really does. Or whether it is nice for aestheticians to speak of the re-creation of art as if that meant that we are to do the artist's work again (instead of allowing the work to reveal *our* need of remaking). It was Nietzsche's highest compliment, costing him most, to say of Luther that he had the courage of his sensuality. It was the courage to marry his desire; to plight *his* troth, prepared, if need be, to conquer the ceremony of heaven. And there is need. To boast now of one's capacity for pleasure bespeaks a greater sanctimony, a more grating irony, than ever trapped the glummest seriousness. The boast of pleasure is the modern hypocrisy.

Dada burlesques the condition of high art, as the lows of culture generally do. (Of course, of course: the highs often need decanting, and the lows are often deeper and more joyful.) It mimics the condition in which the fact of exhibition takes precedence over the quality and meaning of the thing exhibited. Vaudeville, in both its pornography and its clowning, makes that condition laughable.

Movies from their beginning avoided the shadowing of seriousness by exhibition, because they are simply not exhibited (or performed), but distributed and screened and viewed. One print of a movie is as full and authentic an instance of it as any other, so long as it is fair and complete. It is not a substitute for an original, but its manifestation. Photographs can have not merely many prints, but, one could say, many originals: they would be the ones accepted by the photographer as realizations of his picture. Each print of a photograph vies with every other for that acceptance. Unlike the case of photographs, the craft of its maker does not extend through to each instance; when his work is done, he releases it to multiply itself. It is everything a commodity should be: equal instances available to all, regardless of position.

We are told that people seeing the first moving pictures were amazed to see the motion in motion, as if by the novelty. But what movies did at first they can do at last: spare our attention wholly for *that* thing *now,* in the frame of nature, the world moving in the branch. In principle, anyone and everyone could be seeing it now. It is not novelty that has worn off, but our interest in our own experience. Who can blame us for that? Our experience is so coarsened that we can be moved by it only through novelty, and that has lost interest.

It is because movies can still work their original fortune that most good movies are still largely traditional [46]—but not all good movies, and the traditions are borne uneasily. Our sudden storms of flash insets and freeze frames and slow-motions and telescopic-lens shots and fast cuts and negative printing and blurred focusings—unlike the use of such experiments in the early period of film—are responses to an altered sense of film, a sense that film has brought itself into question and must be questioned and openly confessed.

How, specifically, are movies questioning themselves, and what specifically requires acknowledgment in their making? The habitual answer I hear to these questions begins with an idea that the way for a work to acknowledge itself is to refer to itself. Underlying this idea is an indefinite, more or less unexamined notion that modern art is "about" itself, painting about painting, music about music, the novel about the novel. . . . Stranded upon such a notion, you couldn't tell the difference between Mallarmé and Joyce Kilmer. The idea of self-reference recognizes that the artist's self-consciousness has come between his conviction and his work, between himself and the conventions (automatisms) he relied upon, forcing him to justify his works even as he performs them. This is the Protestant malady, and legacy. And it means only that the modernist artist is first of all a modern man: his art is his way of questioning his humanity without forfeiting it—to taste, to appetite, to irony, to boredom, to incitement, to halfhearted skepticism, to halfhearted belief, to scorn of an unknown past, to the mercy of an unchecked future.

My harping on acknowledgment is meant to net what is valid in the notion of self-reference and in the facts of self-consciousness in modern art. The explicit form of an acknowledgment is "I know I [promised; am withdrawn; let you down] . . ." But that is not the only form it can take; and it is not clear why this form functions as it does. We should not assume that the point of the personal pronoun here is to *refer* to the self, for an acknowledgment is an act of the self (if it is one of recognition, then it is not like recognizing a place but like recognizing a government); and it is not done apart from an admission of the existence of others (denial of which made the acknowledgment necessary) or apart from an expression of

124 THE WORLD VIEWED

one's aliveness to that denial (the revelation in acknowledgment). Without developing the philosophy this calls for, it is plain enough that self-reference is no more an assurance of candor in movies than in any other human undertaking. It is merely a stronger and more dangerous claim, a further opportunity for the exhibiting of self.

The specific emptiness of the notion here is its forgetfulness of the film's early capacities for self-reference, both by alluding to other movies and by calling attention to the camera at hand. I think of the moment Groucho Marx came across a snow sled with the name "Rosebud" stenciled across it and remarked to no one in particular, "I thought they burned that"; of an opening shot of Katharine Hepburn in *The Philadelphia Story* walking abstractedly through a room, cradling a sheaf of long-stemmed flowers, saying aloud to no one in particular, "The calla lilies are in bloom again" (see *Stage Door*); of Cary Grant's response, upon being introduced to Ralph Bellamy in *His Girl Friday*, "Haven't we met someplace before?" (they had, in the same juxtaposition of roles, a couple of years earlier in *The Awful Truth*). No doubt these lines were improvisatory; in any case, their sharp pleasure is of the inside joke, and, in addition to that pleasure, they confirm for the insiders a strong sophistication in moviegoing, a proof that their increasing consciousness of movie-making routines will not jeopardize the film's strength for us. So the allusions to Hollywood films in the films of French New Wave directors are not simple acts of piety toward a tradition they admire, but claims to be a continuation of that tradition.

Instead of confirming our conviction, by a gesture of self-awareness whose self-confidence inspires conviction, the gesture may attempt to distract us from our lack of conviction: instead of laughing at himself with a well-deserved appreciation of self, an author (of a work or act) may wish to steal our laughter in order to cover his embarrassment. An instance of this is the moment in *Tom Jones* at which Albert Finney, having rescued the half-naked widow from the bully, uses his cloak to cover the camera instead of shielding her from its gaze. It might have been a good gag, if the film had established Finney's character as one innocently capable of that confusion of courtesy (leaving the woman as naked as ever, merely out of *our* sight). As it stands, Finney's reflex is to shield himself. Since Tom Jones's natural confusions of nature and convention never lead him to protect himself at the cost of another, or to confuse his comfort with another's, we read the act not as Tom's sparing the widow, and us, embarrassment, but as Finney's or Richardson's (whichever thought of this piece of business) cloaking his own. (It's an old conspiracy being called upon. Groucho gets it when he looks into the audience and asks something like, "How did I ever wind up in this lousy picture?")

A striking feature of these self-referential instances is that their effect is comic. This feature is confirmed in three extendedly reflexive movies which come to mind: Fields's *Never Give a Sucker an Even Break*; Olsen and Johnson's *Hellzapoppin'*; and Keaton's *Sherlock Jr.* At some point in the back-and-forth between Fields's reading of his script to Franklin Pangborn and the projected visualizations of it, it dawns on us that what Fields has in his hands is the whole film we are seeing, including his readings and Pangborn's heavenly exasperations. I recall from *Hellzapoppin'* a moment in which either Olsen or Johnson, finding himself caught, as it were, by an off-sprocket film alignment (the frame separation dividing the top and bottom halves of the screen), hoists himself over the frame separation to rest wholly within the upper half of the screen. The virtuoso passage in which Keaton dreams of himself as the great sleuth repeatedly undone by shifting scene placements is more sublime in execution and effect than is knowable without its experience; it is as if every lie ever told by a photographer's

backdrop or prop—from painted hills and waterfalls and foun-
tains in formal gardens, to the comic-strip cut-outs into which
the subjects insert their heads—had suddenly come to life.

In these instances, the comedy arises first from a transgres-
sion of mechanical or conventional conditions upon which coherent narration in film has depended. Beyond that, reversing
the old idea that laughter is a burst of danger miraculously escaped, *Sherlock Jr.* and *Hellzapoppin'* project dangers which
the new art miraculously creates. More specifically, Keaton
uses the fact that in film anything can follow anything, and any
place any other place, to depict our lack of control over both
fantasy and reality—above all, our helplessness to align them.
Never Give a Sucker shows that there is nothing beyond the
power of film to make us accept: man's adaptability, his suck-
erhood, is his greatest trick and his greatest threat. We are at
the mercy of what the medium captures of us, and of what it
chooses, or refuses, to hold for us. This comedy of self-reference satirizes the effort to escape the self by viewing it, the
thought that there is a position from which to rest assured once
and for all of the truth of your views.

17

The Camera's Implication

One can feel that there is always a camera left out of the picture: the one working now. When my limitation to myself feels
like a limitation of myself, it seems that I am always leaving
something unsaid; as it were, the saying is left out. My problem
seems to be that human existence is metaphysically dishonest.

(Maybe this is how Berkeley's metaphysics was intended to keep the world honest, taking it that you cannot imagine a situation without imagining yourself present in it.) It seems that there should be some stronger connection between an assertion and the world it asserts than *my* asserting of it is empowered to make. (Of course, I can precede anything I assert with the formula "I assert . . ."; but that is just a shift on the same plane of assertion.) One almost imagines that one could catch the connection in the act, by turning the camera on it—perhaps by including a camera and crew in the picture (presumably at work upon *this* picture), but that just changes the subject. The camera can of course take a picture of itself, say in a mirror; but that gets it no further into itself than I get into my subjectivity by saying "I'm speaking these words now." I want words to happen to me; my saying of them makes their meaning private.

The camera is outside its subject as I am outside my language. The abyss of ready insincerity is fixed, but that is what makes truthfulness possible— and virtuous. Wittgenstein is known for his emphases upon the publicness of language. But his emphasis falls equally upon the absoluteness of my responsibility for the meaning I attach to my words. Publicness is a shared responsibility; if what we share is superficial, that is also our responsibility.

Such problems perhaps arise most explicitly in documentary films, but the distinction between documenting and narrating blurs here as elsewhere. The documentary film-maker naturally feels the impulse to make his presence known to his audience, as if to justify his intrusion upon his subject. But this is a guilty impulse, produced, it may be, by the film-maker's denial of the only thing that really matters: that the subject be allowed to reveal itself. The denial may be in spirit or in fact, an unwillingness to see what is revealed or an inability to wait for its revelation. But the only justification for the knowledge of others is the willingness for complete knowledge. That is the justice of knowledge. Your position in this is no more localizable before-hand than the knowledge itself is.

If the presence of the camera is to be made known, it has to be acknowledged in the work it does. This is the seriousness of all the shakings and turnings and zoomings and reinings and unkind cuts to which it has lately been impelled. But then why isn't the projected image itself a sufficient acknowledgment? Surely we are not in doubt that it comes by way of a camera. But what is this certainty, this not being in doubt?

Knowing your claim to an acknowledgment from me, I may be baffled by the demand you make for some special voicing of the acknowledgment. Any word of mine should amply make my presence known to you. The experience is not uncommon: I know I am here; you know I am here; you know that I know I owe you the acknowledgment. Why isn't that enough? Why am I called upon to *do* something, to say specific things that will add up to an explicit revelation? [47] Because what is to be acknowledged is always something specifically done or not done; the exact instance of my denial of you. The particular hurt or crudity or selfishness or needfulness or hatred or long-ing that separates us must be given leave to declare our sepa-rateness, hence the possibility of our connection. It is balm, but it must still touch the wound.

What is it the movie's turn to acknowledge? The notion of self-reference suggests that the need is for the camera to tip its hand. That is sensible enough—if the camera must acknowl-edge itself, at least it oughtn't to hide—and more than sensible, indeed, for it recognizes the hard Berkeleyan-Kantian truth that an event in which we participate is not knowable apart from our knowledge of our participation in it. Yet it neglects the Hegelian truth that the actual consciousness of our partici-pation is not assured *a priori*, but can be won only through the paths over which we have arrived at this event, and at this spe-cific placement toward it. The camera cannot in general merely declare itself; it must give at least the illusion of saying something. (Analytical philosophers will recognize an analogous problem. You cannot in general merely say something; there will be a reason for saying just that just then, and saying it implies the reason. You can have the illusion that there is no reason and no implication.)

The long, slow swings Godard maintains for the conversation piece in *Contempt* are clearly enough an original and deep statement of the camera's presence. But by that fact they are also a statement from the camera about its subjects, about their simultaneous distance and connection, about the sweeping desert of weary familiarity. It is sometimes said, and it is natural to suppose, that the camera is an extension of the eye. Then it ought to follow that if you place the camera at the physical point of view of a character, it will objectively reveal what the character is viewing. But the fact is, if we have been given the idea that the camera is placed so that what we see is what the character sees *as he sees it,* then what is shown to us is not just something seen but a specific *mood* in which it is seen. In *Paths of Glory*, we watch Kirk Douglas walking through the trenches lined with the men under his command, whom he, under orders, is about to order into what he knows is a doomed attack. When the camera then moves to a place behind his eyes, we do not gain but forgo an objective view of what he sees; we are given a vision constricted by his mood of numb and helpless rage.[48] (It may be worth calling this view objective, if you know that you have in mind not some unassessed contrast with subjectivity, but a mood in which reality becomes reified for you, a mood of nothing but eyes, dissociated from feeling.) The moral is not merely that the camera will have its assertion, but that a narrator cannot cede his position to his protagonist, and, more specifically, that the protagonist's point of view is not the same as the placement and angle of the camera which records it.

Mere declaration of your presence is specifically called for in cases of physical concealment or of emotional withdrawal; there your acknowledgment is a revelation of your mere presence, however attenuated. Is that the state the camera now finds itself in—concealed, or withdrawn? How can that be, when there is no more complete evidence of its presence than the shown film itself? Is it because the camera cannot be present at the same time that the film is shown? The live television camera overcomes that dishonesty, but only (as mentioned earlier) by giving up connection with the world as such.[49] Is the sense of your or your camera's concealment directed not to your audience, but to your subjects? Then why not attract the attention of the subjects, maybe have them glance over at the lens from time to time? Whatever the possibilities there, they miss the present problem. The subjects still would not know the secret of the camera's presence, the foreign animation it imposes upon them. While filming, you might project what you're taking on a screen in full view of your subjects so that they can see and respond to the image as it is taken from them. But then your camera would be imposing an animation on *that* response.

And how, in the case of spiritual withdrawal, would acknowledgment help? It won't make it any the less a case of withdrawal. If you or your camera suddenly swing into life, that is not an acknowledgment but a denial of your withdrawal. You cannot sidestep the claims of a position with a trick. The question is whether you can choose to occupy any, and do it honor.

The questions and concepts I have been led to admit in the course of my remarks all prepare for an idea that the camera must now, in candor, acknowledge not its being present in the world but its being outside its world.

The world's presence to me is no longer assured by my mechanical absence from it, for the screen no longer naturally holds a coherent world *from* which I am absent. I feel the screen has darkened, as if in fury at its lost power to enclose its content. The opacity of color masks the old brilliance, the answering glow of the black and white screen. Light itself seems to become, of all things, indiscriminate, promiscuous. This is perhaps why good color films restrict or simplify their groupings and expanses. Kubrick's *2001* is a full if eccentric beneficiary of this fact. I think it is the effort to lighten and unify color that produces all those blurred foreground flowers in *Red Desert*. They caused, at any rate, the clearest cases of color shock I've witnessed in an audience. They are by now compulsory attendants of love.

The images keep staying back, as in photographs they will. That we now feel this as a loss of connection, as staying *away,* underlies the camera's efforts to engulf its subjects—by widening its reach, by staying close enough to them to hold their scent (as a blinded man might), by freezing them in their tracks or slowing them down as if to glimpse them before they vanish. The massiveness of sounds and amplifications of figures in works like *Point Blank* and *The Dirty Dozen* are as if so maddened by the threat of nature's withdrawal that they would in vengeance blot it out on the spot.

I have described this loss of connection, this loss of conviction in the film's capacity to carry the world's presence as a new theatricalizing of its images, another exhibiting of them, another replacement of the intensity of mystery with the intensity of mechanism. I have also suggested that this in turn was a response to the draining from the original myths of film of their power to hold our conviction in film's characters. The conventions upon which film relied have come to seem conspiracies: close-up, which used to admit the mysteriousness of the human face, now winks a penny-ante explanation at us. Hitchcock parodies this with the long final close shot of Tony Perkins in *Psycho*, making a mystery of himself. As its final vulgarization my choice is the point in *Ship of Fools* at which, in response to the jocular line "What can Hitler do? Kill all the Jews in Germany?" Kramer's camera pushes into the dwarf's face, which, aided by a musical thunderclap, is supposed to register at a glance an explicit vision and comprehension of the following decade of German history. And staying nose-close to the body serves finally not merely to fragment it (as in the sexual passage of *A Married Woman*) but to stupefy it beyond all expression. One might attribute the bear-hugging of the camera to an influence from television; but that would not account for the movies' preparation to receive it. If in nothing else, the limited ambition of *Mississippi Mermaid* would be valuable in recalling the sweetness of the human body going its ways.

It is for such reasons that I speak of film's growing doubt of its ability to allow the world to exhibit itself, and instead its taking over the task of exhibition, against its nature. But the same techniques which serve to betray it can also be used, and seen, to keep faith with its nature. This is what I mean by saying or assuming that there *are* serious uses of these devices, something beyond chic. I know there are those who deny this, or who dismiss them as "mod." That seems to me as wrong as the claim that any and every newness puts wings to the mind. The interesting question for us cannot any longer be whether a serious impulse or idea will be debased or imitated or skinned for show. Of course the Beethoven Ninth will be used to throw out the news. Nor is it only the leopard which now becomes part of the ceremony, but the stray cat. The interesting question, in a world beset by seriousness—by fraudulent claims to its possession, and by nauseated mockings of those claims, and by hearty or worldly efforts to deny its existence—is whether room continues to be made for the genuine article, and whether we will know it when we see it. (I promise not to mind being told again that solemnity is not really seriousness, on condition that I not be asked to believe that cynicism and slapdash really are.)

Initially, a film-maker may be content to use a device merely to embarrass the hateful complacency of studio production technique, in which every question is academic, in which every triviality is given the same unloving polish. This impulse is hardly peculiar to motion pictures and their academy. What is peculiar to them is their way of allowing new procedures and formats to continue film's particular capacity to reveal only and all of what is revealed to it, to let the world and its children achieve their candidness. From the narcissistic honesty of self-reference there is opened the harder acknowledgments of the camera's outsideness to its world and my absence from it

18

Assertions in Techniques

Let me collect, not quite at random, some uses of the devices I have mentioned. As always, nothing is a "possibility of a medium" unless its use gives it significance. And "the" significance of a possibility is as worth looking for as "the" meaning of a word.

Take slow motion. It may not have needed Leni Riefenstahl to discover the sheer objective beauty in drifting a diver through thin air, but her combination of that with a series of cuts syncopated on the rising arc of many dives, against the sun, took inspiration. The general message is clear enough in everything from the high-jumping children in *The World of Henry Orient* and *Popi* to the floating women in television commercials honoring feminine hygiene. You'd think everybody would have the trick in his bag by now: for a fast touch of lyricism, throw in a slow-motion shot of a body in free fall. But as recently as *Goodbye Columbus*, the trick was blown: we are given slow motion of Ali MacGraw *swimming*. But ordinary swimming is *already* in slow motion, and to slow it further and indiscriminately only thickens it. It's about the only thing you can do to good swimming to make it ugly. (That might have been the point, but this is clearly not a work which knows its own vulgarity.)

A more surprising significance can be found in Mamoulian's *Love Me Tonight*, where a field of horses in slow motion is read as *silent*. I think Kurosawa is counting on this understanding with the slow-motion duel death in *Seven Samurai*: the instant of a mortal thrust followed by the long drop into endlessness. It clarifies, and caps, the nations of dyings in which men suddenly freeze or double and then gravely sink; or in which they cast off their mortal weapons and then tilt and topple from a crevice or parapet. Kurosawa waits out the bounce, illuminated by the shifting flow of the hair, as the body lands. The possibility is invited but fails to materialize in *Point Blank*; but that film does get one lyrical passage from slow motion, in a close-up of bullet shells falling. The lyricism arises first from the counterpoint motion of identical simple objects falling in different attitudes, but also from the surprising intensification which, in conjunction with the magnifying effect of the closeness, slow motion has upon the reflecting color in the metal.

At the finish of *Bonnie and Clyde* the film persists in an elegy of bullets long after the pair are dead. Society is making sure of itself. But art is not so satisfied. The camera is at once confessing its invasion of their existences and its impotence to preserve them, and our pasts in them; it is at once taking vengeance on them for their absence and accompanying them across the line of death. In *Butch Cassidy and the Sundance Kid* this is done in another way: the ending freeze of the two figures, prepared by the stills of the overture and the entr'acte, instantly translates them to immortality.

The uncontrollable tic of the freeze finish, apparently part of the contract in television drama, mimics two old ending *topoi* from movies. The comic epilogue after the mystery is solved or the conflict is over, which lets society breathe a sigh of relief, reassured of its innocence, is now invoked by freezing a face at a point of grimace, a comic "take"—as if the film couldn't afford to let the subject do his own acting. The outside pull-away, up from the house or neighborhood in which the drama has ended, letting the world return, is now replaced by stopping the departing subjects in their tracks—partly returning the figures and their world to their privacy, but unable really to let them go, since otherwise you wouldn't be convinced they had ever appeared.

Or take flash insets. What do they signify? In *Hiroshima, Mon Amour*, the first use of them that I remember, they generally signify what anyone would guess: the presence of the past, the pastness of the past.[50] In this film they represent moments in the consciousness of a woman whose life has become an effort to keep past and present from suffocating one another, and to keep her present and the world's present from betraying one another. It is essential that we feel it is *her* consciousness breaking in upon itself, *her* past on which she sights her monologues. Many people in Nevers had seen the young German soldier lying dead on the bridge that last day, but only she bears in a wall of her memory the impression of the curve his fingers made as his body clotted in the roadbed. And only for her is that place flashed to light by the resting body of her new enemy-lover.

The imitative use of this device in *The Pawnbroker* does not accept this burden of significance but expects the device to provide its own. That is just what it does, to the film's damnation. What the pawnbroker is shown to remember of his experience in the concentration camp is what anybody looking through a grisly picture book of the camp might imagine that people remember. So the flash device deprives this bereft man even of his own memories. Is that the significance wanted? And why do the breasts of the beautiful black woman, offering to trade herself to him, flash to him his wife's suffering at the hands of Nazi officers? Is it something about this particular woman? We know nothing of a relationship between her and the pawnbroker. Then is it something analogous in the situation of the two women? That further denies the humanity of them both. Then is it because being in a position to give money for the precious possessions of others makes him feel like a Nazi? He should have got out of pawnbroking long ago. Then does it perhaps suggest to him that Nazis were acting, given a certain set of opportunities, from human hungers and with human capacities? Unthinkable; they were merely monsters. Then is it because the Harlem boss, a member of an enslaved race, himself behaves something like a Nazi slave master? The phenomenon is not unknown, but does that make the man a Nazi? Are all crimes roughly equatable with torture and genocide? —The thing is hopeless. It is only another instance of the appeal to a favorite speechless horror as a cover for the inability to respond.

In *La Guerre est Finie*, Resnais uses flash insets (held longer than in *Hiroshima* because containing internal motion) to mean specifically the outsideness and insideness not of one time to another, but of one place to another, an equally ancient feature of human separateness, and one of the first to be noticed in film, through cross-cutting. Resnais is counting on the known properties of suspense in cross-cutting, because he does not always cut to the flash inset from Montand's face, so we do not read it as what Montand is at this moment imagining to be happening to his friend under interrogation in Spain. But his friend is *there*, something specific is happening to him *now*. This is the fact upon which Montand is acting. We know that from time to time the absoluteness of his friend's isolation will flash over him, but we do not know exactly what he imagines, nor exactly when. The very objectivity and banality of the flashes we are shown intensify the character's unknownness to us—his privacy, rather, though we know everything. The film does not, to my mind, rise to its idea, but it is the idea of a genuine mind, and some variation of it motivates each of Resnais' works—an idea of the simultaneous gravity and weightlessness of the past, as though our present is merely a shifting orbiting of our memories, perhaps to pass too close to avoid a death-pull back, perhaps too far to avoid a death-drift away.

Or take freeze frames. In *Darling* they show what the world sees of a darling, and the convenience and perversity in having, and having the chance, to pick what the world will see. In *Jules and Jim* they show what Jules and Jim see together in the woman of their world. The pairing of these two films should forcibly prevent our taking any listing of rhetorical devices for more or less than it is worth. *Darling* is a clever film; *Jules and Jim* is a masterpiece. The distinction is worth making not to warn against confusing technique with authority (which is not a very clear warning, and not specifically called for by the dangers of moviegoing). But it may seem that the freeze device in *Darling* is integrated in the movie as a whole, which is after all about the shallowness and the depth of appearances, about fashion; what better motivation for using the technique of a succession of stilled frames than to show them as products of a fashion photographer's hopeful catchings? [51] Whereas in *Jules and Jim*, however good that idea of Jeanne Moreau stopped against the wall, the thing is used out of the blue.

How an automatism is motivated and justified is no simpler a question than how a number is motivated in an opera or musical comedy, or what relations are to be found between the music and the text it sets. The literality of the device's justification in *Darling* is comparable to justifying Astaire's dancing by its being a dance in the world depicted (as when he's doing an act in a theater or nightclub, or dancing in a dance studio). No worry there. But Astaire is also capable of transforming objects and locales at hand—an office with its desk tops and papers, on skates in Central Park, driving golf balls—into a setting for his dance, letting his wish provide the occasion, as in the brave it will. Here the resourcefulness in using his setting is integral to the resourcefulness of the routine as a whole; making the world dance to his music.

In *Jules and Jim* the image private to the two men appears as if materialized by their desire, which freezes her at the height of laughter, from which she then descends. So the image confirms not only her identity with the figure they first saw in her—the statue they had gone in search of come to life (an identity established by the smile as well as by the motionlessness)—but also the fact that she is their creation, their greatest work as artists, the one work on which they could stake their lives. Hence the image is their proof that they are artists, because they have so staked their lives; it is also to be their proof as men. But, whether because they are failures as real artists or incomplete men, or because the muse of heaven and the god in men never will settle together on earth, this proof fails. Or maybe we fail to know success when we meet with it.

It is a story of fidelity, and it is the story of Jules and Jim. The question by which they measure themselves is to what degree the human frame can house the unaligned fidelities which human nature requires. They do well enough at that question: they will not, whatever the world's odds, willingly let comradeship and desire and art and politics destroy the place of each in each. The surprise is not that in the end they fail but that they get so far—far enough to test the world by the test of themselves. It is this last point that determines whether the film holds one's conviction or not. In a world in which it is common to rest assured that a given problem is either neurotic or existential, psychological or political, few works or acts are sufficiently autonomous to testify that the relation between self and community (because they are composed of one another) is an undying dialectic, that you cannot know beforehand whether a given contradiction requires a revolution of self or an adaptation of community.

The woman ("She was all women") *will* not be the statue, the totem of their community, but she *will* be watched, and not merely when they want to see. And she is right—not alone as a woman but as a totem. Even if she is their creation, their success is that she is alive and separate, that there is community among them (community: not just marriage, not just desire, not just comradeship; because there are three). She is the answer to a prayer, not the servant of wishes. When the men's loyalties exclude her, she excludes herself, and draws them after. Her first leap into water comes early, when the men are enjoying Baudelaire's dirty remark on the topic of women in church—as though, being men, there can be no religious differences between them. Her second leap comes at the end, when the men join again, this time on the topic of Nazis burning books—as though, being adults partial to books, there can be no political differences between them. Her final solution is to take Jim for that ride off the earth and to say again to Jules, "Watch!"

You have to decide about that gesture: Is it her vanity working, a neurotic inability to permit a loyalty that is not directed by her? Or is it still her loyalty to the three of them, an obedience to a shared knowledge that, in a world gone to war, they have taken loyalties to the extremest edge open to them, and that this is the last time in which they can end together, salvaging most? In that case, I interpret her position this way: When the three had met, they had agreed upon a try for success, for happiness in love married with freedom in work. If one is faithful to such an enterprise, failure is as honorable as success. But the woman sees, from within her mechanical infidelities, not that the men have failed but that they have broken faith with the original vows of their community. It is no failure as a human being not to be a serious intellectual. Jim's early falterings over Jules's writings may have been only the expression of a lack of vocation for the life of the mind. Some men admire that life who cannot lead it, who are in fact embarrassed by any sense of themselves as leading it (but probably no more than lead it without respecting it). Such a man may be devoted to other men because they seem to lead it without embarrassment and may take the other's ease in it as his call to it, his right to it. You can have such an admiration, and your devotion can make this mistake, and you can nevertheless be a good man, and know friendship. But Jim is at the end not even a serious journalist: he is defeated by the book-burning before he has acted against it, with whatever rage and talent and experience and position he commands. There is every reason to expect failure, but that is different from opting for it. So his conversation with Jules on the subject is a substitute for leading his life, and for accepting the terms of his friendship. It makes a sentiment of horror.

The newsreel footage of the bonfire of books, the young virtuously chanting around it in unison, is ontologically the negation of the newsreels used earlier in the film: there, they had set the scene in Paris at a time in which the little community was in Paris; and the long newsreel passage, halving the film as the First World War halved the characters' lives, sets the battles of that war at a time in which the virtuous young men were in those battles on opposite sides—when, moreover, the meaning and fear of those battles is the knowledge that the friend, the essence of his community, may be there, unknown to him, as he advances against fire, firing. Truffaut uses the nostalgia of the old photographs of Paris streets and houses, and the heartbreaking beauty and terror of the soldiers rising like flowers from their fields, to open us to the knowledge that these mortals whose lives we have been shown and will be shown were there, in the only world we inhabit. It is, to my knowledge, the most elegant, direct, and sustained use of the familiar device of newsreel clips in movies, a possibility of the medium which declares that the world of movies is an extension of the world of news.[52] The clip of the book-burning reinforces this meaning by showing us an event taking place at a time the men are *not* there. It therewith serves to rebuke their absence, or to state that the world has passed them by. The land of their community, in Alsace, neither quite France nor quite Germany, is already overrun. The mind's safety cannot depend upon such regions, but only upon inhabiting with balance the lines between sanity and madness, and between apathy and apocalypse.

Jules has not failed, as anyone might, to write a serious novel. He is thinking of a novel about insects, as though that would be, if something else, just as good; or as if, were it to be serious, it would be easier to write. This cheating of his ambition suggests that his forgoing of his wife is not the natural exclusion there is in separateness, his version of exclusiveness; but has instead become a denial of his responsibility with her. —"Watch!" Not: watch my destructiveness; but: see that your ability to watch and to wait, which was your strength, has become your destructiveness, our destruction. I will do as you ask; that much of our bargain we have always kept.

Upon cremation, the bones of love remain, the genders indistinguishable except in size. As Jules and the child walk away hand in hand, the last words tell us that Jules is "relieved." By what? Of what? Not of fidelity, but of making room for incompatible faiths, faiths called incompatible by the world, by the self's limits in the room of its world, by men of little faith, by men. With the child, Jules knows he can keep faith; and the woman knows this, she could always count on it. It is the affinity he would himself have selected. Patience and nurturance, requirements of motherhood, were always his manly virtues. He gave birth to the mother of his child, who therefore is the grandchild of his friendship. It is not all of faith, but it is faithful; and since all is reflected in each, it is enough to keep the idea alive. At any rate, that is the faith.

To compare the different significances of the possibility of freeze frames in *Darling* and *Jules and Jim* is not to show that in one the device has a simple meaning and in the other a complex one, nor that in the one it is motivated crudely and in the other subtly. It is to show that integrating a device is not the artistic issue, because integration can itself be a device (like motivic unity, or an organization "based" on a lump of mathematics). There is no substitute for integrity. And it is to show that only the integrity of a given work can make out the significance of a given possibility. If the device is integral to what makes a work convincing, it has full importance; without the conviction it has any and none.

One necessity of movies is that the thread of film itself be drawn across light. Is this a possibility of some medium of film? It is obviously noticed in certain stretches of experimental films, meant to hurt the eyes with speedy scratches and continuous cuts. It is present in the epilogue sequence of *Eclipse*, where the motionlessness within each shot acknowledges the continuous current of film necessary to hold one view in view, as if with nature's own patience. This acknowledgment is the reason Antonioni's idea here does not read to me, as it has for others, as more do-it-yourself nihilism. Other things equal, depicted motionlessness feels and looks different from motionless depiction. Whether you read those closing sonorities as a real eclipse or as the eclipse of the human, it is either way an environment in which something more happens—in which instinct is estranged and birds droop at noon, in which strange gods are readied. The passage reminds us that half the world is always eclipsed by the world itself. So it recalls that there is no reason under the sun why a day's business should always be bad (making a place for love by removing each receiver from the litter of office telephones is an original image of the ego's chance for disengagement by sexuality), and it recalls that night is still there for cover or for recovery or for entertainment, and for turning one's thoughts to stars. (Monica Vitti's capacity for fun—in this case shown by her African costume and dance during the evening with the girls—is from the first a factor of her independence, hence of her desirability.) The most beautiful declaration I have seen of the difference between motionless and moving depiction occurs in a science-fiction film by Chris Marker, told in stills except for one late shot of eyes opening.

The camera has to be somewhere; it can be anywhere. Are those aesthetic possibilities, even if no particular advantage is taken of its placement, no significance made of it? In countless passages in which repeated reverse shots are used to follow the back-and-forth of dialogue, you will find at the shifts that the listener's attitude and demeanor are not continuous with what they were when we saw him speaking. They have shifted—like the necktie in old continuity. Obviously there are good reasons for this in the technical matters concerning how such scenes are set up: with different set-ups, either a mismatch of the reverse shot could be hidden, or a way could be found to perfect the match. But the discontinuous, unnaturally altered expression of the listener *could* be intended; e.g., to convey lack of communication. That is to say, some films we care about might undertake to mean something by it. But if no film does, or if it only happens in films we do not take seriously, is it so much as a possibility of the medium of film?

Splitting the screen does not overcome, but multiplies, or fractures, the somewhere of the camera; it might thereby declare it. Focusing that blurs either the foreground or background, as in an intention of the eye, suggests that after the choice of the somewhere, and of horizon, and of distance and tilt, there is still a choice in seeing; resolution is still to be made, which steadies and excludes. (Masking is a different mode of focusing, as in an intention of the ear.)

I think here of the permanent revelation upon which *Grand Illusion* closes: the two figures bobbing through a field of snow, away from us. Somewhere under that one white is a mathematical line, a fiction that men call a border. It is not on earth or in heaven, but whether you are known to have crossed it is a matter of life and death. The movie is about borders, about the lines of life and death between German and Frenchman, between rich and poor, between rich man and aristocrat, between officer and soldier, between home and absence, between Gentile and Jew. Specifically, it is about the illusions of borders, the illusion that they are real and the grand illusion that they are not. That last view carries this weight exactly because Renoir's camera does not take advantage of its possibility to move all the way up to the figures, but asserts its power to remain, accepting some position as its last, its own.

Compare this with another memorable end in the snow of the German-Swiss border, in Borzage's *The Mortal Storm*. There the camera cannot resist a last close look at James Stewart's and Margaret Sullavan's faces, as she lies where she was hit and he refuses to go on without her; what until then has been a history of friendships and family love and young passion broken and cauterized in the fire storm of Nazism, turns into a private tragedy of a failed escape attempt, the privacy heightened by the melodramatic irony of the last words, given to a member of the German ski patrol as Stewart continues the ski run with the dead woman in his arms—something like, giving the signal to cease fire, "They're in Switzerland. They're free."

In *Grand Illusion*, the very success of the escape is a metaphysical irony. That such an action should constitute an escape and that there should have to be such things in our world are facts from which there is nothing like an escape.[53] The reticence of Renoir's camera is more than beautiful tact. It is the refusal to assert what no one is in a position to assert for us: where it is that one man's life ends and another's begins. Or the refusal to manufacture a response, however sweet the complicated pain, which covers our complicity in the metaphysics of exclusions we have willed for our world, which in turn covers the ontological facts of our separateness and commonality, which we will not will.[54]

My reason for speaking of film techniques was that I wanted to specify the difference between a condition of the physical bases of a medium and an achievement of art by means of them.[55] The distinction is familiar in traditional art and in traditional works in the philosophy of art (e.g., Dewey's treatment of it in *Art as Experience* is central in the excellence of that book). But in modernism, when the physical basis is itself the subject of acknowledgment, the distinction between technique and victory is not familiar and is likely to go unnoticed—even when the insignificance of familiar notions of technique is itself declared.

A good reason not to go on with listing the possible significance of given technical possibilities, apart from my inexperience with the machines of magic, is that it suggests a foolish idea of "technique": that its mastery is something other than the endless acquisition of an art. The trouble with the "a great technician, but no soul" formula is not that a great technician has too much technique, but too little; he can do only what his technique dictates, not what his art demands. It is perhaps a fault of the way Wagner draws Beckmesser that one cannot think of him as a Meistersinger at all. His absurdity is not in slavery to technique—that is not absurd, but the condition any serious artist, any person with passion for his life, pits his character against—but the absurdity of the critic putting on the laurels of the artist. The joke is too private.

Nor is technique simply a matter of "attending to details," because the moral of art, as of a life, is that you do not know in advance what may arise as a significant detail. The mechanism of movies all but deliberately misleads about this: it seems to promise that the magic of its results can be had by anyone who rubs its lamp. Good old conservatories and academies turned out their share of freaks, but if they sometimes discouraged true talent they equally discouraged mere curiosity and lazy vanity. The purest statement of the moral (apart from the *Art of the Fugue*) is made by the Chopin *Etudes*, in which atoms of technique are shown to contain their own skies, and in which it is declared that there is no preparation for art which is not already art.

19

The Acknowledgment of Silence

A "possibility" of a medium can be made known only by successful works that define its media; in modernism, a medium is explored by discovering possibilities that declare its necessary conditions, its limits. Let me recall how we got to this point.

Having arrived at an initial characterization of the medium of the moving picture as a succession of automatic world projections, I took it for granted that movies are no longer easy in the nests of wish and myth that gave its media their conviction for us, and also that their modernist fate is not yet sealed. I was detoured into a discussion of some modernist painting as a means for developing the idea of acknowledgment as modernism's faithfulness to its art and the history of its art. I then asked what specifically movies have to acknowledge, what it is that would not exist (for it) unless admitted by it, what it is that the movie can no longer safely assume, but must declare, in order not to risk denying.

My answer was that it must acknowledge, what is always to be acknowledged, its own limits: in this case, its outsideness to its world, and my absence from it. For these limits were always the conditions of its candor, of its fate to reveal all and only what is revealed to it, and of its fortune in letting the world exhibit itself. I took it that the new rush of technical assertions—

whether of sophistication or of crudity—are, insofar as they are serious, responses to a sense of withdrawing candor; and I started to list some of them to try to determine which limits they discover. I find I have emphasized silence, isolation in fantasy, the mysteries of human motion and separateness: such are the conditions of existence that film, in its magical reproduction of the world, tries and tries not to transgress. My hypothesis about the general relative importance of montage and continuity comes just to this: that any such procedures will find their significance within these tasks of acknowledgment.

The new emergence of the ideas of silence and fantasy and motion and separateness takes us back, or forward, to beginnings. For it isn't as if, long after our acceptance of the talkie, we know why the loss of silence was traumatic for so many who cared about film. They may have failed to account accurately for the loss; but that would not mean that their trauma was not an accurate measure of it, and of their caring, which history turned upon. What was given up in giving up the silence of film, in particular the silence of the voice? Why suppose there will be some simple answer to that question, that there was some single spell broken by the sound of the human voice? For the voice has spells of its own.

I think this issue now underlies all the explorations in film to which I have alluded. The technology of sound recording soon overcame the actor's stiff bondage to the microphone, and the camera was free to stray again. But the technology did not free it from a deeper source of bondage, in the idea of synchronization itself. On the contrary, the possibility of following an actor anywhere with both eye and ear seemed to make their binding necessary. No doubt that source has to do with the absolute satisfaction of a craving for realism, for the absolute reproduction of the world—as though we might yet be present at its beginning.

But there is a further reality that film pursues, the further, continuous reality in which the words we need are *not* synchronized with the occasions of their need or in which their occasions flee them.

I have in mind not the various ways dialogue can stand at an angle to the life that produces it; nor the times in which the occasion is past when you can say what you did not think to say; nor the times when the occasion for speech is blocked by inappropriateness or fear, or the vessels of speech are pitched by grief or joy. I have rather in mind the pulsing air of incommunicability which may nudge the edge of any experience and placement: the curve of fingers that day, a mouth, the sudden rise of the body's frame as it is caught by the color and scent of flowers, laughing all afternoon mostly about nothing, the friend gone but somewhere now which starts from here—spools of history that have unwound only to me now, occasions which will not reach words for me now, and if not now, never. I am not asking for more stream-of-consciousness. Stream-of-consciousness does not show the absence of words as the time of action unwinds; it floats the time of action in order to give space for the words. I am asking for the ground of consciousness, upon which I cannot but move.

But why the sense that words are out of reach, that there will never be the right time for them? From where the sense of the unsayable?—time's answer to the ineffable. Out of my obscurity I reach the wish for total intelligibility, as though my words should form for you but remain part of our breaths. As though poetry were lodged in every cave of memory and locked in every object of thought. For poetry is so out of the ordinary that it could not appear unless the world itself wished for it. Not alone the poetry of poetry, but the poetry of prose—wherever the time of saying and the time of meaning are synchronized.

This reality of the unsayable is what I see in film's new release from the synchronization of speech with the speaker, or rather in its presenting of the speaker in forms in which there can be no speech. Speech slowed to match slow motion sinks into moan and grunt. Speeded human actions become the actions of machines, still intelligible; speech matched to them rises to blurts of twittering. You cannot flash a word into a phrase without altering the phrase; you cannot freeze a word without losing it. The tempo and progression of spoken intelligibility are inexorable. The poetry of poetry finds new breath for the world within that inexorability; it does not escape and does not want to escape it; it shows that we may be up to it. The paces of music have their own inexorability, with which for the time being they lift speech out of earthly gravity: melisma puts the word in slow motion but continues the surrounding world as its rod and staff; the soprano's high dominant freezes her word and her world for their descent into one another. The possibilities of moving pictures speak of a comprehensibility of the body under conditions which destroy the comprehensibility of speech. It is the talkie itself that is now exploring the silence of movies.

A silent movie has never been made. We called some silent after others acquired speech; but that was to register the satisfaction of the world's reproduction, as if the movie had until then been thwarted from that satisfaction, as if the actors and their world had been inaudible. But they were no more inaudible than the characters in radio were invisible. The Lone Ranger was no more invisible than his horse or gun, unless you wish to say that what exists as sound is invisible. But no person or object we could be shown could *be* the ones called into existence by those sounds, though you might be interested to know how the sounds were made. No word we could hear could be the word spoken by that figure of silence. We are told that most silent-film stars had to be replaced because his or her voice disappointed our expectations, but that a few satisfied us and crossed the boundary intact. No; no one did; all were replaced, some by themselves. We were universally disappointed. The new creations of synchronized sight and sound were merely powerful enough to distract us from the disappointment, and they deserved to. Now the disappointment is waking again.

Movies, before they spoke, projected a world of silence, as the radio beamed a world of sound. Those who miss serious radio will say that, unlike television, it left room for the imagination. That seems to me a wrong praise of imagination, which is ordinarily the laziest, if potentially the most precious, of human faculties. A world of sound is a world of immediate conviction; a world of sight is a world of immediate intelligibility. In neither is imagination called upon.

With talkies we got back the clumsiness of speech, the dumbness and duplicities and concealments of assertion, the bafflement of soul and body by their inarticulateness and by their terror of articulateness. Technical improvements will not overcome these ontological facts; they only magnify them. These ontological facts are tasks of art, as of existence. The advent of sound broke the spell of immediate intelligibility—a realistic renunciation, given the growing obscurity of the world. Then the task is to discover the poetry in speech.

It will not be the poetry of poetry. It seemed at first as if it ought to have been, as if when the filmed world expressed itself in speech it would have the same absolute intelligibility as its exhibition to sight. But every art wants the expression of the world, to speak the being of it directly, and none can simply hand its own powers to the others. The poetry of synchronized speech arises from the fact that just that creature, in just those surroundings, is saying just that, just now. The best film dialogue has so far been the witty and the hard-nosed, apparently because the lines are fast, or laconic. But wit and clip are in themselves not always of the highest interest. They work, I think, because they provide natural occasions on which silence is broken, and in which words do not go beyond their moment of saying; hence occasions on which silence naturally reasserts itself.

For the world *is* silent to us; the silence is merely forever broken. Poems and music incorporate that silence when they speak the world. Film speech can merely imitate it, backed by the world. Generally this imitation has relied upon the fact that movies, unlike performances in a theater, will contain long stretches without dialogue, in which the characters can be present without having to say anything (not: without having anything to say). We can observe the activities that involve them at points that precede or succeed the words surrounding them— their fights or their struggles with objects and places, or their criminal or military tactics. It has also relied upon some conventionalized sense of the best distance at which dialogue can be overheard. Orson Welles's speech tracks go beyond registrations of natural speech, to form a class almost by themselves. Not merely in his use of overlapping dialogue. That seemed on second thought, after one was at first simply overcome by it, a simple trick. But I have never seen the trick successfully duplicated by anyone else. I think the reason is that other directors understand the overlapping merely as one set of sounds bleeding into another or serving as background for another, whereas for Welles each of the different origins of speech attempts to maintain its individual meaning and coherence, so that they vie for significance. Beyond this, Welles explores and declares the fact and variation of distance between the speaker and the hearer of a line. Here he justifies the sound of high theater for film. I think of the dream-strange passage in *The Lady from Shanghai* in which the husband's partner, circling in a motorboat the yacht on which Welles and Rita Hayworth are alone together, calls out to them his loony singsong razzes. In *Citizen Kane* there is Kane's repetition of the name "Geddes" down a lengthening stairwell; and there is the transition from the reading of his campaign speech in the presence of a small gathering to his delivery of it on the platform at a mass meeting—a transition so shocking and yet smooth that one recognizes the platform as an inner distance from which Kane always speaks. His money, not made by him in competition with others but fallen upon him from an incomprehensible distance, causes and expresses his distance from individual others, and equally from the reality of his own inner life, which takes place on some isolated platform he cannot mount.[56]

How hard it is to let silence resume, how frightening it is, is registered early in the years of talkies, in *King Kong*. The words are not many, and those which are there are either arty ("It was beauty killed the beast") or are delivered as artily as can be. But most of the soundtrack is continuous Wagnerama and almost equally continuous screams; you finally feel the film is more afraid of silence than Fay Wray is of the beast. The whole film is an artless confession of film: film-makers on location discover that a thing of nature is more wondrous than any film; and when they trap this nature and bring it back, it is displayed crucified.[57] Movie music remained in genuine continuity with its soundless era. It continued to cartoon the emotions it could accompany, and continued to use that as an excuse for the general deadening of the pain of silence.

In my experience the most perfect provisions for the breaking of silence by speech are made in two of the greatest films on anybody's count. In *Children of Paradise* Arletty breaks the silent conventions of mime with Baptiste's name, the one word drawn from her with his appearance; later, off the stage but staged by a proscenium window onto the balcony of a theater, she again speaks his name as the window curtain is ripped aside revealing them to each other. The speaking of the word in those times and at those places collects to itself the fantasies it expresses and shatters them against the reality it shatters. In *Rules of the Game* the fact that the triumphant aviator's first words are over the public radio, to a watching world, but addressed to the absent woman whose presence is thereby made cause and accompaniment of his solo flight, gives his words the power of Shakespearean soliloquy.

There is another half to the idea of conveying the unsayable by showing experience beyond the reach of words. It is conveyed by freeing the motion of the body for its own lucidity. The body's lucidity is not dependent upon slowing and flashing and freezing it and juxtaposing it to itself over cuts and super-impositions. It was always part of the grain of film that, however studied the lines and set the business, the movement of the actors was essentially improvised—as in those everyday actions in which we walk through a new room or lift a cup in an unfamiliar locale or cross a street or greet a friend or look in a store window or accept an offered cigarette or add a thought to a conversation. They could all go one way or another. Our resources are given, but their application to each new crossroads is an improvisation of meaning, out of the present. These trivial facts take us back to the idea of acting on film. Earlier, I objected to calling the subjects of film "actors" at all. But obviously they are actors the way any human being is. The ontological fact that actions move within a dark and shifting circle of intention and consequence, that their limits are our own, that the individual significance of an act (like that of a word) arises in its being this one rather than every other that might have been said or done here and now, that their fate (like the fate of words) is to be taken out of our control—this is the natural vision of film.

To act without performing, to allow action all and only the significance of its specific traces, the wound embracing the arrow and no self-consciousness to blunt or disperse that knowledge—that has been the explicit wish of human action since Kierkegaard and Nietzsche summed up Protestantism and Stanislavsky brought theater into line. Brecht automatically gets an unanticipated version of his wish for the epic in theater and the alienated in acting: not the dissociation of actor and character, but their total coalescence, allowing a dissociation or freeing of action from speech. He does not get detached lucidity directly issuing in effective action for change. He gets "the turning of the spectator into somebody who just looks on" (i.e. the absence of "involvement" of the spectator as in the events on a stage), but without "forcing him to make decisions." [58] But then art alone is not going to achieve the changes of consciousness which its own reception also requires. It ought to be part of epic theater to contain the confrontation of its own continuous failing—every night our knowing the truth of our condition and every day dawning just the same— in order to make this failing neither palatable nor bitter, but to make it something we can live with faithfully, in consciousness, and with readiness for the significant detail when it really is ours to act upon. And he gets the vision that everything in the world other than nature is a human construction, humanly open to change.

The impact of movies is too massive, too out of proportion with the individual worth of ordinary movies, to speak politely of involvement. We involve the movies in us. They become further fragments of what happens to me, further cards in the shuffle of my memory, with no telling what place in the future. Like childhood memories whose treasure no one else appreciates, whose content is nothing compared with their unspeakable importance for me. St. Augustine stole a pear; lots of children have. Rousseau got a spanking with his pants down; lots of little boys have. Why seems it so particular with them? Everybody has his stolen pear, and his casual, permanent seductions; if they are to know their lives, those are to be known. Parents are forever being surprised at their children's memories. Some find it amusing or quirky of them to remember such details; some boast, on that evidence, of their child's intelligence. The parents do not know what is important to the child; and their amusement and boasting mean that they are not going to try to learn.

The movie's power to reach this level must have to do with the gigantism of its figures, making me small again. (For all the times the motif of a character watching a movie has been used, that is a possibility of the medium I remember acknowledged only once: when in *Saboteur* a man chased through Radio City

Music Hall runs across the stage in front of the screen, his human size in comparison with the size of the screen character seems that of an entirely other race—about the size of Fay Wray wriggling in the sky-blown hand.) It must also have to do with the world it screens being literally of my world.

I have said elsewhere that in a theater we do not occupy the same space as the actors on a stage but that we do occupy the same time.[59] That is rather superficial. But I have been told that it is obviously false: in a theater we obviously are in the same room as the actors, whereas at a movie we obviously are not. That idea comes from wrong pictures of how the spaces can be entered. It imagines that you could enter the actors' space in a theater by crossing the footlights. But of course all you would accomplish would be to stop the performance. And it imagines that you cannot enter the world of a movie because breaking through the screen is of no use. But you are headed in the wrong direction. (As in Plato's Cave, reality is *behind* you. It will become visible when you have made yourself visible to it, presented yourself.) The actors are *there,* all right, in your world, but to get to them you have to go where they are, and in fact, as things stand, you cannot go there *now.* Their space is not metaphysically different; it is the same human space mine is. And you are not, as in a theater, forbidden to cross the line between actor and incarnation, between action and passion, between profane and sacred realms. In a movie house, the barrier to the stars is time.

The sacredness of the stage still holds. Not any longer because certain figures are authorized to be there, but because the characters in a play have a past and future that you could never have been part of. If you wander over and they address you in character, that will alter their future and so destroy them; and if the actors address you in person, that will suspend their characters. (Of course, there may be forms of theater that will wish to incorporate just such possibilities.)

The world filmed is all profane, all outside. They and we

could have been anywhere, may be anywhere next. The discontinuities in the environment of a film are discontinuities not of space but of places. You do not discontinuously *go from* one place to another. How you get from one to another place need not be told, any more than it must be told how they got from one place to another; that is up to the tale. The discontinuities are those of *attention*. You are given bits of the world, and you must put them together into those lives, one way or another, as you have yours.

The fact that we are in a given place on earth is as utterly contingent as the fact that we are on earth. The fact that we are in one place at any given time is as necessary as the fact that, once on earth, we are until the end earthling. I think everyone knows odd moments in which it seems uncanny that one should find oneself just here now, that one's life should have come to this verge of time and place, that one's history should have unwound to this room, this road, this promontory. The uncanny is normal experience of film. Escape, rescue, the metamorphosis of a life by a chance encounter or juxtaposition— these conditions of contingency and placement underpin all the genres of film, from the Keaton and Chaplin figures who know nothing of the abyss they skirt, to the men who know too much.

Because the absolute reality and placement of these people are conditions of their appearance to us, film has an absolute freedom of narrative. It escapes Aristotelian limits according to which the possible has to be made probable. It was a great achievement of realistic theater when Ibsen created an event, a suicide, in itself so improbable and in the character so right, that he could rely on his play to rebuke the curtain line—"But people just don't do things like that"—with the force of fact. That is the ordinary condition of the audience of film. Things like that don't happen in the world we go our rounds in—your father does not turn out to be a foreign spy, one's life does not depend upon finding a lady with a strange hat whom no investigation or headline can unearth, one man does not hold another by his sleeve from the top ledge of the Statue of Liberty, people do not (any longer) turn into werewolves and vampires just because someone says they do. But there they are. There is nothing people do not do, no place they may not find themselves in. That is the knowledge which makes acceptable film's absolute control of our attention.[60] It is the knowledge, together with the visible incarnation of character into star and of star into successive characters, that we exist in the condition of myth: we do not require the gods to show that our lives illustrate a story which escapes us; and it requires no major recognition or reversal to bring its meaning home. Any life may illustrate any; any change may bring it home.

The knowledge of the unsayable is the study of what Wittgenstein means by physiognomy. His continuous sketches of it occur in Part II of the *Philosophical Investigations*, in the long set of pages beginning with an investigation of the concept of "seeing as." It is a region, I believe, less worked on than others. But the idea of "seeing as" has for some reason been picked up by more than one theorist of art as the key to the subject of art, at least so far as Wittgenstein is relevant to that subject. I do not wish to argue against that, but to warn against a false idea of its importance—namely the idea that "seeing as" is some fancy species of seeing. The ideas Wittgenstein enters with that concept have to do with my relation to my own words and with the point at which my knowledge of others depends upon the concepts of truthfulness and interpretation. Empirical statements that claim truth depend upon evidence; statements that claim truthfulness depend upon our acceptance of them. My acceptance is the way I respond to them, and not everyone is capable of the response, or willing for it. I put this by saying that a true statement is something we know or do not know; a truthful statement is one we must acknowledge or fail or refuse to acknowledge.

It is particularly worth cautioning against useless simplicity about this because Wittgenstein's discussion of interpretation has what looks like a ready-made application to our knowledge of the subjects of film. He gives various examples in which some drawn figures (like some words, in some places) can be taken variously. One of the examples, now a bit fingered, is the duck-rabbit; another is an acute triangle, long side down, which can be read as "fallen over"; others are line drawings of faces and descriptions of postures which can be taken various ways—in which, as Wittgenstein puts it, different aspects of them can dawn, and in dawning strike us. (The relevance of this to the new sense of *series* is self-evident.) The application I have in mind is to the widely quoted experiment of Kuleshov in which the same frame of a man's face alters its aspect depending upon the image which precedes it. Bazin, in a set of fine passages on the topic, turns this fact against what its admirers have taken it to show, *viz.,* the omnipotence of montage in film narrative. Bazin takes the demonstrated power of montage to show its weakness, because the inherent ambiguity or mystery of the human face is denied in presenting a context which forces one definite interpretation upon us. We could study the issue this way: shown (a photograph of) a human face, I might, as in the case of the duck-rabbit, be struck right off with one of its possible aspects. This is unlike the case of the triangle, in which, to read it as "fallen over," I have to imagine something in connection with it, surround it with a fiction. But like the triangle and unlike the duck-rabbit, I *can* surround the face with a fiction in order to alter its aspects. And unlike the triangle and the duck-rabbit and all other optical illusions, I must surround the face with a reality—as though the seeing of a reality is the imagining of it; and it may itself either dictate or absorb the reality with which I must surround it, or fascinate me exactly because it calls incompatible realities to itself which vie for my imagination. The fact of recurrence of an actor in his type both limits his range of expression, the physiognomical aspects which may dawn (one film working in montage to another), and also threatens the limit. It can be internal to a character that he threaten his own limit. This does not require the explicitness of *Dr. Jekyll and Mr. Hyde*. The threat is present when Harpo inevitably finds his harp. Then the usual frenzy of his information and gluttony and satyromania are becalmed in the angelic sounds with which the man of whistles and honks and noiseless roars and sobs can also express himself, the camera doting on the innerness of that face. The special use of unknown faces for their sheer impression upon us (as, familiarly, in Dreyer and Fellini) serves both to invite and to refuse the imposition of imagination. The inflection of meaning available to a type is the background against which the inflexibility of a face commands its power of mystery. Film's promise of the world's exhibition is the background against which it registers absolute isolation: its rooms and cells and pinions hold out the world itself. The fullest image of absolute isolation is in Dreyer's *Joan of Arc*, when Falconetti at the stake looks up to see a flight of birds wheel over her with the sun in their wings. They, there, are free. They are waiting in their freedom, to accompany her soul. She knows it. But first there is this body to be gone through utterly.

To satisfy the wish for the world's exhibition we must be willing to let the world as such appear. According to Heidegger this means that we must be willing for anxiety, to which alone the world as world, into which we are thrown, can manifest itself; and it is through that willingness that the possibility of one's own existence begins or ends. To satisfy the wish to act without performing, to let our actions go out of our hands, we must be willing to allow the self to exhibit itself without the self's intervention. The wish for total intelligibility is a terrible one. It means that we are willing to reveal ourselves through the self's betrayal of itself. The woman in *Hiroshima* is almost there: "I betrayed you tonight," she says in a monologue to her dead lover, looking at herself in the mirror, confessing her new lover. It does not mitigate the need for acknowledgment that her old lover is dead, because what she has betrayed is her love for him, which is not dead. As things stand, love is always the betrayal of love, if it is honest. It is why the path of self-knowledge is so ugly, hence so rarely taken, whatever its reputed beauties. The knowledge of the self as it is always takes place in the betrayal of the self as it was. That is the form of self-revelation, until the self is wholly won. Until then, until there is a world in which each can be won, our loyalty to ourselves is in doubt, and our loyalty to others is in partialness.

A world complete without me which is present to me is the world of my immortality. This is an importance of film—and a danger. It takes my life as my haunting of the world, either because I left it unloved (the Flying Dutchman) or because I left unfinished business (Hamlet). So there is reason for me to want the camera to deny the coherence of the world, its coherence as past: to deny that the world is complete without me. But there is equal reason to want it affirmed that the world is coherent without me. That is essential to what I want of immortality: nature's survival of me. It will mean that the present judgment upon me is not yet the last.

Note (1979)

The following essay, along with Alexander Sesonske's essay to which mine contains responses, originated in a symposium held on *The World Viewed* at the meetings of the American Society for Aesthetics in the fall of 1972, at New College in Sarasota, Florida. The essays were published together in *The Georgia Review,* Winter 1974. My remarks at the symposium were drawn from a manuscript which then, reworked and expanded, became the basis of a Sloss Memorial Lecture at Stanford University in November 1973. Still further expansion resulted in the essay reprinted here. So while, especially in its first third, I let what I say be prompted by criticisms I quote from Sesonske, I use his puzzled remarks—as I understand him mostly to have done—as examples of puzzlements that I knew or imagined others to share, and of course that I might also sometimes share, or that I was otherwise glad to develop; yet the essay was from the beginning conceived as an independent addendum to my book. I should like to record my indebtedness to an intellectual association with Alexander Sesonske that dates from our first years in the study of philosophy. This has encouraged me to believe in the sincerity of his closing invitation to "indicate how the true course of [my] thought runs around . . . the shoals threatening the course of our understanding of *The World Viewed,*" in particular to believe him prepared to accept the condition that such indications as I can give can only proceed by continuing to run—not away from my territory, but further along the shoals of it that I know are there, and courting others that I have not yet found the resources or the heart to fathom. I am also indebted to Professor Ted Cohen, who chaired the symposium, for his closing comments, whose reverberations helped guide my rewriting.

More of The World Viewed

I have been told, and by friends sympathetic to the issues of *The World Viewed* and patient with the difficulty of their expression, that I have made a difficult book, a sometimes incomprehensible book. I have no choice but to believe this and, since I also continue to believe in the book, to attempt to account for its difficulty and do what I can to alleviate it, at least do what I can not to discourage a genuine desire to assess it sympathetically. I persist in the feeling asserted in the book's Preface, that its difficulty lies as much in the obscurity of its promptings as in its particular surfacings of expression. Given the feeling that a certain obscurity of prompting is not external to what I wished most fervently to say about film (and hence cannot have been cleared up before I commenced writing, nor at any time before I called the writing over), the commitments I set myself as I wrote were, first, to allow obscurities to express themselves as clearly and as fervently as I could say, and, second, to be guided by the need to organize and clarify just these obscurities and just this fervor in the progression of my book as a whole. These procedures would be pointless unless the obscurities I allowed myself were accurate responses to the nature of film and unless the expressions I found for them were accurate to those responses; and unless I did in fact manage, in the progression of the book, to bring some order and to do some justice to these expressions.

Such procedures differ from, almost reverse, the procedures I had followed in my previous philosophical writing. There my hope for conviction from the reader was placed in my ability to motivate assertions, and objections to them, and to voice them in such a form and at such a time that the reader would have the impression that he was himself thinking them, had been about to have said them—not about to have said something generally along their lines, but as it were to find himself thinking those specific words just when and just as they were appearing to him. (Naturally this need not, even when done well, occur on a first perusal. Then what in a first should encourage going back?) Whereas in writing about film I felt called upon to voice my responses with their privacy, their argumentativeness, even their intellectual perverseness, on their face; often to avoid voicing a thought awaiting its voice, to refuse that thought, to break into the thought, as if our standing responses to film are themselves standing between us and the responses that film is made to elicit and to satisfy.

Perhaps the plainest of my intentions, certainly the intention least hidden from me from the outset of the writing, was to demonstrate that movies may be written about, and that some are worth thinking and writing about, with the same seriousness that any work of art deserves, with the same specificity of attention to the significance of the work at hand and to the formal devices of the work by means of which this significance is achieved. I knew from the outset, accordingly, certain of the issues that awaited me. (1) I would immediately have to say why so grotesquely obvious a point as the worth of certain movies is worth the making. It is worth making, to my mind, not alone because making it implies a commitment to specify the grounds of worth in particular cases, but because it implies that not all movies are in fact worth this attention and that there is next to no agreement among those who speak of movies over the canon of movies to which their speaking must be accountable and by which standards are thus far set against which to weigh worth; nor over the cinematic grounds there may be in terms of which to argue worth or worthlessness. These lacks in agreement are a function, I believe, less of the comparative "youth" of the art of film than of the sociology of film criticism and theory. One might compare, for better and for worse, the contemporary state of film criticism and theory with the state of literary criticism and theory at the time of the establishment of the newspaper or of the literary-political Reviews; a time, that is to say, before the professionalization of scholarship and the academicizing of criticism. (2) I would have at some point to begin to specify what I took to count as "formal devices" of film, and in particular to say why a rehearsal of the technological properties of lenses, filters, shutters, film exposures, etc., does not in itself constitute specifications of aesthetic properties of film. (The common appeal to technological properties is caused in part by a sense that the sheer *power* of film is unlike the powers of the other arts. I share this sense, and I agree that this power is essentially related to film's technology. But the aesthetic role of this technology is no more specified by studying it apart from its specific achievements in significant films, than, say, the role of electronic amplification in rock music is specified by studying electronic amplification apart from its specific results in the sounds of rock, indeed, apart from its role in determining what counts as a "sound." (3) I would have to say why a general declaration of the nature of film's "differences" from other artistic media—a declaration of cinematic "essence" —was apt to be called for and likely to be fruitless. Whatever one may mean by the "essence" of a medium of art, its sense can only be specified by the achievements of that art itself. The declaration of film's essence I had heard most frequently was that it consisted of "light and movement." That seems the natural, the only, answer to the isolated and persistent question, "What is the essence of the medium of film?" Since the answer seems to me more or less empty, I take the question to be more or less the wrong question to ask. In particular, I have seen no objects consisting essentially of light and movement (and essentially of nothing else) that have struck me as having the force of art. And since the objects of film I have seen which do strike me as having the force of art all incontestably use moving pictures of live persons and real things in actual spaces, I began my investigation of film by asking what *role* reality plays in this art.

There is at least a double cause for finding it natural now to resist the pressure of reality upon art: there is a more or less vague and pervasive intellectual fashion, apparently sanctioned by the history of epistemology and the rise of modern science, according to which we never really, and never really can, see reality as it is; and there is an interpretation of the history of the representative arts, especially the history of painting and of the novel contemporary with the invention of photography and with the advent of motion pictures, according to which art had been withdrawing from the representation of reality as from a hopeless, but always unnecessary, task.

I was counting on its being found equally natural to resist these causes for resisting the pressure of reality: if for no further reason, a general dismissal of reality depends upon theories (of knowledge, of science, of art, of reality, of realism) whose power to convince is hardly greater than reality's own. I was not unaware that, in my case, resistance to this resistance is colored by my readings of Wittgenstein and of Heidegger, each of whom I understand to be writing within the threat of skepticism, out of a philosophical necessity not so much to deny its conclusion (which it may be fashionable to do, or not to do) but to determine the place of skepticism's inspiration, as though its threat is as revelatory of human thinking as science itself is. I wrote in hopes, however, that my reading of these philosophers was not overly idiosyncratic and that I could, besides, keep them from overlying what I had it in mind to say about film.

The issue of reality for film was, in any case, forced upon me by the experience of Panofsky and of André Bazin. I felt that, whatever my discomforts with their unabashed appeals to nature and to reality, the richness and accuracy of their remarks about particular films and particular genres and figures of film, and about the particular significance of film as such, could not, or ought not, be dissociated from their conviction that film bears a relation to reality unprecedented in the other arts. I was therefore interested to discover that they had significantly misspoken themselves, or spoken unnecessarily, in speaking of film as "a dramaturgy of Nature" and in speaking of "the medium of movies [as] reality as such." They both wish, correctly, to emphasize that on film reality is not merely described or merely represented. But obviously it is not actually present to us either (anyway, obviously not present with us) when it appears to us on the screen. So I was led to consider that what makes the physical medium of film unlike anything else on earth lies in the absence of what it causes to appear to us; that is to say, in the nature of our absence from it; in its fate to reveal reality and fantasy (not by reality as such, but) by projections of reality, projections in which, as I had occasion to put it, reality is freed to exhibit itself. —I cannot say that I was entirely surprised to find that my emphasis on reality has caused a certain amount of unhappiness among readers of my book.

In the Sarasota symposium, Alexander Sesonske raised questions about this topic of reality which he intended as specifying a number of causes for unhappiness likely to be shared by others. I propose to concentrate my remarks here along a series of such causes, as I have so far understood them or shared them. I shall want to account for the way in which, at each point, the issue of reality poses itself at once as too obvious to mention and too obscure, or false, to argue. I will also have it in mind to respond to certain suspicions aroused by my limitation to the canon of talkies at my disposal as I wrote: at one extreme, by my over-indulgence of Hollywood's contributions to the history of film; at another extreme, by my all but complete neglect of contemporary experimental film making. The former limitation is thought to distort my account of what I call "traditional" movies; the latter neglect is thought to falsify my account of film's relation to modernism in the other arts, on the ground that the real modernism of the art of film is spoken for by its experimentalists, present and past.

About halfway through my book (p. 72) I give a provisional, summary characterization of what I call "the material basis of the media of movies." I say that this basis is "a succession of automatic world projections." The remainder of the book then works out some consequences of each of the major terms of this characterization. But these consequences may seem misconstrued from the beginning, because there is one whole region of film which seems to satisfy my concerns with understanding the special powers of film but which explicitly has nothing to do with projections of the real world—the region of animated cartoons. If this region of film counters my insistence upon the projection of reality as essential to the medium of movies, then it counters it completely. Here is what Sesonske says about cartoons (he is thinking specifically of Disney's work, which is fair enough: if any cartoons are obviously to be thought of as movies, even to the point of their containing stars, these are the first candidates):

> . . . neither these lively creatures nor their actions ever existed until they were projected on the screen. Their projected world

exists only *now,* at the moment of projection—and when we ask if there is any feature in which it differs from reality, the answer is, "Yes, every feature." Neither space nor time nor the laws of nature are the same. There is *a* world we experience here, but not *the* world—a world I know and see but to which I am nevertheless not present, yet not a world past. For there is no past time at which these events either did occur or purport to have occurred. Surely not the time the drawings were made, or the frames photographed; for the world I know and see had not yet sprung into existence then. It exists only now, when I see it; yet I cannot go to where its creatures are, for there is no access to its space from ours except through vision.

Each of these remarks is the negation or parody of something I claim for the experience of movies. But of course they do not prove that my claims are false except on the assumption that cartoons are movies, and that, therefore, what I said about movies, if it is true, ought to apply to cartoons in the way it applies to movies. But on my assumption (which I should no doubt have made explicit) that cartoons are not movies, these remarks about their conditions of existence constitute some explanation about *why* they are not.

Since this is merely logic, what is the moral to be drawn from the fact of cartoons? I take the moral to be something like this: A good case can be made out, using the very terms of *The World Viewed* (about a world present to me from which I am absent, about various kinds of succession or motion, about conviction and memory, etc.) that cartoons are movies. It would, therefore, in a sense not be surprising to me if someone likes to think that that is what they are. Then there is this asymmetry between his position and mine: He does not have to show that cartoons *are* movies because he has no theory which his taste contradicts. He can simply say "the two are not that different." Whereas I do, apparently, have to show that cartoons are *not* movies, or anyway show that the differences between them are as decisive as my emphasis on reality implies.

And of course I cannot show this, in the sense of prove it— any more than I can show that a robot is not a creature or that a human is not a mouse or a dog or a duck. If someone is convinced that humans are not that different from mice or dogs or ducks, he can bring a great deal of evidence in his support. There are probably more citable similarities between them than differences. To affect someone's conviction that cartoons are movies, all I could do would be to provide some reflections on cartoons. I imagine they would contain considerations of the following sort.

The chief inhabitants of the world of animated cartoons (the ones I am imagining and the ones Sesonske's remarks seem to have in mind) are talking animals—anthropomorphic, we might say, in everything but form. The human figures in them seem, in comparison with the animal figures, out of place or in the way. I think the reason for this is that there is less room, so to speak, in these human figures for our fulfillment of their animation, i.e., for our anthropomorphizing of them. If it proves to be true that human figures are thus generally problematic, then it becomes of interest to determine how the human figures that occur are made fit to occur, i.e., made to live the laws of animation.

The world inhabited by animated creatures is typically also animated; it may not remain the stable background of the actions of the live figures, but act on its own. It is animistic. There is, of course, no general problem of achieving conviction in such a world; it taps perhaps the most primitive of our convictions about the world. If I say it is essentially a child's world, I hope I will not be taken as belittling it, nor as denying that it remains an ineluctable substatum of our own, and subject to deliberate or unlooked for eruption. The difference between this world and the world we inhabit is not that the world of animation is governed by physical laws or satisfies metaphysical limits which are just different from those which condition us; its laws are often quite similar. The difference is that we are uncertain when or to what extent our laws and limits do and do not apply (which suggests that there are no real *laws* at all).

The most obvious abrogations of our limits and laws concern those governing physical identity or destruction. The possibility of metamorphosis, even a tendency toward it, is familiar enough. The abrogation of gravity is manifested in everything from the touching movements of these creatures as they trace their arabesques in the air or climb upon a friendly petal, to the momentary hesitation before a long fall and the crash which shakes the earth but is never fatal. (The topos of the hesitation suggests that what puts gravity into effect is a consciousness of it.) Or rather, what is abrogated is not gravity (things and creatures *do* fall, and petals are sometimes charmingly difficult to climb up to) but corporeality. The bodies of these creatures never get in their way. Their bodies are indestructible, one might almost say immortal; they are totally subject to will, and perfectly expressive. (Reversing the economy of human expressiveness, their bodies bear the brunt of meaningfulness. Their faces are more or less fixed, confined to two or three attitudes. This condition captures and expresses the condition, the poignance, of real animals.) They are animations, disembodiments, pure spirits.

Apparently it is natural for the animation to be of *small* animals, perhaps because they most immediately convey animatedness, quickness; perhaps because they can be given an upright posture without appearing grotesque or parodistic of the human (like chimpanzees dressed in cute clothes). The horse and the large dog (the usual principals of movies about animals) either have to be taken seriously or else they are merely comic. (Obvious exceptions here are Bambi—whom I have not seen— and Dumbo. But they are both children, and the former is an animal known for its expressive eyes and the uncanny beauty of its motion, while the latter is redeemed by its almost unbelievable discovery that it can *fly*.) Beasts which are pure spirits, they avoid, or deny, *the* metaphysical fact of human beings, that they are condemned to both souls and bodies. A world whose creatures are incorporeal is a world devoid of sex and death, hence a world apt to be either very sad or very happy. At either extreme its creatures elicit from us a painful tenderness.

If I pursued such thoughts much farther, I would perhaps start sounding theoretical. I would, at any rate, wish to locate the specific moods, emotions, and subjects which are natural to (narrative) animation. Natural is no more than natural, and may change with historical or cultural change. It does not mean that no other art *can* convey the moods and emotions, or employ the subjects, of cartoons; nor that cartoons which compete with movies cannot change. It means that each art and each change will convey and employ these moods and subjects in its own way. For example, cartoon violence can be funny because while it is very brutal it cannot be bloody. (Silent slapstick can achieve this logic; but its violence is often under-cranked, which feels semi-animated; and it is often more imminent than actual; and where active, often occurs between humans and objects, not between humans; and where between humans, often inadvertently or spasmodically.) Cartoon tenderness and loss is tenderness and loss maximized, or purified. Cartoon terror is absolute, because since the body is not destructible, the threat is to the soul itself. (This is different from horror movies. There the threat is not of isolation through abandonment or annihilation, but of isolation through unacknowledgeable disfigurement. They play upon the fear that cartoons laugh at: irreversible metamorphosis.)—Does Popeye have a soul? Well, does he have a human body? A sailor is nicely suited for exaggerated forearms; and for the rest, Popeye's body survives, or ignores, everything that brute human strength can deliberately inflict upon it—if, that is, it at some point receives its magic infusion of canned fuel. His body is not so much fed as stoked, and with a substance for herbivores, anyway for creatures of non-violence, for mythical children. (His timid acquaintance is also associated with a childish food, ground meat, no real amount of which satisfies his need. Which other human figures are indecorous enough to be shown eating?) Steam up, his body acts on its own, unaligned with, and not affecting, other avenues of expression: his face remains, through violence, preternaturally fixed; his voice goes on with its continuous static of undecipherable commentary; at last his pipe releases a whistle or two of satisfaction.

In cartoons, sexuality is apt to be either epicene or caricatured. I suppose this is because cartoons, being fleshless, do not veer toward the pornographic, although, given a chance, they may naturally veer toward the obscene. Of course, overlaps and affinities may be expected among various media. A cartoon of Garbo or Dietrich or Marilyn Monroe will miss what is truly attractive about them—not simply their specific physical presences but the animation of those presences by the human female's exemplification of independence and profundity and wit. A cartoon of Mae West, however, may really capture her genius, because she is already a caricature of sexuality; the caricature of sexuality is her subject. It is the essence of her deflationary comedy that her blatant presence signifies nothing special. She is the woman of *no* mystery, or the woman whose interest has nothing to do with mystery. The invitation of her gait and voice are not suggestive, but epicene—nothing permanent ever happens. The stuffing of her dress is no more revealing than the giant hanging member on the front of an old clown. It is not arousing, but funny and obscene. Her constant self-possession and good humor mock our obsession with the subject of sexuality, both our cravings for it and our evasions of it.

Have I missed Sesonske's point about cartoons? Is the point that my characterization of movies as successions of automatic world projections rules out the consideration of cartoons altogether as a species of film—that, so to speak, according to me they ought not to exist, or ought not to be able to exist? That would be bad. Then I might say that cartoons are successions of animated world projections. And I would expect this characterization also to be no more helpful, and no emptier, than what it is meant, and may prove, to summarize.

Perhaps I am unduly solemn. Perhaps Sesonske's point— when he says that "the two are not that different"—really is confined to the joke in it: not that movies in general and cartoons as such are "not that different," but specifically that Hollywood feature films are mostly mickey mouse. I think that our experiences may really disagree here; if they do, I cannot afford to laugh this off.

Everything I wrote in *The World Viewed* about Hollywood films is perfectly compatible with a claim that most of them are childish or worthless. (Though I am still willing to bet that this is true of no greater a proportion of them than of, say, French or Russian films, a part of whose prestige comes from our knowing so few of them, I assume the best.) My problem was rather to understand, if the accidents and stringencies of Hollywood production were the wholly baneful things that devotees of non-Hollywood films suggest, how so many of them could have been so good. (I am not prepared to argue with someone who is prepared to say that all are worthless.) People sometimes say, when their experience of some of these films cannot be denied, that they are good in spite of Hollywood's bosses and agents. But what reason is there to believe this? Does it make any sense at all to think of figures like John Ford or Howard Hawks or Frank Capra or Preston Sturges as *limited* by Hollywood? (Perhaps others could have made better Hollywood movies. No; theirs are perfect of their kind. Then other people could have made better movies of different kinds and were kept out by Hollywood commercialism. I do not doubt it, but this is not a problem peculiar to America and its Hollywood.) Shall we blame Hollywood moguls for the obsession with happy endings? We can hear some maddening stories along this line. But this gossip will not account for the good films which call for, and earn, their happy endings. All that the prevalence of the happy ending shows—to the extent that it prevails and to the extent that it is more common in American than in foreign films—is that Hollywood did its best work in genres which call for happy endings. Of course it is arguable that the genres and conventions of Hollywood films are themselves the essential limitation. But to argue that, you have to show either that there are no comparable limitations in other traditions or else that their limitations (say a Russian tendency toward the monumental and operatic, or a French tendency toward the private and provincial, or a German tendency toward the theatrical and claustrophobic) are less limiting. Hollywood films are not everything; neither is American fiction at its greatest. But it is not clear to me that American films occupy a less honorable place among the films of the world than American fiction occupies in world literature.

It is typical of my procedures in *The World Viewed* to invite words or concepts which are common, all but unavoidable, in speaking about film, and then try to discover what there is in these words and in my experience of these objects that they should go together. This means that I must often say things that will sound more or less familiar. The obvious risks here are that I will either not be credited for saying something new or else not be saying something new. Neither seems to me unbearable.

Sensing an accuracy in the idea of a type, and feeling that film creates new access to drama's ancient concern with types, I traced these intuitions to the fact that on film the type is not primarily the character but primarily the actor. The sets of "fixed attitudes and attributes" by which types are defined—as these are at work in the experience of film—are established by the individual and total physiognomy (of face, of figure, of gait, of temperament) of the human beings taking part in the drama. For this reason, a type on the screen need not be established in theatrical tradition, by the recurrence of a role in a corpus of plays; it can be established by the recurrence of an actor in a corpus of films. (This is why, in my sketching a list of Hollywood types [p. 36], I mixed together the names of characters and of stars.) This helped explain to me why I find that the distinction between actor and character is broken up on the screen; and I was led to speak of the individuals projected on the screen as individualities and, implicitly, to deny in the experiencing of them the distinction between types and well-rounded characters. So I am not likely to be much impressed by the statement that European directors (Sesonske mentions Renoir, Vigo, and Pagnol), unlike Hollywood directors, concern themselves with characters and *not* types. I will hardly deny that the major European directors have made different sorts of movies than the major American directors have made; nor am I interested to deny that their films are on the whole better than those made in America. But their differences are not touched, or they are obscured, by saying that the American keep to a concern with types and the European do not.

I would find it hard to believe that anyone admires *Grand Illusion, Rules of the Game, Zero for Conduct* and *L'Atalante* more than I, but it seems to me more accurate to their intention and effect to say that they are explorations of types rather than explorations of characters. Naturally this could be "proven" only in the specific analysis and experience of the individual works themselves. But just think of the obvious surface of their content. The figures in both of the Renoir films are insistently labelled for us: the Aristocrat, the Jew, the Officer, the Professor, the Good Guy, the Poacher, the Wronged Wife, the

Impetuous Lover. The shared subjects of the films depend upon this; both are about the arbitrariness and the inevitably of labels, and thence about the human need for society and the equal human need to escape it, and hence about human privacy and unknownness. They are about the search for society, or community, outside, or within, society at large. So are the films of Vigo. And if four of the greatest films ever made are about the same subject, it gives one to think that film has here found one of its great subjects. It is the subject I found to underlie the Western as well as American thirties' comedies and musicals, and therefore to begin to account for the remarkable fact that works within just *these* genres are among the highest achievements of the art of film. The terms I used were different: I spoke of individual autonomy and its resemblance to outlawry, and of the claims placed upon autonomy by society and by love.

Let us suppose that *L'Atalante* is the best film ever made about the idea of marriage, specifically about the ideas of taking in marriage and being given in marriage. The richness and the beauty and the convincingness of the film have nothing to do with anything I understand as a study of character. Compared to Desdemona and Othello, Vigo's bride and groom are, well, mere types. We know and learn next to nothing about them; nothing they do need puzzle us. She is a village beauty who expects to find excitement in the world outside; he becomes frightened and jealous of her attention to attractions which are not within his power to provide; she leaves, more or less innocently; he retaliates by abandoning her; they long for one another; they are happy when they are reunited. The character of the old man is somewhat more developed, but Vigo's concern with it is not to explore it very far. We learn that the old man is superstitious, appreciates women and is successful with them, that he is capable of natural courtesy but also of crudity and selfishness, and that he has been around. In short, an old sailor. We know that he somehow holds the key to the plot or plight of the little community, but this is a function of his actions rather than of his character (if we are to have that distinction): If this marriage is to take effect—which the Church, and the community of the village, and apparently satisfactory sex, have all failed to insure—then the old man will have to effect it. That is, he will have to *give* the bride. He has authority in this because we have seen him win her for himself.

This is a nice little yarn and, as in any nice little yarn, there are any number of treasures to be found, any number including zero. They are found here by the resonance that Vigo's camera, with wit, with tact, with accuracy, elicits from these temperaments in those actions in these settings at those times. From that we learn more than we knew of wedding processions, how they can feel like funeral processions, presumably because they commemorate the dying of the bride to her past; we know more precisely and memorably than we had known of the daze and remoteness of brides, of the innocence of grooms, of the daze and remoteness of a husband who recognizes that he has been no husband; we know more certainly that a man wins a beautiful young girl only when he wins her imagination, i.e., only when he can share his imagination with her, and that if he can do that he may even be ugly and not young; we realize—for the first time or the fiftieth, it makes no difference—that one's responsibility to one's desire is to acknowledge it, and acknowledge its object, i.e., acknowledge its object's separateness from you. The power of these last ideas, as they find incarnation in the image of the husband searching under water for his love, is finally as inexplicable as the power of a phrase of music or of poetry. And the ideas are nothing without that power. Of course there is a sense of character explored. It is our own.

I am reminded here—and there are passages in my book which show that it kept being reminded—of Thomas Mann's description, in his essay on Freud, of the "point at which the psychological interest passes over into the mythical," and of his assertion that "the typical is actually the mythical." Mann speaks of the step he took as a novelist when his subject-matter moved "from the bourgeois and individual to the mythical and typical" and he finds that "the mythical knowledge resides in the gazer and not in that at which he gazes." Mann locates this knowledge and gaze within "the mythically oriented artist," and what he says seems applicable also to major writers of this century otherwise different from him. What he finds to be an achievement for the novel I find to be the natural mode of revelation for film. That gaze of knowledge is the province of camera and screen; it is the power with which the director, in his pact with his audience, begins. —The mythical in the typical. I am not claiming that that is clear. I am explaining why I would like for it to be made clear. Beyond accounting for the irrelevance of character and individual psychology in assessing the significance of screened figures, it suggests the right level of explanation for the familiar fact that mediocre novels often make good film scripts and that great novels almost never do.

Sesonske writes: "In the days of silent film it was necessary, of course, to be content with mere types . . . [because] speech is so deeply implicated in the formation and expression of our character, our identity as individuals. . . . One has to search hard among serious American slient films to find a single credible or really interesting character. But as soon as the actors began to speak, the possibilities changed." Two brief remarks about this. (1) As soon as the actors began to speak, an immediate new possibility was exactly the definition of a type through his particular attitude and attribute of speech: one need think no further than of the best comedians of the early talkies—for example, of Groucho and of Harpo (whose muteness, as well as his particular repertory of sounds, most brilliantly declares the new medium), and of Mae West and W. C. Fields—characters unthinkable apart from their singular voices. (2) It must have been Sesonske's impatience with my views that caused him, I assume, not to consider Chaplin in this light—the Little Man, the Tramp, who is a type, and reenacts types, as deep as comedy. (Enid Welsford, in her study of folly, more than once emphasizes particular actors in the development of comic stage types. It suggests itself that the early affinity of film with comedy is an expression of their respective latitudes and appetites for the actor's individuality, something that suits each of them for being "popular.")

Having spoken of Renoir and Vigo, and remembering afresh the vividness in their films of Michel Simon and Dita Parlo and Jean Gabin and Marcel Dalio, I can hardly avoid recurring to the topic of acting and performance for film. I agree with Sesonske that a number of my remarks on this topic are weak and unconvincing. And he has called me on a couple of stupid slips. He finds that I had written, "The audience in a theater can be defined as those to whom the actors are present while they are not present to the actors." That is a conflation of two ideas. The first records a theme of some earlier essays of mine in which I define the audience in a theater as those to whom the *characters* are present while they are not present to the characters; the second contrasts the audience in a movie house as those present neither to the characters nor the actors. Again, I was wrong, in discussing the different ways in which an actor's role is explored for the screen and for the stage, to put this as though it was always the actor who did the exploring and not the director; what I was saying does not depend on any such general division of labor.

Sesonske writes: "De Sica and Bresson have not shown that film does not require actors but rather that there is something of the actor in us all. . . ." I say that particular people who are successful subjects for the screen may also be accomplished actors. The implication is that whether their accomplishments as actors are relevant to the screen is up to the screen; it cannot be determined *a priori,* i.e., without experiencing them on the screen. And the same is true of the non-professional's native gifts for acting. When, late in my book, I go back to my initial resistance to the idea of film's subjects as actors, what I say is: "But obviously they are actors the way any human being is" (p. 153). Does this say less than "there is something of the actor in us all?" It says that we are all ineluctably actors, leaving it open—as the word leaves it open and as our lives leave it open—how far that means we theatricalize ourselves and how far we are naturalized, fated both to motion and to motive; and it suggests that our condition as actors is shown not particularly by De Sica and Bresson, but by film itself. One might say that what De Sica and Bresson (and others) have shown is that there is something of the type in us all, something of the singular and the mythical. It is not merely that we occupy certain roles in society, play certain parts or hold certain offices, but that we are set apart or singled out for sometimes incomprehensible reasons, for rewards or punishments out of all proportion to anything we recognize ourselves as doing or being, as though our lives are the enactments of some tale whose words continuously escape us. The mismatch of intention and consequence was the natural province of tragedy in theater. On film it is the natural province of comedy, and of something that is neither tragedy nor comedy, exemplified by *Bicycle Thief* or by *Nights of Cabiria* or by *The Diary of a Country Priest,* in which the mismatch appears as the distance between the depth to which an ordinary human life requires expression, and the surface of ordinary means through which that life must, if it will, express itself. One may call such forms secular mysteries.

De Sica and Bresson are directors, along with Dreyer and Fellini, famous for their interest in unknown physiognomies. One might take this interest as incompatible with my emphasis on the recurrence of actors across their roles. But why? I do say that the use of unknown faces is a special possibility, and

I relate its special power to the different powers of recurrence (p. 159). A further way to see its specialness is to compare it with the casting of unknowns in the theater. There the fact of unknownness is artistically more or less irrelevant; you take the person best for your conception of the part, or most reliable, or one whom you can afford, or one forced upon you by the management. These considerations are also at play in casting films. But sometimes a film director, some film directors in particular, require physiognomies for their subjects which not merely happen to be unknown but whose point, whose essence, is *that* they are unknown. Not just any unknown face will do; it must be one which, when screened, conveys unknownness; and this first of all means that it conveys privacy—an individual soul's aliveness or deadness to itself. A natural reason for a director's requirement of this quality is that his film is itself about unknownness, about the fact and causes of separateness or isolation or integrity or outlawry. The greatest use of this quality, in my experience, is found in Dreyer's *Passion of St. Joan*. One of the burdens of my book is that a film of such depth must be giving deep significance to conditions of the medium of film itself. (This is, or ought to be, the meaning of "cinematic.") Dreyer's film above all declares at once the power of the camera to interrogate its subjects and, for all its capacity for pitilessness, its final impotence to penetrate the mystery of the individual human face. —The force of this declaration is to be measured against the use of known faces, as known, to the same effect, which generally means placing them in unanticipated environments. I give sufficient examples of this in my book to attest to my conviction that this is a tendency of film as such, adjoining its tendency to discover at any moment the endless contingency of the individual human's placement in the world, as though nothing could be more unanticipated than one's existence itself, always in placement. The physiognomies of Chaplin, Keaton, Garbo, perhaps Gary Cooper, consistently explore this experience; they are at home everywhere and nowhere. The mystery of the familiar is caught memorably in the faces of Henry Fonda in *The Wrong Man,* Cary Grant in *Suspicion* or in one of his Hawksian disguises, Ginger Rogers in *Roxie Hart,* Joan Crawford in *A Woman's Face,* Billy Burke in *The Wizard of Oz,* Joe E. Brown in *A Midsummer Night's Dream,* Rita Hayworth in *The Lady from Shanghai,* Montgomery Clift in *From Here to Eternity,* Burt Lancaster in *The Leopard,* Clark Gable in *The Misfits,* and, trailing off, John Garfield in *Gentleman's Agreement,* and Kirk Douglas in *The List of Adrian Messenger.*

The difference between stage and screen acting cannot be determined apart from determining the differences between stage and screen, between the nature and participation of their audiences and the role of their directors; above all, by the first fact about acting that I looked at in my book—that in a stage performance the actors are present, live, and in a screen performance not. Is this important, or trivial? Mostly it is obscure.

What is the screen actor not, if he is not live? Is he dead? Not necessarily, but he *could* be. He could also be sitting next to me, which he could not be if he were on stage (and I not). —These seem stupid mysteries. Of course it's not *him* on the screen. Nothing is *on* the screen, but, at best, moving light and shadows. It's the *performance* which is live. —As contrasted with what? Since the use of sound transcription and videotaping, "live" performances contrast with recorded performances. And it seems that there ought to be this same contrast between what is presented to us on the stage and on the screen. From here it will occur to someone to ask, Then what is a movie a recording of?; to which the answer is apt to be, Nothing. From here, in turn, it may seem to follow that the issue of reality is settled, that movies are "something on their own"; the only thing they *could* be recordings of—real events happening as they are transcribed on the screen—have simply never taken place. Film *can* be used as a sort of recording device, as in newsreels. But the events in a movie are ones we can never be, or can never have been, present at apart from the movie itself. So the issue about the presence of the world and the actor, raised by Panofsky and Bazin, and modified by me, is a false issue. Movies and their actors are what they are. —With this last assertion I shall hardly disagree. What are they?

First of all, movies are not recordings. It is worth seeing why they are not. In calling something a recording (say of a piece of music), two criteria are in play: (1) there is an original, separate event of which this is a recording and to which one can be present directly, so to speak; anyway, present apart from the recording; (2) the recording is in principle aurally indistinguishable from that event, where "in principle" signifies that the essential virtue of a recording is fidelity. Now when someone says that we cannot have been present at the events projected on the screen apart from that projection itself, *nothing* follows about what *is* apart from that projection itself. In particular, it does not follow that reality has played no essential role in the origin of that projection. All that follows is that any role reality has played is not that of having been recorded. But reality is not so much as a candidate for that role, because the projections we view on a screen are not in principle aurally or visually indistinguishable from the events of which they are projections— what could be more distinguishable? So to say we cannot have been present apart from the projection does not settle the question of reality; it does not so much as raise it. (Someone may say "can't have been present" because they believe that the issue *oughtn't* so much as be raised; or they may say it to me in particular because they imagine that I have asserted that one *can* have been present. We will have to get closer to both of these claims.)

Then the state of the present question is this: If reality does play an essential role in understanding the medium of film, and if its role is not that of being recorded, then what *is* its role? My book gives a series of answers to that question. I describe the role of reality as one of being photographed, projected, screened, exhibited, and viewed. (These answers are the paths of my differences from Panofsky's and Bazin's emphasis on "reality itself.") The significance I attach to these terms can be assessed, I believe, by nothing short of my book as a whole.

Take my speaking of the fate of the camera as one of revealing all and only what is revealed to it. Sesonske calls this a myth of immaculate conception, i.e., one more way of denying the human role in human conceiving. My description certainly was mythological, as the terms "fate" and "revelation" in this context declare. But the mythological point of the description was not exactly to describe purity. My use of the term "camera" in this context, to begin with, stood for the entire physical apparatus which comes between what is before the camera and what results after it, on the screen; it stands for the camera, plus its lenses and filters, plus its film, plus the light required to expose its film, plus the physical procedures of preparing the film for projection. (I am defining the word "camera," so to speak, in terms of its final cause.) Now when I speak of the camera, so understood, as revealing all and only what is revealed to it, I do not limit what is revealed by it merely to the subject which has passed before it. The revelation can, as it were, come from inside. Before the camera, let us say, stands a white building. If what results on the screen is a shaky white building, or a blurred or deformed one, or two identical ones moving past one another, this does not prove unclean conception—unless, perhaps, it prompts us to believe that the building itself is shaking, or is subject to deformation as in a cartoon, or is capable of self-locomotion and spontaneous self-duplication. The mythological point about the camera's revelations is twofold: first, that the camera has no choice either over what is revealed to it nor over what it reveals; and second, that what is revealed to and by it can only be known by what appears upon the print or screen.

The first fold of the point, about the camera's lack of choice, is not an emphasis on its chastity but on its sterility. To say it has no choice is to say that it is a species of machine, a contrivance, and a reasonably simple one at that, compared, say, with a TV set. You can call its work immaculate, not because its conception is produced inhumanly (i.e., automatically), though the extent to which it works automatically is an essential fact about its work; but because it has no conception whatever of its own. (A camera is a kind of room, not a kind of womb.) It does all and only what it is made to do. It tells no lies, any more than a typewriter tells lies; not because it is perfectly honest but because it is perfectly dumb. Unlike your use of a typewriter, however, you cannot know what you have made the camera do, what is revealed to it, until its results have appeared. This was the second fold of my mythological point about it: that the mysteriousness of the photograph lies not in the machinery which produces it, but in the unfathomable abyss between what it captures (its subject) and what is captured for us (*this* fixing of the subject), the metaphysical wait between exposure and exhibition, the absolute authority or finality of the fixed image. The weight of this point is not reduced if some director is in fact able to predict his results with assured accuracy. Hitchcock is famous for this. One might say that he has the gift of photographic prophecy. Or one could explore the possibility that he limits beforehand what he shoots to what he can thus assuredly foretell. I mean explore the possible consequences upon his style.

Film turns our epistemological convictions inside out: reality is known before its appearances are known. The epistemological mystery is whether, and how, you can predict the existence of the one from the knowledge of the other. The photographic mystery is that you can know both the appearance and the reality, but that nevertheless the one is unpredictable from the other.

Take again the project I cited in which Edward Steichen took a thousand shots of the same cup and saucer. Each shot, let us suppose, is different, each has a different physiognomy. But do what he will—change lenses, use different film or filters, vary the lighting, the angle, the distance—it is still the same cup and saucer. Therein lies the fascination of the thing of photography, like the fascination in faces. The art of the thing lies in the capacity for finding what will cause what, and for finding what is wanted.

I said that the camera has no conception of its own. But it can be said, unlike a recording apparatus, to lead a life of its own, with its own possibilities of variation and inflection. (A tape recorder may also be said to "lead a life of its own." This would mean, apart from certain specific manipulations to improve the quality of its sound, that it is no longer reproducing independently recognizable sounds, and perhaps that it is not attentive to any sounds at all apart from its own powers of originating them.) These are original with it, and they create its particular temptations, but they are not its sins. They are either its stupidities or its glories, depending upon who is using it. Here is where sin gets a foothold. (The situation is described by Descartes when he is rehearsing the contents of the mind. They may be distorted, but in themselves they are not erroneous. Error arises when you make judgments on the basis of them.) This is the specific topic of the sections of my book called "The Camera's Implication" and "Assertions in Techniques." It is the topic, in my terms, of *giving significance* to a possibility of film.

I say, in effect, that any and every gesture of the camera may or may not mean something, and every cut and every rhythm of cuts, and every framing and every inflection within a frame —something determined by the nature of film and by the specific context in which the gesture occurs in a particular film. I call such possibilities of the physical medium of film its automatisms. They are the bearers of the film maker's intentions—like syntactical and lexical elements of a language. Unlike speakers of a language, film makers can construct not merely, as it were, new sentences, but new elements of sentences. This intentionality of film's automatisms dictates the perspective from which a critical understanding of a film must proceed. It is a perspective from which a certain level of description is called forth, one in service of the question, "Why is this as it is?"—the critical question—which may be directed toward works of art as toward any of the acts and works of human beings and of their societies. Suppose that it would be true to describe what is shown on the screen as a shot of a stairway. This description may or may not have a point (beyond cataloging the shot). If one calls what is shown a "point of view shot," one may go on to say that such a shot may be established by, for example, cutting to it from the face of a character and cutting from it back to that face. This can seem a sort of syntactic remark, like saying that, in English, in standard declarative form the object of a verb follows the verb. Its usefulness will depend upon how many further remarks of that sort you are able to offer, and how systematically you arrange them. (The analogy with syntax is extremely thin. The term "verb" carries systematic implications on its face, like the term "subdominant," but unlike the terms "travelling shot," "medium shot," "point of view," etc.). If, however, you go on to say why *this* way of establishing a point of view is used, and why *here,* and why with respect to *this* character, and why by way of *this* content, then you are proposing a critical understanding of this passage. Its interest will depend upon its faithfulness to the intention of this work. But what will you be saying if you say, speaking about this work, that this shot is a point of view shot, and you go on to say nothing further about this shot in this work? Unless your words here are meant to correct a false impression, they do not so much as add up to a remark. They are at most the uttering of a name, which, as Wittgenstein puts it, is a preparation for going on to say something. No narrative device is more common than a cut from and to a character as he enters or leaves a room. In *Grand Illusion,* a film obsessed with the entering and leaving of rooms, with the relations between the inside and the outside of a dwelling, with the impassability of sills and frames, this most common of devices is actively avoided until the beginning of the last act, at the farm. Then we cut from Gabin entering a doorway away from us, still in the cold and foreign night, to Gabin entering through that doorway towards us, into a bright kitchen. The very commonness of the gesture yields to, and acknowledges, the commonness, the anonymity, of the need for warmth and food.

Good directors know how to mean everything they do. Great directors mean more—more completely, more subtly, more specifically—and they discover how to do everything they mean. The gestures of bad directors are empty—they speak, as it were, nonsense. The implication of this theme is the absolute responsibility of the artist for the actions and assertions in his work. It is an instance of the human being's absolute responsibility for the intentions and consequences of his actions, and a kind of solace for it. (The human condemnation to intention and consequence is the sequel, if not the meaning, of original sin.) My impatience with the idea that photographs and paintings never really project or represent reality (when, that is, they obviously do) expresses my sense that, as elsewhere, a fake skepticism is being used to deny that human responsibility.

We may need freedom from this responsibility, but the denial of its claims is no route to that freedom, except within the bounds of comedy or of religion. Film is a moving image of skepticism: not only is there a reasonable possibility, it is a fact that here our normal senses are satisfied of reality while reality does not exist—even, alarmingly, *because* it does not exist, because viewing it is all it takes. Our vision is doubtless otherwise satisfiable than by the viewing of reality. But to deny, on skeptical grounds, just *this* satisfaction—to deny that it is ever reality which film projects and screens—is a farce of skepticism. It seems to remember that skepticism concludes against our conviction in the existence of the external world, but it seems to forget that skepticism begins in an effort to justify that conviction. The basis of film's drama, or the latent anxiety in viewing its drama, lies in its persistent demonstration that we do not know what our conviction in reality turns upon. To yield here to the familiar wish to speak of film as providing in general an "illusion of reality" would serve to disguise this latent anxiety—as does the conclusion of philosophical skepticism itself. This idea of the illusion of reality dims the differences in the role of reality posed in painting, in theater, and in film, and it closes out the wish of art to address reality in order to combat, or suspend, our illusions of it. The "sense of reality" played upon in comedy and by religion, or searched by philosophy and in tragedy, is neither enforced nor escaped through film; one might say that it is there entertained.

The moral of film's image of skepticism is not that reality is a dream and not that reality confines our dreams. In screening reality, film screens its givenness from us; it holds reality from us, it holds reality before us, i.e., withholds reality before us. We are tantalized at once by our subjection to it and by its subjection to our views of it. But while reality is the bearer of our intentions it is possible, as I put it in my book, to refuse to allow it to dictate what shall be said about it (p. 120). Flanked by its claims to speak for us, it is still open to us in moments to withhold it before ourselves, so that we may see for ourselves and may gladly grant that we are somewhat spoken for. To know how far reality is open to our dreams would be to know how far reality is confined by our dreams of it.

One will perhaps wish here to distinguish between natural and social reality (or between epistemological and political "givenness"). But I doubt that we yet know what becomes, on film, of the distinction, hence the relation, between nature and culture, or between individual and society. Nature is naturally projected as the scene of specific human occupation; contrariwise, society tends to be projected in human relations which are either wholly personal or wholly anonymous. I mentioned in *The World Viewed* the tendency of film to project the idea of community in the form of male comradeship (p. 48), as though the sense of belonging together as citizens could only appear as an intimacy of discipline, and only after the nation had been threatened (as by war) or exercised its rejection (as by prisons). (Work can provide pools of comradeship if it has an internal drama and involves the adventure of danger—rigging and drilling for oil comes to mind; but the possibility of comradeship within factories seems available only for propaganda, as an image of mobilization, or for the explicitly fantastic.) It is common enough for social evil to be projected as the deliberate product of melodramatic aging villains. Capra's *It's a Wonderful Life* most innocently reveals a further range of this fantasy. The hero's ruin is averted when the good people, the little people, band together with their individual contributions, returning personal favors done for them over the years by this man. The sentiment in the scene is very deep. It has been constructed as cunningly as a Keaton gag; what caps it, finally bursting the dam of tears, is the crowding of this band of goodness into this hero's house, each member testifying individually to his or her affection for him; so that the good society, the good of society at large, is pictured as this man's family (personally sponsored, what's more, by a denizen of heaven). This justice, hence this society, is poetic or nothing. The film adopts the terms, and at least equals the effect, of *A Christmas Carol,* told as it were from Cratchit's point of view. I would forego its effect if we had something to equal, say, *Bleak House.* But in that case the effect would not be so worrisome.

One may think to settle the issue of reality by saying something like this: "Let us agree that movies are made of incisions, ingestions, projections, and what not, of reality. Then it is just a matter of emphasis whether you go on to study the significance of the fact that the ingestions and projections are manipulated and arranged (e.g., edited) or whether you go on to study the fact that the manipulated and arranged projections are of reality." This sounds sensible enough, and I do not wish to appear unreasonable; but I cannot accept this idea of alternative and noncompeting emphases, for two main reasons.

1. Generally, because a difference of emphasis may, in philosophizing, make all the difference in the world. Whether you emphasize nature's likenesses or unlikenesses to an artifact may determine whether you wind up with a proof for the existence of God. Whether you emphasize the likenesses or the unlikenesses between men and women may determine what you take their relationship to promise. Whether you emphasize liberty or equality may determine whether you are a liberal or a socialist. The question is why your emphasis falls where it does, and whether it makes sufficient and exact room for the competing emphasis.

This is a theoretical question, anyway a philosophical question, which only means that it is not going to be settled by any given set of instances alone. Take, for example, Dziga Vertov's *Man With a Movie Camera,* which is at the least a brilliant anthology of the tricks a loaded camera and fixed and refixed film can play. It is a natural example for someone to appeal to who wishes to emphasize film's independence of reality. But it is fully open to me to say that what this film shows is precisely the inescapability of reality, its fixed point within every brilliance of technique. It would not in fact be so good an instance for my emphasis unless its technique were an extreme of brilliance, for only then would it suggest that the extremest bound of technique is still leashed to reality. It is only within this theoretical issue that a simpler fact about this film's declaration of reality can make itself felt, viz., that all virtuosity of technique is quite overwhelmed, or silenced, by a shot of childbirth.

2. My more specific reason for rejecting the sensible proposal about alternative emphases is that there is no sensible alternative of the kind proposed. To speak of reality photographed, projected, screened, exhibited, and viewed, just *is* to speak of the specific *ways* in which—arrangements in which and successions by which—reality is projected, screened, etc. This is another way of emphasizing what I called "giving significance to specific possibilities and necessities of the physical medium." Whereas, alternatively, to speak of the arrangements and successions of projections apart from the fixed point of reality is to block comprehension of why the arrangements and successions are as they are. Such a claim can only be proven in the analysis and criticism of particular films; that is the only source of evidence there is for any theory of film—but as usual only the theory can tell you what to look for, or what counts, as evidence. If, as suggested, someone believes that we never see reality as it is, with or without a camera, on the basis of some epistemological or scientific theory of vision, then immediately he owes us a presentation of this theory. (If one believes that projection inevitably distorts what is seen, then this must be compared with cases in which one is convinced that projection alone can reveal what is seen—as, for example, in a slow-motion shot of a moment of impact, or a time-lapse sequence of a gathering storm.) Whether or not this theory is forthcoming, however, I am content to proceed on the assumption that the camera is no better off epistemologically or scientifically than the naked eye—that the camera provides views of reality only on the assumption that we normally do, apart from the camera, see reality, i.e., see live persons and real things in

actual spaces. (The fact that one and the same cup and saucer can appear in continuous variations and inflections of light and of angle *may* play a role in the conclusion that we never see objects as they are. But as it stands this fact is as unexceptional as the fact that you could not see the cup and saucer were they in total darkness. What else would you expect? —There is also no end to the ways these objects may be picked out in words; but variations and inflections among alternative words are not naturally continuous. This difference will affect what counts "as possibilities" in photographing and in writing, hence what counts as giving or showing the significance of these possibilities in what you choose them to say.)

If, again, one denies that it is reality which is projected, on the ground that spatial or temporal relations within and among projections are not the same as spatial or temporal relations within and among real things and persons, I may not be much moved to disagree—as long, that is, as one sees that such a remark says either practically nothing or practically everything ambiguously. To say that spatial and temporal relations in reality are not what they are in the projection of reality would be a way of saying at least two things. It would repeat and begin to specify the point that projections are not recordings, they do not reproduce what they are of—in the sense that a reproduction of a statue reproduces the dimensionality of the statue (is another statue), or the reproduction of a painting reproduces the dimensionality of the painting. And it would stress the fact that the physical medium of film, like the physical medium of painting (paint on a two-dimensional surface), or like an aesthetic medium of literature (e.g., one of its genres), obeys its own laws, has its own autonomy—even when it is also a representation of reality. So, for example, you can compose a slow-moving narrative of a fast-moving horse race, and you can represent a horse rearing in a painting which itself does not rear. You merely have to know, or find out, how to do it; and your audience merely has to know how to read what you have done.

You might, having now stressed the autonomy of the medium, its obedience to its own laws, then go on to discover and publish what those laws, or some set of them, are. You might, for example, discover some syntactical laws (as it were) governing this medium's power of narration (but then, of course, one will have to know what you understand its lexicon to be). Or you might really discover particular ways in which the two-dimensionality of the projection, or of the screen, is organized in order to capture certain dramatic or fictional qualities of the three-dimensional space it projects. Such laws, whose promulgation I could only welcome, will take their place in position with the other facts about this medium which we know, or believe, to enter into its working, e.g., with the fact that it is photographic, and therefore, to draw one further inference from this proposition, that the general relation between a projection and what it projects is not an achievement within the medium (as in the relation between a visual representation and what it represents) but constitutes the inception of the medium altogether, so that exploring the physical basis of the medium is not, as in the case of painting, like exploring and mastering the uses of tools but rather like exploring and mastering the powers of an instrument, such as the Hammond organ. The possibility invites one, accordingly, to become a virtuoso of the instrument without, so to speak, being able to say anything upon it of any significance. The moral is merely that if one is to discover laws for the artistic medium which takes the medium of film as its physical basis, one will first of all have to know which players of the instrument have been able to speak significantly upon it, and what it is they have been saying.

A further motive for denying the fixed point of reality is the supposition that this leaves no room for the art of movies. A poor reason for the supposition is that this seems to leave no room for the work of the cinematographer. This pictures the cinematographer in terms of his manipulations of his equipment and images. Whereas I have wished to insist upon his, in principle, incessant exercise of insight and choice, for example, upon *whether* to manipulate, and how, and how much; and to emphasize that this exercise begins before there is anything to cut or pan or freeze, and continues until he has the insight, and the choice, to stop. A better reason for supposing the fixed point of reality to crowd out the art of movies is that, as remarked, realism had become, at the time of the advent of photography and continuing through the advent of the motion picture, the central issue in the practice of the other major representative arts. This is why I felt drawn into a discussion of modernist painting, beginning a couple of centuries ago, as a history of responses to the loss of connection with reality and a consequent history of painting's ways of reestablishing this connection, which in practice required a self-conscious reestablishing of its connection with the past of its art. I described the artistic significance of the motion picture (whatever its new powers of entertainment and documentation) as its apparent and unpredictable solution of the problem of reality at a stroke, by its miraculous neutralizing of the need to connect with reality through representing it, by its stroke of acquiring this connection through successive projections of reality itself. And I went on to say that this had also not solved the problem of reality but brought it to some ultimate head, since the connection is established by putting us in the condition of "viewing unseen," which establishes the connection only at the price of establishing our absolute distance and isolation. And this is exactly the price of skepticism. —My complaint against the complaint against me to the effect that I am naive about reality is that it is naive about reality.

There are more obvious reasons for taking my emphasis on reality to be misguided. I mention two of them. (1) My insistence seems just to deny the obvious fact that what appears on the screen may not be real from the beginning; the props may be fake and the backgrounds painted. (2) It seems to neglect the decisive role, in our experience of film, of composition within the frame.

1. Let us distinguish between the counterfeit and the artificial, between cases in which the fake props and painted backgrounds are meant to fool the camera into thinking that what is revealed to it is reality, and cases in which their point is explicitly their non-reality.

Explicit artifice is, first of all, quite rare; not just rare, but specialized. The instances I cite in my book are from German expressionism and from technicolor make-believes. Suppose that the only point of reality in these films is the ultimate point in any film, namely the actors—not a real animal or tree or sky or meadow or body of water to be found. Then what happens is that the locales of such films are given a specialized psychological or spiritual interpretation; we interpret them as projections of the characters', or some character's, state of soul, as their dreams, their fantasies, their madness. We interpret them in one direction or another, that is, as *competing* with our sense of reality. This means that the acting must be as stylized as the locale; dictated by it, so to speak. I assume this is obvious in *Caligari*. In *The Wizard of Oz* you have, within the dream, just two characters who are not of this artifice, whose sense of reality is ours, a young girl and her dog. The unmasking of the Wizard is a declaration of the point of the movie's artifice. He is unmasked not by removing something from him but by removing him from a sort of television or movie stage, in which he had been projecting and manipulating his image. His behavior changes; he no longer can, but also no longer has to, maintain his image, and he demonstrates that the magic of artifice in fulfilling or threatening our wishes is no stronger than, and in the end must bow to, the magic of reality; that, for example, Margaret Hamilton on a broomstick in the sky of Oz and Margaret Hamilton on a bicycle in a black-and-white projection of Kansas, taps one and the same source of power, call it the human craving for reality, call it the craving for our fantasies and reality to complete or to project one another.

The case of counterfeiting reality is the typical case. Here we have the whole history of movie production technology, with its special effects, back-projections, miniatures, false fronts, etc. Doesn't all of this just immediately go to show how unnecessary the fact of reality is? On the contrary, it goes to show just how necessary it is, or how it is necessary. For the point of all this elaboration of machinery is exactly that it shall serve for reality, from the camera's point of view. To unmask such tricks is the treat for certain sensibilities; they will delight in production shots which show a half-constructed tree-trunk next to an actor standing on a box to give him more height than his leading lady. But all such facts, however interesting they are, like gossip, and however necessary the knowledge may be to certain makers of film, is of no more significance in viewing and assessing a film than it is, in reading and assessing the achievement of a novel, to know the working habits of the novelist. —I do not mean to confine the natural interest there is in technology to the level of gossip, or to the level of pleasure in unmasking achieved by the inside dopester. Nor would I wish to slight the fact that technology plays a role in the cinematic art unlike its role in any of the other arts. Because of its natural interest, and this role, one may well include, one often has included, the technology of movie making as part of the *mise-en-scène* of movies. The technology of architecture is at least as complex, and it has an appeal which plays directly into the artistic appeal of architecture—not merely an intellectual appeal to the engineers who participate in its invention and construction, but an appeal as spectacle and drama to those who watch its structures being raised or felled, or their sites excavated. The technology of painting has lately appeared to be the business of non-

painters, but its mastery—say yoking colors, or staining them
in—remains part of the work of a lifetime. The technology of
writing is nothing in comparison, yet the relation between constructing a line and constructing a sentence has provided study
for more than one millenium of poets. The interest there may
be in the fact that all writing is visible, is made with, say, ink
on paper, or successive letters, is less interestingly declared in,
say, Mallarmé's *Un Coup de Dés* than in Bresson's *Diary of a
Country Priest* (in which the physical commitment in writing
is brought under investigation in full-frame shots of a school-
boy's notebook being filled with silent thoughts, and the act of
writing is shown, through an identification of ink and wine, to
be this Priest's sustenance and suicide).

The artistic moral of all the machinery of fakery is the same
as the moral of photographic projection itself: that only what
appears within the projected frame counts, exists for the film.
The rest is mere convenience. What you can get away with,
or have a real need for, are empirical matters to be discovered,
as with everything else to do with film, only by screening it.
When a convenience is no longer convenient, it drops out of
use, like an out-house. Of course certain survivors from an
older generation will persist in thinking that only the out-house
is proper, or worth the inconveniences of distance and bad
weather. And when you see the results of the newer technology
and social developments which made the studios at the same
time unnecessary and too expensive, you realize that the older
generation is not, in all cases, wrong. But then mere convenience was never the whole issue.

The insistence on reality is not a matter of ethical purity but
of cinematic fact. It does not alter this fact if, to place your
characters in a particular house, you build from scratch as
much of the house as you need for the camera to see, or whether
you start with an actual house and tear down as much of it as
you need for your camera to move around in as you wish it

to. On the stage, two trees may constitute a forest, and two brooms the two trees; for the screen, this would yield only two brooms. A stage empty of everything but a couple of platforms may be made to constitute everything from the Roman Senate to the bedroom of Caesar's wife, to a field of battle; on the screen, it is an empty stage with a couple of platforms on it. (You may wish to exploit this fact on the stage itself, e.g., use the naked back wall of the theater building, and the radiator suspended from its middle, and the theater work-lights and work-ladders, as impersonations of themselves. This is not the denial of theater but a simple-minded declaration of it. In any case, it requires a new bargain with the audience; it remains in each case to be seen whether it is worth their while.) The screen contracts for its powers of illusion by destroying incompatible powers, sometimes by turning them to its own necessities, as in the other arts. On the screen, a view horizontal to the action reaches all the way to the horizon, unless its visibility is stopped—not by convention but in fact, say by an interposed object or atmosphere or by darkness or by a close-up which wholly or almost wholly fills the frame and blurs or obscures what is left. You can—if you can—fool the camera by *giving* it the horizon through painting it or back-projecting it. But this *trompe l'appareil* is no more essential to cinema than *trompe l'oeil* is essential to realistic painting. And either may be in service of an art which is not "realistic."

2. A second obvious feature of film that my emphasis on reality may seem to deny, or not so much to deny as to neglect, is the importance of the way reality is shaped on film, not merely by the juxtaposition of shots but by its ordonnance within the individual frame. Some theorists of film will wish to lay their emphasis on this fact, or rather on an interpretation of this fact, viz., that what is within the film frame is composed, as if the frames of which movies consist are to be read as paintings, certain kinds of paintings. Now it is certainly compatible with

what I have written that a cinematographer should *treat* the frame as if it were the frame of a painting. This is, for me, *one* possibility of film, one more fact of the medium whose significance is to be discovered. Let us try briefly to locate this discovery.

I start by reminding myself of the significance of the film frame generally, of the sense in which, as I put it in *The World Viewed,* it has the opposite significance of the frame in painting. Following Bazin's suggestion that the screen works as much by what it excludes as by what it includes, that it functions less to frame than to mask (which led me to speak of a photograph as of a segment of the world as a whole), I interpreted the frame of a film as forming its content not the way borders or outlines form, but rather the way looms or molds form.

The frankest acknowledgment I remember of the camera's exclusion, hence of its continuous implication of what is beyond the frame, occurs in George Cukor's *Adam's Rib.* There the camera is trained for a whole scene on Tracy's and Hepburn's bedroom, now empty, save intermittently, of their commanding presences, attending motionlessly as they shout to one another across the vacant space from one dressing room to the other, hers just left and out of the visual frame, his just right. The effect is the opposite of speaking across a void (a different director may want that effect and be able to get it with something like this set-up); here it projects an intimacy which does not require visible presence. The effect is to increase our intimacy with these figures because their invisible and pervasive presence to us puts us in the same relation to each of them in this passage as they bear to one another. It is not every marriage that one would care to become that intimate with. This scene is prepared by the longer one which precedes it, where the camera was also unmoving throughout, and at the same unobstrusive angle, but with its frame filled with three characters sitting at a table talking; yet nothing is significant here but what is, apparently routinely, shown. So the camera can do this too, and be equally interesting—if, that is, you have at your disposal, and dialogue with which to dispose, Katharine Hepburn and Judy Holliday and a supporting actress strong enough to bear up in such company, and if you see how to open the field behind these figures by placing a witness to them against a far wall. (Cukor's "implication beyond the frame" in the empty bedroom scene is just beyond it to the sides. It thus exploits the typical region of cinematic narrative implication, in which a definite visible something is explicitly denied our view. This possibility has provided cliché devices for local suspense—as when the camera moves in upon a woman's listening face, limiting the view, hence widening the area, of the regions from which something may pounce—or for cowardly or tactful withdrawals from a scene of sexuality or violence. So suspicious have we become, in our freedom, of this mode of implication that any avoidance of the visually explicit may be felt as cowardice. I assume this to be under discussion in the long back-tracking of Hitchcock's camera in *Frenzy,* recoiling from a scene of implied violence after the shutting of a door in its face. What is implied is not beyond the sides of the frame but beyond its blocked horizon, and the horrified wittiness of the backing gesture is capped when, later showing us what went on behind that door, Hitchcock shows us practically nothing at all of the event, which is again happening beyond the side of the frame or rather below it.[61])

My suggestion, once again, is not that composition has no significance, but that any significance it has can be assessed only on the basis of what it is a composition of—in movies, that it is one of a succession of automatic world projections. For the idea of "composition" to carry for film anything like its weight in speaking of paintings, the various degrees of motion in the succession of projections will have to be stilled, at least the motions of the camera and the motions of its subjects at a given moment. For if either the frame or the subject budges, the composition alters. This is of course, even so, the merest of analogies, for the current of frames through the projector cannot be stilled (unless for analysis), so that the liveness of a motionless camera on a motionless subject remains altogether different in its significance from the stillness of a still depiction—as is trivially declared on film by the possibility of freeze frames. The liveness itself suggests that what we are shown on the screen is always only one of an endless number of equally possible views, that nothing the camera does can break out of the circle of viewing; we are always outside; there is no perfect, or most significant, view. This is one of the meanings of the 360 degree track Hitchcock's camera traces around the embracing couple in *Vertigo*. We see them from every angle—at least every angle from a certain head-high height—and the effect is to accept as final their privacy with one another.

Again it is well to insist that this meaning is a function of *this* 360 degree track, in *this* context, in *this* film. It is doubtless to be expected that all 360 degree tracks enforce some range of significance in common; but it is certain that if there is some range of common significance in this automatism it can only be discovered empirically, after the critical analysis of all individual 360 degree tracks. (All? Well, a goodly corpus of all to date. All that matter, that is; all that native viewers accept as significant. Enough to guide the empirical discovery of the *a priori*. Why not? Criticism, as part of the philosophy of art, must aspire to philosophy. Its goal is the native view; the desophisticated.) In *Vertigo,* the circling track cocoons the couple within the man's fantasy, which the woman cannot share but is drawn to realize. The world is circling and the couple are circling and the man is circling alone—a compounding which befits a climate and climax of vertigo. The succession of the man's images are neither really seen nor merely imagined nor simply remembered by him. They are projections and successions of the reality he enacts. They invoke the status of film images. But they simultaneously violate this status. They do not proceed from a position outside the world whose perspective is in principle shareable; they do not imply the world as a whole, but select fragments from it whose implication is for him alone. They are not therefore meaningless but, as in madness, destroy the distinction between meaning and loss of meaning, between possibility and impossibility. They thus declare this woman's reality for this man, who invokes and violates her presence. If one thinks of the Romance, say of *The Winter's Tale,* as the satisfaction of impossible yet unappeasable human wishes, and hence as defining a presiding wish of movies generally, one might think of *Vertigo* as a declaration of the end of Romance. *Rules of the Game, The Children of Paradise, The Earrings of Madame de . . . ,* and *The Birds* are other instances.[62]

The incompleteness, or outsideness, or contingency of the angle of viewing, the fact that each is merely one among endless possibilities, is most perspicuously declared, in my experience, in the work of Carl Dreyer. In the *Passion of St. Joan,* whose subject is so much the human face, the face in *profile* is given particular significance. The judges in profile are revealed as conspirators, whispering into an ear, or hiding their expressions; whereas it is in profile that Joan is revealed as most lucid to herself. It is in profile that she becomes the accuser of her accusers, turns upon them; and in profile that we last glimpse her Passion at the stake. The general implication is that one view of a face eclipses all others, and that we can be given only one at a time. (In case someone supposes that we could defeat this fact by the use of mirrors, it should be said that the doubling of view by a mirror can serve first of all to distract us from the experience of either view, and perhaps to show that two are, in this case, no better than one, that two are just as far from completeness. But the particular significance of the mirror will arise from the individual case.) How Dreyer specifically manages this significance of the profile in this film can only be determined, once again, by an analysis and criticism of the elements and of the whole of this film; and because it is a masterpiece of the medium of film, this analysis should result in an analysis of the possibilities of film itself.

Another of the elements of this film arises from the possibility of zoning the screen space; in particular the left side of the screen, and more particularly the upper left quadrant, is zoned for special intensities of mood. —But how do you know what an "element" of cinematic significance is? You do not know in advance of critical analysis. Nothing—no variation or combination of angle, distance, duration, composition, and motions between—can be ruled out in advance as a sign of significance. Nothing would count as a nonsense syllable or as an ungrammatical sequence, except perhaps after something that would count as a semantical analysis. From a linguistic point of view, this seems backwards, or incomprehensible. It suggests that film has neither a lexicon nor a grammar. Then why try to think of film as a language? Because the gestures of the camera are, or are supposed to be, significant, and because there is no known end to the significance they may have. If one thinks of a grammar as a machine for generating sentences, then perhaps one will wish to speak of the camera and its film as a machine for generating idioms. Then when one of its proposals is in fact used significantly, you will have a specification of the cinematic. This will be a specification of the cinematic not as that which is grammatical but as that which is idiomatic to film. One welcome consequence of this undisguised nonsense is that one would not then think of the cinematic as conveying significance that *cannot* be conveyed in another medium but as conveying a particular significance in *this* (critically specified) way.

Dreyer's last film, *Gertrud,* made some thirty-five years after

Joan, trades on and refines—with the refinement and concentration at the command of a lifetime of work—the fact of the limitedness, or arbitrariness, of the single view. The significance in this film depends upon a procedure which brings composition within the frame of motion pictures to its maximum analogy (excluding the use of stills) with the composition in paintings. The camera, once placed, is typically stilled for long minutes at a stretch, so that there is something recognizable as *a* frame; and it remains about as still as a camera following the motions of speaking, listening human beings can be. Just as the characters depicted are about as still as speaking, listening human beings can be. They pose and repose themselves against a total, simplified environment, as for a painting or a still portrait, and the result is not the commemorative or candid significance of paintings or still photographs, but the opacity of self-consciousness. The emotion conveyed is of theatricality, and the cause of the emotion lies not in the drama of the characters' words and gestures but in our sense that they are characters before themselves, that our views of them are their views of themselves. Their views are not caused by ours, by their awareness that they are being watched from outside; their awareness is of being watched from inside. After God, they are God to themselves. Our views of them come after the fact. Here is one view, or one form, of the life of the mind, or the life of the love of the mind. The idea of love is itself eroticized and becomes part of the fact of love, so that faithlessness is faithlessness to the idea, i.e., a heresy.

I call this the opacity of self-consciousness to distinguish it from the lucidity of self-consciousness, the capacity to exist for others, to acknowledge and accept the limitedness of the others' views of oneself, most perfectly expressed, as I claimed in my book, by the greatest of the courtesan figures of film, Garbo and Dietrich; to them I would now add, in all seriousness, Mae West. The idea raised in *Gertrud* is that the condition of privacy, of unknownness, of being viewed—the human condition—is itself the condition of martyrdom, the openness to interrogation and rejection; the question raised is whether a refusal to accept this condition causes greater suffering than the suffering of martyrdom itself—whether martyrdom is as necessarily the cause as it is the effect of intolerance. The sense of constriction about these characters—the sense that they are limited or condemned to the same views of themselves that we are given—produces a sense that it is they who are selecting these views, as if their spiritual energies are exhausted in the effort to find some perfect or complete view of themselves to offer and to retain. The freedom of the courtesan figures I have contrasted with them lies in their indifference to such a question, in their sense not so much that they are invulnerable as that there is no interrogation or rejection whose terms they cannot dictate, or afford. They may be taken, but never unawares.

Defining their individualities would require defining their individual handlings of their authority over intrusion, settling the terms upon which they yield. Each has her own relation to solitude, to dominance, to sensuality, to gazes, to reputation, to laughter, to innocence. They seem (thinking of them from the thirties) to triangulate the classical possibilities outside of marriage. If Garbo is the human female at her most private and West the human female at her most public (and the extreme terms could be reversed), Dietrich is the human female awaiting both—vulnerable to change, to mutual knowledge. She is at home on the stage but also prepared to give it up. Change for Garbo is world-changing mood, or death; change for West is repetition. West's songs are not confessions and not addressed to an unknown one, but are part of her instruction; singing them does not display her wares but collects the options at her disposal. West mocks the glamour of the others; Garbo mocks the familiarity of the others; Dietrich mocks the rigidity of the others, permitting herself indignity if she chooses. Garbo suffers the solitude that is not overcome by love, Dietrich the solitude that is. Neither Garbo nor West have secrets, in the former case because her secrets are the world's, in the latter case because the world has no secrets. And neither is subject to gazes, Garbo because she is beyond them and determines them, West because she is before them and disarms them. Unlike Dietrich, the others have no rivals, Garbo because she has no challenger, West because no man is worth the challenge. Dietrich's perversity declares her privacy and her willingness to share her tastes. Her donning of the man's hat is not an offer of dominance but an act of identification. It is a term of equality. West offers to share her favors, and her terms propose equality with all others. Garbo will share her realm, and the terms require the ceding of the wish for equality. Each acknowledges her need for yielding, for partaking of a man. West yields for the moment, out of interest or sympathy; Dietrich out of trust and for as long as it lasts; Garbo for the yielding itself, and forever. West suggests and invites; Garbo recognizes and commands; Dietrich looks and, if she likes, leaps.

Dreyer's power with cinematic stillness, with the stasis of the frame, suggests that one significance of Eisensteinian montage may lie fundamentally not in the juxtaposition and counterpoint of images but in the fact which precedes that juxtaposition or counterpoint, viz., that it demands, and is demanded by, individual images which are themselves static or which contain and may compound movements that are simple or simply cumulative (for example, the inexorable movements of the sea or of a tremendous construction, or of a group or a crowd of persons) and which unify the entire reach of the frame, left to right and bottom to top. If, say, the design of light and shadow made by certain frames of the Odessa steps is less significant than the fact that this design fills and simplifies the entire frame, then the sense conveyed may be that any pose of nature or society is arbitrary and subject to human change, that no event is humanly ungraspable, and that none can determine the meaning that human beings who can grasp it are free to place upon it. Now suppose that this significance is destroyed if this reach of content is budged from just *this* frame; and suppose further that how *long* this may or must be held, to yield this significance, is determined by just this reach. (As how *large* a particular series of canvases must be may be determined by the reach of a continuous hue.) Then the fact that this frame must, at a particular instant, be jumped from, discontinuously, to another frame (of a similar or dissimilar species) will be determined not by any inherent necessity of montage for film narrative but by the necessities of this species of frame. It would follow that montage is necessary to film narrative only on the assumption that a certain species of frame is necessary. This is clearly subject to experimentation. It is worth at least mentioning, however, because on a certain favored form of experimentation this question cannot be tested—I mean the form which takes a particular strip of film (say, the Odessa steps sequence) and re-arranges its shots. However much you will learn about the internals of montage procedure from such exercises, you cannot answer from them what may be an equally intelligible and basic question, viz., what it is about certain species of frames that requires stasis and discontinuity; there is no continuous material of the right kind to contrast with what is on this strip.

If I am right about this, it suggests itself that Eisenstein's theories of montage are responses as much to the giving of instruction in film making as they are to film making itself. This would not be surprising. In *Must We Mean What We Say?*, I had occasion to remark a comparable feature in the development of the New Criticism (at the opening of "The Avoidance of Love") and in the practices of ordinary language philosophy (at the close of "Austin at Criticism"). Since good instruction has goals beyond itself, and since its goals are internally related to the goals of the subject under instruction, the moral I draw is not that the methodical pursuit of an art is fruitless, but that the pursuit of no one method will yield everything. The richness of Eisenstein's observations equally suggests that the pursuit of no method will yield nothing.

I have left for last one further way, I suppose the most blatant, in which my appeal to reality may seem false or misguided: it neglects the fact that the events of movies are fictional. So they *cannot* from the beginning be real or have happened, except perhaps by the purest or most miraculous of coincidences.

My book contains next to nothing about the specific problems of cinematic narration or dramaturgy. My justification for this lack is nothing more than my sense that the problem of cinematic dramaturgy—of the ways in which its stories are comprehensibly related—can only correctly be investigated subsequent to an investigation of the medium of cinema itself. That movies are fictional is not what makes them different from operas, plays, novels, some poems, some paintings, some ballets, etc. Since I assume that film's modes of dramaturgy are as specific to it as the modes of dramaturgy in the other arts of fiction, I assume that discussing the dramaturgy of a film apart from the nature and structure of the specific possibilities of film itself which are called upon in it, is equivalent, say, to discussing the dramaturgy of an opera apart from the nature and structure of its music. I equally assume that there are ways of analyzing music which will fail to show how it works in the drama.

One or two of the preoccupations of my book do bear directly, however, on the concept of fiction. The idea of a type, for example, is raised as a way of grasping the particular ways in which the human being is fictionalized—which is to say, molded —by film. The creation of a fictional presence (like the presence of nature) is not an achievement of the medium of film (as it is an achievement of novelists and playwrights and actors on a stage), but is given by the medium itself. (Perhaps the same could be said of the puppet or marionette theater.) Again, my speaking of the non-existence of the screened world is fairly obviously a way of characterizing part of what is meant by fictionality. It is true that I do not equate this idea of non-existence with the particular artifice of fiction, partly because I do not know what the particular artifice of fiction is, and partly because my intuition is that fictionality does not describe the narrative or dramatic mode of film. There are broad hints in my book that I think the mode is more closely bound to the mythological than it is to the fictional.

My formal reasons for this intuition revolve around my obsession with the particular mode of presence of the figures on the screen and the particular mode of absence from them of their audience. I speak of "a world past," and the idea of pastness threads through my books, as does the idea of presentness and of futurity. But I do not say that this is *the* past, that it is history. I do say that in viewing a movie I am "present . . . at something that has happened" (p. 26). The context is one in which I am contrasting the audience in a theater with the audience in a movie house. Both audiences are present at fictions. When I say, in this context, that the audience in a theater is present at something happening, I do not wish to imply that the events on the stage are taking place, as it were, in real life, nor that they are inevitably set in the present. Just so, when I say that the audience in a movie house is present at something that has happened, I do not wish to imply that the events on the screen have taken place, as it were, in real life, nor that they are inevitably set in the past. I grant that the words themselves may seem at first glance to imply this, but at second glance they imply an impossibility: How can one be *present* at something that has happened, that is over? And this is as much a question whether the events in question are fictional or are historical; the contrast of fiction and history is irrelevant here.

(One can have dreams and have hallucinations. But it makes no apparent sense to speak of being present at dreams or at hallucinations. This suggests why it is wrong to think of movies in terms of dreams or hallucinations.) To speak of being present at something that is over is not to state a falsehood but, at best, to utter a paradox. At worst, it is an unilluminating or unnecessary paradox. Whether it is illuminating or necessary depends upon whether the experience it is intended to express is really expressed by it; and whether, if it is expressed, it has the significance I attribute to it; and whether, if it does have this significance, this significance can be expressed some better way. Its illumination or necessity also depends upon how the paradox is interpreted, specifically upon whether it accurately and memorably encodes the various concepts and descriptions I elicit from it—e.g., about our displacement from the world, about the significance of viewing and exhibition, about the significance of the absence and presence of actors and audience, etc.; and of course it depends upon whether these concepts and descriptions are in turn illuminating and necessary. When at the end of my book I say, "The actors are *there* . . . in your world, but . . . you cannot go there *now*. . . . In a movie house, the barrier to the stars is time," I was counting on having earned the right to expect my reader to take these expressions symbolically, as mythological descriptions of the state of someone in the grip of a movie. Perhaps the writing fails, or I had failed to earn the right to such an expectation, but those expressions cannot in justice be taken to mean that I think someone in the grip of a movie can literally go to the events it depicts at some time other than now. Not just common sense rules this out, but my repeated emphasis on such notions as the projected world's not existing, as the projections of the world as such (which is not the same as the representation of specific locales), as my absence from the world, as its being complete without me. These notions are meant to correct, or explain (of course, mythologically to correct or explain), what is wrong and what is right in the idea of the pastness of the projected world. I relate that idea most immediately to my passiveness before the exhibition of the world, to the fascination, the uncanniness, in this chance to view the manifestation of the world as a whole.

In the sentence preceding the sentences I just quoted from myself concerning "the barrier to the stars," I relate the movie house to the geography of Plato's Cave. The point of the relation is exactly that presenting yourself to these events cannot be a matter of walking out and literally going somewhere else. There is no time for me but the time I am in and there is no specific elsewhere to go. —Then why suggest that there is? —But I claim to be *denying* that there is. —Then why bother to so much as deny it since anyone with common sense cannot fail to deny it? —Because common sense is, and ought to be, threatened and questioned by the experience of film itself; and because the nature of our absence from the events on the screen is not the same as the nature of our absence from an historical event or from the events in a cartoon or in a novel or on the stage; and because the differing natures of our absence are internal to the differing natures of the audiences of the different arts; and because the nature of the audience of an art, its particular mode of participation and perception, is internal to the nature of that art.

In the closing pages of my book I note a certain anxiety in the participation and perception of the audience of a film and I characterize that as an experience of my contingency. This sense of contingency may express itself mythologically as the contingency that I am not *there*—as though my absence requires an explanation. Writers about film are, I believe, responding to the sense that such an explanation is required when they speak of movies as if they were hallucinations or dreams. If they are speaking literally they are wrong. I have indicated that I think they are wrong mythologically as well, but it is not easy to say why. They are responding to the fact that I am seeing things, things not there, experiencing them as overwhelmingly present. You cannot snap me out of this mood by telling me that what I am seeing is the projection of photographs or that I am misusing the word "seeing," because I will tell you that you do not realize what the projection of photographs is. You might as well tell me that I do not see myself in the mirror but merely see a mirror image of myself.

The sense of contingency may express itself unmythologically as the sense that I am *here*, that it is my fate to exist and while I exist to be one place rather than any other. You may not find this to be much of a fate, or you may not credit the existence of such a thing as "the sense of contingency," or you may feel either that I have misdescribed it or overemphasized its importance. Then one of us is wrong.

In line with what I called these formal reasons for the intuition that the dramatic mode of film is the mythological, there are reasons having to do with the content it projects. I do not interpret this content as promising us glamor, magical resolution, and the association of stars, though I do not deny that such wishes are often excited and pandered to, not alone by movies. But movies also promise us happiness exactly not because we are rich or beautiful or perfectly expressive, but because we can tolerate individuality, separateness, and inexpressiveness. In particular, because we can maintain a connection with reality despite our condemnation to viewing it in private. It is, after all, not merely a couple of unintelligible German philosophers of the early and middle part of the nineteenth century who were speaking, at the establishment of the industrial age, of the human being's estrangement from the world; nor, in its closing years, was a crazy European philologist speaking merely for himself (even if mostly to himself) when he announced the Death of God—by which he meant to record an altered relation in which we have placed ourselves to the world as a whole, to nature and to society and to ourselves. The myth of film is that nature survives our treatment of it and its loss of enchantment for us, and that community remains possible even when the authority of society is denied us.

For movies are inherently anarchic. Their unappeasable appetite for stories of love is for stories in which love, to be found, must find its own community, apart from, but with luck still within, society at large; an enclave within it; stories in which society as a whole, and its laws, can no longer provide or deny love. The myth of movies tells not of the founding of society but of a human gathering without natural or divine backing; of society before its securing (as in the Western) or after its collapse (as in the musical or the thirties' comedy, in which the principals of romance are left on their own to supply the legitimacy of their love). It shares with any myth the wish for origins and comprehension which lies behind the grasp of human history and arbitration. In myth the past is called before us, reenacted, and in its presence we are rededicated. On film, the past which is present is pastness or presentness itself, time itself, visually preserved in endless repetition, an eternal return, but thereby removed from the power to preserve us; in particular, powerless to bring us together. The myth of movies replaces the myth according to which obedience to law, being obedience to laws I have consented to and thus established, is obedience to the best of myself, hence constitutes my freedom—the myth of democracy. In replacing this myth, it suggests that democracy itself, the sacred image of secular politics, is unliveable.

By opposite means, the myth of democracy is found unliveable (at least without prior, visionary transformation of ourselves) in the best of American literature. There we find the absence of romance, of the individual woman and man free to consent to one another; in particular, unable to imagine the bearing of a happy family. It is the land which had refused its full expression to the novel which gave rise to the first dramatic films of major artistic ambition, and to the greatest of the film comedies, which take their form as satires of authority.

The anarchism of movies is already contained in the condition of viewing unseen. For the *polis* can be affirmed only in present speech, the members live for one another, each explicit, the city gathered within earshot of itself. I speak here within the condition of the doubt expressed earlier that we yet understand the relation, on film, of individual and society. I might say that we have yet to understand the images of society we offer ourselves. For of course we can be *shown* a gathering of persons—say around a leader—meant as a gathering of the city within earshot of itself. But what city would this be? Who might these individuals be for one another? What future can a collective image affirm as their common happiness? Such images will suggest that film's natural alternative to an anarchic response to social existence is a utopian one. —Which is more important, for us to know our society to be just, as least open to justice; or for us to know that even in the absence of justice we may enact and satisfy our private need of one another? Which would you rather have, a mind or a brain?

Before finishing with these additions and multiplications, I would like to modify, if not quite to retract, what I said in my book about the delayed encroachment of modernism upon the art of film. Reacting against what I regarded as empty and prejudicial announcements appointing film as the major modern art, hence against certain definitions of that art, I insisted that the historical interest of film lies rather in its condition as the last traditional art, which means in part the last to find itself pushing itself to its modernist self-questioning. I was amply tentative about this, but it may well be too soon to be so much as tentative about such a question, too soon conceptually as well as too soon artistically. It may be that the art itself and, more directly, the concepts in which one attempts to grasp its behavior, are too chaotic to allow of any such perspective now —except one taken upon the platform of a manifesto, which is not my business.

One may share the sense of change in the art of movies over the past fifteen or twenty years, and even agree that this has something to do with the encroachment of modernist problems, but then account for this encroachment in at least two ways I have not considered: as a repetition, more or less farcical, of film's first and most serious modernist phase, expressed, say, in revolutionary Russia; or (non-exclusively) as the new emergence of experimental film making.[63] I am not now interested to adjudicate this issue but to emphasize that its adjudication is a matter essentially and simultaneously of the value and understanding one places on the particular objects in question and of the value and understanding one places on the concept of modernism. I have used the term modernist, not originally, to name the work of an artist whose discoveries and declarations of his medium are to be understood as embodying his effort to maintain the continuity of his art with the past of his art, and to invite and bear comparison with the achievements of his past. The term is not meant to cover everything that may be thought of as advanced or *avant-garde* in art. On the contrary, it suggests to me a wish to break into (certain uses of) the concept of the *avant-garde* at at least three points: into its implication that advanced art looks away from the past toward the future; into its tendency toward promiscuous attention to any and all claims to advancement, together with a tendency to cede the concept of art altogether, at any rate, to cede the idea of the arts as radically distinguished from one another, which is the sensible significance of the "pure" in art; and into the military-political image prompting its title, which suggests that an art can advance, or survive, in some way other than through its faithfulness to itself, and in particular that what prompts this advance, or promotes this survival, is a synchronized or imminent social advance. (*Arrière-garde* is more like it. The modernist critic is not penetrating more territory but more time.)

These may prove to be grounds on which to regard, say, Eisenstein's work as *avant-garde* but not as modernist. I hope it is clear that this in itself would not imply that his work is less good than any other. (And because I mean to be keeping open the relation between art and politics in a given generation, I would not like to give the impression that I take them as having no relation. One may still hope, almost above all, that the dream of the good city will not be lost, without forgetting that it is a dream, and hence just the beginnings of responsibilities.) They are also grounds on which to regard certain recent experiments in film making as inheritors, or relatives, not of modernism in the other arts, but of (what I called) their modernizings. I do not know this work well or extensively enough for my judgments of it in individual cases to be much use. But if there is a genuine artistic movement in question, and if claims concerning the state of the arts of film are to be based upon it, then it is worth saying that the role of experimentalism in film making is as specific to it as any other of its features, so that one cannot assess its significance apart from an assessment of the significance of film as such. Two features in particular seem to beg for assessment. (1) In the arts of the novel, of music, and of painting contemporary with the establishment of the art of film, the major experimentalists have generally proven to be the major artists of their period, i.e., their "experiments" have been central to the development of the art itself, not more or less peripheral attacks upon it. One can, of course, claim that this will prove to be true of the art of film as well, that the dominant position of movies with their famous directors and stars and their mass audiences will ultimately be shown to have been an aberration of the art from almost its beginning, caused and maintained by historical, economic forces essentially external to its autonomous development. We should be able to convince ourselves of this about a century from now. (2) Film has from the beginning aroused, and throughout its history has inspired, lines of experimentation with its physical basis. This is another way of seeing the unique role played in this art by its technology. An apparently significant fact about its early experimentors is that their results provided devices for particular kinds of comedy, e.g., for animation and for burlesques of magic.

What I have been saying makes out the concept of modernism to be in service of an art that is in battle not particularly against Goliaths (which is not new, and which waxes and wanes), but against false Davids. The concept is called for in specific stages of culture. Naturally its application will appear prophetic, since it will depend upon distinguishing among claimants to art those which play at liberation and those which play for it, those which are documents and symptoms of their time and those which are also valid diagnoses and statements of it. This motive for the concept bears on what I have written about movies only more or less eccentrically, mostly so far as I have felt impelled to make the Hollywood case against what I considered to be bad briefs against it (finding, if you like, Davids in Goliaths' clothing). The concept will be at home, and will then shed what is then unnecessary in its dogmatism, only within a believable critique of culture, call it a critique of historical judgment, which is able to schematize the emergence and the features of a stage of culture that calls for such a concept as modernism at all—a stage in which everything and nothing seems to matter, for example, that some say that everything new is significant and others that nothing significant is new; in which diagnosis has replaced dogma, hence institutions have no inside and culture is an unmasquerade; in which art and politics and religion forget themselves, and will covet one another's leavings; in which conscience seems bad manners, faith an indulgence, and nihilism our amusement.

In the meantime, I am prepared to modify my claims about film's modernism by saying either that movies from their beginning have existed in a state of modernism, from the beginning have had to achieve their power by deliberate investigations of the powers of their medium; or else that movies from their beginning have existed in two states, one modern, one traditional, sometimes running parallel to and at varying distances from one another, sometimes crossing, sometimes interweaving; or else that the concept of modernism has no clear application to the art of film. My feeling is that none of these modifications need weaken my insistence on film as the last traditional art, but on the contrary that each would be a way of explaining that insistence. I hold on to the critical hypothesis which runs through my book as well as through this continuation of it, that pride of place within the canon of serious films will be found occupied by those films that most clearly and most deeply discover the powers of the medium itself, those that give fullest significance to the possibilities and necessities of its physical basis. Placing this significance in individual cases is an act of criticism. —Perhaps what I just called a hypothesis is more accurately thought of as a definition of, or as a direction for composing a definition of, "the powers of the medium itself." The idea, in any case, is empty apart from placing its significance in individual cases.

I conclude with a sketch of such an act of criticism, somewhat more elaborated than those which have so far affected my remarks. It deals with certain of my experiences, as they have so far developed, of *Rules of the Game,* and directs itself toward accounting for one of its frames.

The frame I have in mind figures in the last sequence of the film. Its view fronts upon the façade of the chateau in and around which the events of the film have played themselves out, and includes its terrace with its balustrade, the set of steps leading up to the terrace, and a segment of the entrance court from which the steps lead. The Marquis, at the center of the terrace and at the head of the steps, framed behind by the entrance portals to his house, is making a little speech of explanation to his guests, assembled at the bottom of the steps. He is saying something like: "There has been a deplorable accident, that's all. My keeper Schumacher thought he saw a poacher, and he fired, since that is his duty. Chance had it that André Jurieu should be the victim of this error." There follows a final isolating closeup of the Marquis as he concludes his speech and suggests to the company that they go inside to avoid catching a chill; then a longer shot to show a servant opening the portals behind him to receive the guests. Then a medium close-up of the homosexual and the general for the last of their typifying exchanges: "A new definition of the word 'accident.'" "No, no, no, no, no. La Chesnaye [the Marquis] has class. That is a rare thing these days." These two then quit the frame and the camera holds its position as shadows of the guests file across the façade of the chateau, leaving us with the looming balustrade, and, beneath it, a line of cypresses in their brightened tubs; upon which the film ends.[64]

The sequence is a kind of summary epilogue, gathering together the characters as well as the themes of the production we have witnessed. If this production had merely copied rather than absorbed to its own purposes the tradition of eighteenth-century comedy which it consistently invokes, this sequence would serve to beg our pardons for any offense, celebrate the timely conversion of a miscreant (*The Marriage of Figaro*) or his timely riddance (*Don Giovanni*), and permit the cast jointly to ask our blessing with our hands. Instead, the Marquis speaks alone, in confusion, to, not for the cast; they face him, their backs to us; and they file away from us, in clumps, as if their production had not been concluded but been interrupted. As if to declare: this production has from the beginning had no audience, none it has not depicted; no standing group of spectators will have known what they were watching. (Such a declaration inspires the most public in-joke of the film, in the line addressed by the Marquis to the head of his household staff: "Corneille, stop this farce!"—to which this chief servant replies soberly, as befits his name, "Which one?")

I emphasize two critical features in the formal tableau of the Marquis' speech: (1) the position of Schumacher, the gamekeeper, notable by his awkward posture and by his zone of isolation, halfway up the steps, between the Marquis and the Marquis' audience; (2) the absence of Octave, the part played by Renoir, notable in this moment of general assembly.

Schumacher's posture is slightly hunched, turned largely from us but aware of the audience, as over his shoulder, and inflected toward the Marquis. His torsion might present a posture of contrition, but his gamekeeper's shotgun is again in place, strapped across his back, as we had always seen it before the masquerade party. Here the gun happens to be pointing exactly at the Marquis' head. (I mean no more than "happens to be"; the meaning will be clear without this.)

Let us recall that we already knew something about the significance of the camera's fronting upon the entrance to the chateau, in particular something about the terrace and its balustrade. The terrace had recently been established for us as a stage—when Octave, pushed by the mood of a late interview with Christine, the friend of his youth and now the Marquis' wife, enters the terrace from its side, as from the wings, to re-enact the manner and moments in which his old teacher of conducting, Christine's father, used to make his entrance as head of the orchestra in Vienna and bring his performers to attention. So the Marquis, standing on that spot, is giving some further sort of performance, and his chateau has become a piece of theatrical decor, a backdrop, situating him.

This merely underlines what is in any case obvious, but it

impels us to ask more closely what the nature or point of this further performance is. It is one in which the Marquis is constructing a particular form of lie (he says that his gamekeeper mistook his guest for a poacher, whereas the Marquis had earlier that night discharged his gamekeeper, and exactly on the ground that he had endangered his guests); but in this lie he is telling a truth (because his gamekeeper had, in shooting the aviator, shot a poacher on the Marquis' preserves and hence acted on the Marquis' behalf). Telling the truth by lying is, however, a way of defining fiction: the Marquis is not only giving a performance but composing a play or the ending of a play, or starting a further game. In tacitly accepting the gamekeeper back into his service and thereby conspiring to cover the accident, the Marquis places himself at the mercy of the gamekeeper. In explicitly accepting the gun as the lawful defense of his domain (i.e., his domain inside the house, his private life), he has submitted himself to the gun's dominion. (The little poacher had said to the Marquis during their first encounter that while the Marquis may be master inside the house, outdoors Schumacher is boss.)

Schumacher had worn that shotgun strapped to his back throughout the set-piece of the shoot, as he tracked the rabbits and birds into the guests' range of fire. After the shoot, but still within the shoot's locale, the action centers around a particular object, the small telescope or eye-piece. We are told or shown three main features of this object: it is fun, even fascinating; when you look through it, reality is suddenly revealed, or made accessible, in an otherwise unavailable manner; it is deadly, it penetrates to the inner life of living creatures. Omitting further detail, I will simply assert that the eye-piece is a sort of figure of speech, or synecdoche of sight, for both a gun and camera. (When the wife spies through it and sees her husband with his former mistress, this is already a kind of shooting accident.) Outdoors, outside, the camera is boss. It dictates what you may see and the significance of whatever you do. What the camera has killed, or breached, is the rule of theater. It uses theater, dominates it, locks it indoors. It participates in the subjugation of the Marquis, the ending of his game. For him, now, newly, all is but toys. He has become the Midas of amusement; everything he touches he winds; and he has laid hands upon himself. The camera, however, is out of his reach; it is behind his audience, witnessing them as well as his performance for them.

This is part of what Octave-Renoir's absence from this concluding scene means. He has taken his place behind the camera. His absence declares his responsibility for what has happened; that is to say, for the act of interfering in the events of this society (he had, for the beginning, arranged for the presence of the poacher-rabbit; for the ending, he had directed and costumed the events which cause the accident), in particular, for interfering by exposing it, which is what finally discomfits this comity.

I was criticized in one recent discussion of these matters for, in effect, failing to see that Jurieu, the poacher-rabbit, was from the beginning fated to be expelled by this rule-intoxicated society, and that, presumably, his riddance, if extreme, all the more extremely testifies to the power of the Marquis' game, which remains in full sway. The ground of this criticism must be the thought that Renoir's film merely condemns the Marquis' society (merely condemns, and merely this one), showing his toys of moral scruple always to have worked behind the gun of reality. But this seems to me to deny the facts and the mood of the frame from which my reading has begun. One set of facts depends upon remembering who the Marquis is, I mean recollecting what his rules are. Of course he had wished all poacher-rabbits to be kept out, but there were limits to what he would do to keep them out. He would not, for example, permit fences. He had, again, fought in person for his wife, honorably; but it was also a point of honor with him to acknowledge the rights of love and of friendship and to respect his wife's wish to leave. Sincerity was as much a point of honor with him as the safety of his guests.

The poacher-rabbit was expelled, if by mistake, according to the rules of Schumacher's game—not his game as the Marquis' gamekeeper but his own game of honor ("A shot in the dark, in the woods, and no questions asked," as he described his honor to his wife. It remains a question for us why the Marquis accepts, and protects, this foreign rule of honor. The answer cannot simply be that it has fulfilled his wishes. If that were all, there would have been for him no rules in the first place. He accepts Schumacher's rule because he is afraid not to, finally unable to confront him and judge him. This reflects an inability, no doubt, to confront his own guilt. But his guilt and his fear have not begun with his implication in this act of Schumacher's. We know from the first scene with the literal little poacher that the Marquis is afraid of Schumacher. There the Marquis had entered into a conspiracy with the little poacher exactly to spite Schumacher. One result of this is that the poacher feels free, during the masquerade, to ask the Marquis to do him "a little service"—feels free because the service amounts, again, to a conspiracy against Schumacher. The Marquis thus becomes the servant of his servant. The final result is that the Marquis, as if confessing this conspiracy, enters into a conspiracy with Schumacher, and so becomes an accessory against his own authority. (The absence of the little poacher from the final tableau signifies, accordingly, that the Marquis is no longer able to protect him from Schumacher.)

I said just now that a certain criticism of my reading seemed to me to "deny the facts" of the frame I was reading. But the way I have tried to read my way into that frame shows that facts of a frame, so far as these are to confirm critical understanding, are not determinable apart from that understanding itself. It shows, further, that questions prompted by one frame are not answerable from within that frame alone. Take so plain a matter as the presence of those tubbed cypresses beneath the balustrade. Are they significant, i.e., are they "facts of a frame," so far as these facts are meant to confirm critical understanding? The concluding shot of the film undeniably emphasizes these tubs. They now gather the intensest patches of light within the frame; and they seem to *be* the source of the light which draws those shadows. Are we to understand in this allusion to footlights a final statement of the terrace as an abandoned stage, and a capping ambiguity about the source of illumination—a question whether it reveals as for an audience in a theater or for an audience in a movie house? A convincing answer would have to take its place among the answers to the other questions this film raises about the relations between society and theater and cinema.

That *Rules of the Game* is interested in theater is about as obvious as that Marx is interested in money. Its adoption of the look and manner of traditional French comedy depicts the social role of theater as its extremest point, the point at which theater and society are absorbing one another, dissolving in one another. I account for its perspective upon this condition as one achieved through Renoir's declared faithfulness to the perspective of cinema. This dialectical step could be summarized as follows: When society has become fully theatricalized (conscious of its rules but inaccessible to their backing, the fool of its own artifice, of its peculiar compacts), cinema reestablishes our sense of reality by asserting its own powers of drama. —This is more or less what I say, in *The World Viewed,* happened historically (pp. 89–94). I need not, I think, be told that this is very obscure. My excuse for the obscurity, I mean for voicing the idea in its obscurity, is my intention to counter, or question, the familiar claim that "cinema has changed our ways of looking at the world"—to question this, generally, by suggesting that such a claim is no less obscure than any claims of my own, merely unquestionably fashionable; and to question it, specifically, by claiming that cinema entered a world whose ways of looking at itself—its *Weltanschauungen*—had already changed, as if in preparation for the screening and viewing of film. —Film's easy power over the world *will* be accounted for, one way or another, consciously or not. By my account, film's presenting of the world by absenting us from it appears as confirmation of something already true of our stage of existence. Its displacement of the world confirms, even explains, our prior estrangement from it. The "sense of reality" provided on film is the sense of *that* reality, one from which we already sense a distance. Otherwise the thing it provides a sense of would not, for us, count as reality. —Documentary immediacy, should it be desired, cannot, I assume, deny this condition though it may negate it through acknowledging it. This will require defining what it is that you, as this film maker, proposing this immediacy, must acknowledge—your position in it; and it will require defining the position of the audience to whom you are proposing to make it known. Godard's *Two or Three Things I Know About Her* is a rich exploration of the former of these requirements. (Is it needless to say that the satisfaction of such requirements will not, of itself, insure the quality of the work that contains it?) (It will not count as an acknowledgment of your being late for you to register your knowledge that there is tardiness in the world; nor will it count if you register your knowledge to the company you are leaving rather than to the company you have kept waiting. It must not be an excuse; it need not be an apology. If, however, what you wish to acknowledge is something about *us,* then you must define our positions accordingly, e.g., presume an acknowledgment from me of your right to speak for me. If you proceed without it, rebuking me for my ignorance or my cowardice, then you risk, or seek, my rebuke. You may thus achieve dissociation from me, the company you are leaving, through a betrayal. What cause justifies you—not in leaving, but in leaving this way?)

I mention two further issues whose settlement will, I believe, have to enter any account of *Rules of the Game* that I would find convincing. One concerns the significance it gives to the camera's frontality, say in the shot of the tableau at the terrace; the other concerns the significance of the *danse macabre* which ends the theatrical inside the chateau. (If someone wishes to say that the former is a "formal" issue, then I would like to ask what particular contrast he has in mind.)

I. Frontality, or perpendicularity, in this film (as in *Grand Illusion*) is the angle of theater, both of its establishment and of its questioning. *Grand Illusion* twice employs a cut from full front to full back, across 180 degrees, on a centered figure. It happens first on the figure of Rosenthal (played by Dalio, who will play the Marquis, a connection openly alluded to in *Rules*), as he for the first time invites his companion prisoners to partake of a feast he has arranged. The gesture of this cut carries a sense of Rosenthal's pride in his providence, his wish to preside at this festival of his making; but equally, as we find ourselves at his back, a feeling of his vulnerability, his humanity, his sincere willingness to please. Such a gesture opposes any hurried contrast between theater and sincerity. The second occurrence of this front-to-back cut is on the figure of Carette (in *Rules*, the little poacher), during his song in the theatrical for the other prisoners. This makes more explicit the frontal acknowledgment of theater and the camera's declaration, as it shoots from behind the scene, showing its facing audience, of its absorption and command of theater; it also establishes a connection between the figures of Dalio and Carette which is elaborated in the later film. This much seems to me relatively uncontroversial. In *Rules of the Game,* perpendicularity more openly defines the ascension of cinema over theater. A central piece of evidence for this is the great tracking shot of the beaters, headed by Schumacher, as the shoot begins. It is, as it were, shot from the side, from the wings, and it is as if Schumacher, characteristically a bit hunched over, with the tool of his trade

strapped to his back, is not so much guiding the action as following it, tracking it, filming it. This idea interests me, beyond
itself, for the role it might play in a full reading of the film.
Much as I regard it as obvious, I also expect it to be resisted.
Must I, as a reader, leave this point to the sheer agreement of
others, or can it sensibly be argued?

2. If it can be argued, some terms of argument will have to
emerge from the other scene of a dance of death, the one inside,
for the masquerade. There the camera is at its freest and the
characters spill from the stage into the audience, entangling
them in the performance. There is good reason to take *this* as
this film's way of declaring its cinematic perspective: the audience (i.e., the depicted audience) is kinaesthetically assaulted
by this performance, frightened and thrilled by the Saint-Saëns
skeletons and the roving points of light, frightened and alarmed
by not quite knowing whether this is or is not a performance
(which is the obvious surface of the plot at this point, with
Schumacher entangling the audience in his private hunt for his
poacher); and the scene is as pure a realization of the cinema's
vaunted "patterns of light in motion" (distinctly all black and
white) as a movie is likely to admit. Still, we know this dance
to be a piece of theater. So the scene reads to me as a parody
of a particular *theory* of cinema. As if to say: if kinaesthetic
patterns of light and motion is what you want, theater can satisfy
you as well as cinema; it is as specialized a claim for cinema
as it would be for theater; as either may, and neither need,
explicitly show the walks of life united in the dance of death.
(A parody of a particular theory of theater can be heard in the
late line from the Marquis to Schumacher: "Get Corneille to
deal with the formalities, the telephone calls and all the rest.")

The simultaneous spilling over of the stage and spilling over
of the scene below-stage, both into the arena of the audience
—the simultaneous break-down and break-up of both lively and
deadly realms of artifice, forming a chaos of artifice—exempli-

fies the film's pervasive theme of "accident," and comments upon it. In a theater, the actors appear in person; it is part of the latent anxiety of theater that anything can happen to break the spell—a cue missed, a line blown, a technical hitch. The abyss between actor and audience is not bottomless, unless convention is bottomless. In a movie house, the actors are not present in person and the screen is metaphysically unbreachable; the abyss between actor and audience is as bottomless as time. This does not mean that accidents are out of the question. One can say, as I have implied, that everything caught by film is accident, contingency. Then one must equally say that every accident on film becomes permanent (like the existence of the one world, in the midst of all possible worlds). —These are consequences of the ontological fact that two screenings of the same film bear a relation to one another absolutely different from the relation borne to one another by two performances of the same play, I mean two performances of the same production of a play. This is the same fact as that a screening of a film is not a performance of it. —There is no essence of the difference between stage and screen. They are essentially different, as like one another, and systematically unlike, as tragedy and comedy, or as two stages of society.

It can seem an accident of culture (while perhaps a necessity of the art of theater, certain theater) that a theater director relinquishes his influence upon a production; whereas it seems a matter of physical law that the movie director call his work finished and step absolutely aside. One could imagine it otherwise. A theater director might invite audiences only to "rehearsals"; a movie director may insist upon showing only "rushes." Such practices might be guided by particular conceptions each has of his art; and they might serve in the achievement of new forms of success within the works of these respective arts. In *Rules of the Game*, the movie director's absolute absence from his work (accented if, *per accidens*, he appears in it) is fictionalized as Octave's departure from its scene of accident. Following his reenactment of his old teacher, he had told Christine of his longing to have had a public as a "conductor." As a movie director, absence from the public view is accounted for. So Octave's departure can declare Renoir's success as a director of movies. Is it also Renoir's confession that he knows himself to be a public failure as a director of movies? Evidently there is a wave of self-pity here. But as usual in the history of comedy, the clown's self-pity functions within the highest ambitions and achievements of his art: it is the natural tendency of his pity for the world, and his pitilessness towards it, refusing his own exemption from it; it expresses his knowledge of the cost in its falling just to him to embody his displacement from society as society's disfigurement of itself. Specifically, here, self-pity is an acknowledgment of the writer's hectic sense, at least since the eighteenth century, of the burden of his art, not knowing whether it is the root or the height of his displacement, nor whether it signifies his greater purity or impurity, measured against the state of his public. Renoir identifies himself through Octave as both cause and casualty of the accident, and therewith identifies himself through Jurieu—the artist as poacher and poached, groundling flyer, a soloist. —The loss of a public is in fact the artist's withdrawal from his public, as a consequence of his faithfulness to his art. The public is lost to art because they are readying themselves for war, for life by the gun. They are also lost because of art, because art maintains itself against their assaults, and because, almost against its will, it unsettles the illusions by means of which civilized people conduct themselves. It is in this loving brutality that Renoir declares film's possession of the power of art.

Notes

1 (p. 7). See René Wellek, *A History of Modern Criticism* (New Haven: Yale University Press, 1955), I, 184; II, 56.

2 (p. 7). Although André Bazin is the central figure in this policy to discover the director, what I know of his writing is too individual in its clarity and passion and resourcefulness to permit much in the way of a generalization to a school. A convenient and interesting place from which to form an idea of the *auteur* ideology may be found in Andrew Sarris, *The American Cinema* (New York: E. P. Dutton, 1968).

3 (p. 13). William L. Hedges, "Classics Revisited: Reaching for the Moon," *Film Quarterly*, XII, No. 4 (Summer 1959), 27–34; James Kerans, "Classics Revisited: *La Grande Illusion*," *Film Quarterly*, XIV, No. 2 (Winter 1960), 10–17; Annette Michelson, "Bodies in Space: Film as 'Carnal Knowledge,'" *Artforum*, February 1969, pp. 54–63.

4 (p. 13). Warshow's essays on film are collected in *The Immediate Experience* (New York: Doubleday, 1962 [paperback edition, 1964]). I hope my indebtedness to them is obvious.

5 (p. 13). See Michael Fried's contribution to a symposium held at Brandeis University in 1966: William C. Seitz, ed., *Art Criticism in the Sixties* (New York: October House, 1967).

6 (p. 16). Erwin Panofsky, "Style and Medium in the Moving Pictures," in Daniel Talbot, ed., *Film* (New York: Simon and Schuster, 1959), p. 31.

7 (p. 16). André Bazin, *What Is Cinema?*, trans. Hugh Gray (Berkeley: University of California Press, 1967), p. 110.

8 (p. 17). Certainly I am not concerned to deny that there may be, through film, what Paul Rotha in his *The Film Till Now* (first published in 1930) refers to as "possibilities . . . open for the great sound and visual [i.e., non-dialogue sound, and perhaps non-photographically visual] cinema of the future." But in the meantime the movies have been what they have been.

9 (p. 20). Bazin, *op. cit.,* p. 12.

10 (p. 21). *Loc. cit.*

11 (p. 21). See Michael Fried, *Three American Painters* (Cambridge, Mass.: Fogg Art Museum, Harvard University, 1965), n. 3; and "Manet's Sources," *Artforum*, March 1969, pp. 28–79.

12 (p. 22). See Michael Fried, "Art and Objecthood," *Artforum*, June 1967; reprinted in Gregory Battcock, ed., *Minimal Art* (New York: E. P. Dutton, 1968), pp. 116–47.

13 (p. 25). When painting found out how to acknowledge the fact that paintings had shapes, shapes became forms, not in the sense of patterns, but in the sense of containers. A form then could *give* its shape to what it contained. And content could transfer its significance as painting to what contains it. Then shape *pervades,* like gravity, or energy, or air. (See Michael Fried, "Shape as Form," *Artforum*, November 1966; reprinted in Henry Geldzahler's catalogue, *New York Painting and Sculpture: 1940–1970* [New York: E. P. Dutton, 1969].)

This is not, as far as we yet know, a possibility of the film or screen frame—which only repeats the fact that a film is not a painting. The most important feature of the screen format remains what it was from the beginning of movies—its scale, its absolute largeness. Variation of format—e.g., CinemaScope—is a matter determined, so far as I can tell, by questions of convenience and inconvenience, and by fashion. Though perhaps, as in painting, the declaration of color as such required or benefited from the even greater expanses of wider screens.

The idea may seem obviously false or foolish that the essential ontological difference between the world as it is and as it is screened is that the screened world does not exist; because this overlooks—or perhaps obscurely states—a fully obvious difference between them, *viz.,* that the screened world is two-dimensional. I do not deny the obscurity, but better a real obscurity than a false clarity. For *what* is two-dimensional? The world which is screened is not; its objects and motions are as three-dimensional as ours. The screen itself, then? Or the images on it? We seem to understand what it means to say that a painting is two-dimensional. But that depends on our understanding that the support on which paint is laid is a three-dimensional object, and that the description of *that* object will not (except in an exceptional-or vacuous sense) be the description of a painting. More significantly, it depends on our understanding of the support as *limiting* the extent of the painting in two dimensions. This is not the relation between the screen and the images projected across it. It seems all right to say that the screen is two-dimensional, but it would not follow that what you see there has the same dimensionality—any more than in the case of paint, its support, and the painting. Shadows are two-dimensional, but they are cast by three-dimensional objects—tracings of opacity, not gradations of it. This suggests that phenomenologically the idea of two-dimensionality is an idea of either transparency or outline. Projected images are not shadows; rather, one might say, they are shades.

14 (p. 25). This idea is developed to some extent in my essays on *Endgame* and *King Lear* in *Must We Mean What We Say?* (New York: Scribner's, 1969).

15 (p. 26). Bazin, *op. cit.,* p. 97.

16 (p. 27). Panofsky, *op. cit.,* p. 28.

17 (p. 30). "The Film Age," in Talbot, *op. cit.,* p. 74.

18 (p. 30). Panofsky, *op. cit.,* p. 18.

19 (p. 32). *Ibid.,* p. 24.

20 (p. 33). *Ibid.,* p. 25.

21 (p. 41). Within that condition, objects as such may seem displaced; any close-up of an object may render it *trouvé*. Dadaists and surrealists found in film a direct confirmation of their ideologies or sensibilities, particularly in film's massive capacities for nostalgia and free juxtaposition. This confirmation is, I gather, sometimes taken to mean that dadaist and surrealist films constitute the *avant-garde* of filmmaking. It might equally be taken to show why film made these movements obsolete, as the world has. One might say: Nothing is more surrealist than the ordinary events of the modern world; and nothing less reveals that fact than a surrealist attitude. This says nothing about the

value of particular surrealist films, which must succeed or fail on the same terms as any others.

Ideas of displacement (or contrasted position), of privacy, and of the inability to know are linked in my study of the problem of other minds, "Knowing and Acknowledging," in *Must We Mean What We Say?*

22 (p. 41). *The Painter of Modern Life* was first published in 1859. My references are to a volume of Baudelaire's prose selected and edited by Peter Quennell, *The Essence of Laughter* (New York: Meridian, 1956), pp. 32, 21, 33, 21.

23 (p. 42). The significance of this idea, and related ideas, in understanding Manet's enterprise is worked out in Fried's "Manet's Sources." My justification for mentioning Courbet in this connection comes in part from the references to him in Fried's writings, but primarily from his detailed analysis of Courbet's work in a course of lectures given at the Fogg Museum at Harvard in the spring of 1966 on French painting from David to Manet.

24 (p. 42). This *Salon* can be found in *The Mirror of Art* (London: Phaidon Press, 1955), a selection of Baudelaire's critical studies translated and edited by Jonathan Mayne, pp. 217–99.

25 (p. 42). See Beaumont Newhall, *The History of Photography* (New York: The Museum of Modern Art, 1964), p. 34.

26 (p. 43). Baudelaire, *The Painter of Modern Life*, p. 61.

27 (p. 44). *Ibid.*, p. 54.

28 (p. 47). *Ibid.*, pp. 50–51.

29 (p. 49). What is the psychic desperation that produces the chronic image, in television's situation comedies and comic commercials, of the husband as a loutish, gullible, lazy, monstrous child? What horror is this laughter trying to contain? What is the wife trying to clean, what traces is she wiping away? It goes beyond obedience to a Protestant message that the body is to be eradicated, the body that a monstrous husband has further defiled. It is as if she is asked to cleanse herself and her environment of the evidence that she has produced this monster. He of course in turn produced her, and gave her the power to produce monsters, in return for depriving her of freedom. No doubt it is a power both wish she did not have to have. Some bargain; some immaculate conception.

30 (p. 55). Baudelaire, *The Painter of Modern Life,* pp. 46–50.

31 (p. 56). It is characteristic at once of the cleverness and the limitedness of Bernard Shaw that he realized Pygmalion as a dandy—as though the artist, or hero, brings his world to life with the power of his mind and his hands, rather than through his touch and his love. Professor Higgins is the Frankenstein of modelers, creating not an idol but an idolizer.

32 (p. 59). I had been content to let my impressionistic scholarship in these matters speak for itself, but an essay I recently came across suggests that more detailed study will bear such lines of thought further than I can take them. In "Greek Tragedy: Problems of Interpretation" (in Richard Macksey and Eugenio Donata, eds., *The Language of Criticism and the Sciences of Man* [Baltimore: The Johns Hopkins Press, 1970]), Jean-Pierre Vernant speaks of the situation of Greek tragedy as a moment in which two ideals of conduct clash: the hero necessary for the establishment of justice must disappear after its establishment, and because of it. He also speaks of the women of Greek tragedy possessing individual "character" despite their lack of social character, i.e., citizenship. In Westerns, this is true of the bad woman, not of the good woman. (If the woman is not bad but nevertheless mildly interesting, she is a "visitor from the East," usually Boston, and usually serving as the schoolteacher.) The inner relation between the hero and the bad woman lies in their relation to their own feelings. They are real to themselves, and their feelings are strong and clear enough to judge the world that thinks to size them up. They know that their inner lives are unknown to the world at large, and because they are unmoved by the opinion of others (which, whether good or bad, is too compromised to value seriously), their respect for themselves demands scrupulous respect in the way others treat them. The inner code they share is the opposite of the bully's. They are not contemptuous, i.e., afraid, of weakness; they come to its protection. They do not force or buy feeling, in particular not love from one another. This is more important as an impediment to their marriage than something called the Hollywood code. The sanction they lend one another outside society cannot function within it. Inside, there is no room for absolute autonomy; the opinion of others must be ceded some control over one's conduct. This is the end of the woman, whose sense of worth depends upon an absolute freedom from the control of reputation; but it merely limits the man, in favor of society's future,

with his children in it, to whom, to perpetuate his name, he must limit his autonomy. Naturally there is an indictment of society in this, a questioning of its capacity to provide the means for any honest living. But the indictment is lodged earlier than in the man's desire to enter society, and hence to forgo the woman. It is implied in the value of that relationship itself, in society's incapacity to provide, or to live according to, the terms in which honor can be honored. Society cannot produce the hero; he must find its boon outside its limits. That he must leave the woman outside, permanently questions whether the light of civilization is worth the candle. The impediment to this marriage is a psychic incestuousness; they are halves of one another. Their relation, in its combination of mutual independence, lust, knowledge, and narcissism, is a serious modern equivalent of the Platonic.

33 (p. 72). When television is not permitted its special capacity for covering actual events as they develop, it shows most perspicuously the impersonation of personality I speak of. Its most successful serial, over a period of several years, was *Mission: Impossible.* It at first seemed that this was merely a further item among the spies-and-gadgets cycles that spun off from early science-fiction movies or serials, mated with films of intrigue. But it went beyond that. Its episodes contained no suspense at all. Because one followed the events with interest enough, this quality did not show until, accidentally reverting to an older type, a moment of suspense was thrown in (say by way of an unplanned difficulty in placing one of the gadgets, or a change of guard not anticipated in the plan of operation). This felt wrong, out of place. The explanation is that the narrative had nothing to do with human motivation; the interest lay solely in following out how the gadgets would act. They were the protagonists of this drama. Interest in them depended not merely on their eventual success, this being a foregone conclusion, but on the knowledge that the plot would arrive at that success through foregone means, absolutely beyond a hitch, so that one was freed to focus exclusively on how, not whether. Then one noticed that there were no human exchanges between the characters in the mission team, or none beyond a word or two exchanged at the beginning, and a faint close-up smile here and there as the perfect plan was taking its totally envisioned course. The fact that the format required the continuing characters to pass as foreigners and, moreover, required one of them to use perfect disguises so that he could temporarily replace a specific foreigner, itself disguised the fact that

these characters were already aliens, disguised as humans. This displacement permitted us something like our old conviction in spy movies. (*The Man From U.N.C.L.E.* tried to get this by suspending or distracting our disbelief with attempts at humor and self-parody. The old swashbucklers—Douglas Fairbanks, Errol Flynn—laughed out of confidence and pleasure at their abilities, not out of embarrassment at the projects to which they put them in service.)

I should add, noting that I have described *Mission: Impossible* in the past tense, that I have watched it several times over the past two seasons, and the features I have mentioned are no longer there; it is now quite without interest.

34 (p. 72). See Clement Greenberg, "After Abstract Expressionism," in *Art International*, VI, No. 8 (October 1962); reprinted in Geldzahler's *New York Painting and Sculpture: 1940–1970;* pp. 360–71. The passage I refer to is on p. 369.

35 (p. 90). This is a major theme in Fried, "Manet's Sources."

36 (p. 95). See Fried, "Art and Objecthood," n. 19.

37 (p. 105). Of all the relations between movies and painting that have cried out for attention, the connection with nonobjective painting may seem the least fruitful to pursue. I do not, of course, deny that one needed line of investigation is to trace out the specific painters who have in fact influenced the look of particular films and of certain moments in film; or perhaps more important, the influence of less monumental forms of graphic art—caricature, poster, engraving, cartoon. But the implication of my procedure is that no such investigation is likely to bear much weight until we have an internal history of the relation of photography and painting generally. It is not much help to know that, say, Degas learned something about the edges of a picture by looking at photographs, until we know why in him painting was ready to look to that information for its own purposes. I seem to remember a shot in an early Cecil B. De Mille Christian offering which looked more or less like a Rembrandt etching (or was it Piranesi?)—light emerging from darkness, baroque diagonals, a long view and lots of architecture. . . . And of course to say it "looked like" Rembrandt here implies that it equally looked like any number of different imitations of Rembrandt, on religious calendars or by arty photographers. Such a use of painting would show about the same respect for it as was shown for ancient Egyptian culture in *The Egyptian,* where thousands were spent making sure that a cuneiform inscription was accu-

rate. (I expect any night to have a dream about a gnat swallowing a camel.) The direct inaccessibility of the powers of painting to the powers of movies seems to me declared, or betrayed, in the pretentious ballet which ends *An American in Paris.* There the perfection of the life-size imitations of, as I recall, canvases by Renoir, Utrillo, and Lautrec merely reaffirms at once that the technological accomplishments money can buy are unlimited, and that the emotional range of this accomplishment may be roughly that of a cheap gag.

38 (p. 105). Or "paradigm," as in Thomas Kuhn's *The Structure of Scientific Revolutions*; or "formula," as in studies of oral literature; or "schema," as in Gombrich's *Art and Illusion*? My understanding of what I call "media" within the various arts is related, and indebted, to such studies. My use of the term is meant (1) to contribute to a characterization of modernist art (as when I suggest a sense in which the search for a medium replaces the search for a style); (2) to characterize the continuity between a modernist art and the past of its art (or, to show what it is which modernism becomes, so to speak, self-conscious or single-minded in the search for); (3) to emphasize the individual fates and faiths of the individual arts. I have said a little more about this in the first part of "A Matter of Meaning It," in *Must We Mean What We Say?*

Kuhn's idea of "paradigm" is especially pertinent in two major respects. First, it shows, in exemplary cases, that revolutionary change (as well as insurrectionary turnover) may result from conservative motives, from a necessity to conserve the identity of a community's enterprise in the face of circumstances that fragment or undermine its authority over itself. In normal science, paradigms do not conserve its identity, but manifest it; to follow the science is to follow its paradigms of procedure and understanding. In a science in crisis, an old paradigm no longer retains this authority, but requires (what comes to seem to be) external justification, or force, for its dominance. From here, the question is raised of the origin of a new source of authority—which, because the community is in disarray, must be the work of certain individuals—around which the unity or identity of the community's enterprise can be reformed. (The Reformation was in the work of a faithful, initially reluctant, priest.) Phenomenologically, this new authority will not present itself (to those accepting it) as innovation, but as rededication. Secondly, it suggests that in re-establishing a profession's identity, not only does one not know *a priori* who will belong to it, but also one does not know how different it may be from other professions. This goes, I believe, against the grain of certain ecumenical ideas about "the unity of science" and "the unity of the arts" and "the unity of science and art." It suggests that an exemplary science or art cannot be joined on its high ground (or knocked from it) by aping (or opposing) the paradigms it has won for itself, but only by taking inspiration from that separate realization of human seriousness and conviction, to discover the necessities of one's own concern.

39 (p. 108). William Rubin, *Dada, Surrealism and Their Heritage* (New York: Museum of Modern Art, 1968).

40 (p. 110). That an acknowledgment is responded to by acknowledgment, and that acknowledgment is the mode in which knowledge of mind appears, are subjects of my essay "Knowing and Acknowledging," and the concept of acknowledgment is thematic throughout *Must We Mean What We Say?* But when I said just now that I followed Michael Fried in speaking of modernist painting's acknowledging of the conditions of painting, I meant more than that I add his application of the concept to various applications I have already thought about. For in both his writing and in mine the concept of acknowledgment is immediately related to issues of presentness, and of theatricality, in aesthetic, epistemological, and theological contexts.

The concept of acknowledgment first showed its significance to me in thinking about our knowledge of other minds, in such a way as to show (what I took to be) modern philosophy neither defeating nor defeated by skepticism. It showed its significance to Michael Fried in characterizing the medium or enterprise of the art of painting, in such a way as to characterize modernist painting as the continuation of that art. Because of this disparity in origin, the resulting confluence of concepts struck me (struck us both, I think I may say) as something more than a confirmation of an already surmised hypothesis. It was a provocation to further study, and a sanction for it. And one of the first regions I began restudying was Fried's own writings in the criticism and history of painting.

I mention this explicitly because I am sometimes asked about it by people who have noticed the references we have made to one another's writings and classes over the past six or seven years. There is no mystery here. It is perhaps usual to find in academic writing that when a name recurs often, it signifies either repetitious disagreement or monotonous alignment. But other relations are possible, e.g., a continuing discovery of mutual profit.

41 (p. 112). See Fried, *Three American Painters*, n. 13.

42 (p. 113). Greenberg, *op. cit.,* pp. 369–70.

Hence to speak of modernist painting as the International Style is, at best, empty. One style is an alternative, or exists in contrast, to another (red-figure vs. black-figure style, Old Style vs. New Style, Baroque vs. Renaissance). Creating or adopting a style is, in modernist art, replaced by discovering a new medium, or failing to. The members of a series are too close, one might say, for their relation to be described as sharing a style; a series as a whole is too far from a different series as a whole for their differences to be described as a difference in style. The difference between two artists is not a difference of alternatives, alternative ways of doing something. What each is doing can only be known in finding what each is acknowledging. Two or more may acknowledge flatness, but the force of revelation lies exactly in its being *this* which reveals it. A medium of painting is not a manner in which it is made, but its unearthing. (Various anti- or quasi-art figures—in particular minimalists or literalists—can, on the other hand, be said to share or deal in a style. Not, I think, directly because of the ways the materials in question are handled, but because of the way emotion is handled, in particular its mass conversion into mood. The premises they propose are to the ending of industrial society what *ruins* were to its beginning: that we work our contempt and fear of the present into a nostalgia directed to the future.)

43 (p. 113). Ludwig Wittgenstein, *Tractatus Philosophicus*, 6.44.

44 (p. 118). Henry David Thoreau, in "Spring" and "Higher Laws," in *Walden*.

45 (p. 121). Certain religious and artistic concepts of exhibition and of theatricality are traced in a very informative essay by Jonas Barish, "Exhibitionism and the Anti-Theatrical Prejudice," *ELH, A Journal of English Literary History*, XXXVI, No. 1 (March 1969).

46 (p. 122). They even allow for serious minor works, like Truffaut's *Soft Skin*, which relies mostly on the attractiveness and individuality of its observations. After a million miles of stock shots of airplanes taking off and landing, Truffaut notices the moment at which a sky giant ends its climb and almost imperceptibly tips level; and he calls the flight over when the dials wind down. The excited disorientation in finding a woman familiar in one place become a total and interesting stranger, is given in the deft pianissimo of gesture by which the

stewardess nudges one heel against the other to slip off the flats of work and then step into her terms of privacy.

47 (p. 128). Ways in which a version of this question has exercised such philosophers as St. Augustine and Jonathan Edwards are discussed in Gareth Matthews' essay "Bodily Motions and Religious Feelings," forthcoming in the *Canadian Journal of Philosophy*.

48 (p. 129). This would not deny that the effect has also to do with the camera's being (as I remember) hand-held and wide-lensed. The general point here is not new. That a shot intended as the vision through a particular pair of eyes is colored by the state of consciousness behind those eyes is what produces those cliché weavings and blurrings we are given to express such states as drunkenness, or the effects of drugs, or, generally, the passage from consciousness to unconsciousness or from unconsciousness to consciousness.

49 (p. 130). This might, of course, itself be taken as a further specific virtue, as a relief or release. In one direction, it could free you for commitment to revolution; in another, it could free you for complete absorption into the culture as it stands. I have heard—I do not remember the source—that Godard has expressed the wish to become a television reporter.

50 (p. 135). A television commercial for some deodorant soap gives us in one case a handsome happy youth, in another a rare maiden, running about the beautiful nothings of their lives, with punctuating flash insets of their joyful showers with the magic bar in question. The rapid juxtaposition of the same body dressed and undressed (if only implied below the shoulders) has a distinctly, perhaps not unintentionally, pornographic effect. A gentle consequence here, but perhaps its range may be expanded. (Since noting that, I have seen a variation of the same thing—similar device and same soap—which lacks the effect.)

51 (p. 137). I see from the *Late Show* that the freeze device, motivated by a setting of fashion photography, was anticipated in Stanley Donen's *Funny Face*. This film, in addition, serves as an instance to characterize the end of a genre of film. It seemed to me absolutely unconvincing—not exactly because Audrey Hepburn conveyed too much intelligence for us to believe that she was charmed by the sweet nothings of the songs and lines directed to her, but because those songs and lines had become bitter somethings to be swallowed. In every Astaire film, his first ballroom duet with the woman contains the *topos*

in which, as the woman turns from him in an effort to leave the scene of their mutual desire, he throws a magnetic Svengali gesture at her retreating figure, upon which she halts and backs back into the dance. We do not read this as an external control of her by foreign suggestion, but as her accepting the desire she had already admitted when she accepted the invitation to dance. She is not altered against her nature by the coupling, but satisfied. (This is clearest in the early and rudimentary *Gay Divorcee*. At the end of their first dance, Ginger Rogers collapses into a state of inner attention or entrancement. What she is saying to herself is not, as it were, "Who am I?" but "So that's what it's like!") He wants her as he finds her. But in *Funny Face,* the woman has to be bullied or joked out of her youthful dreams of intellect and social justice before she is a worthy object of affection. When the routine is no longer motivated by the man's acceptance of his feeling and of the object of his feeling as she is, when it is no longer formed from his wish to attract her interest by showing himself, in his sweetness and resourcefulness and faithfulness, worthy of her feeling, then this form of happiness is past. The dance-serenade under her window—the old virtuosity intact, here in service of a bullfight number with a cape —is not a passionate request, but a claim of dominance. Virtuosity is no longer an expatiation upon virtue, but a mask for its absence. In the trio about Paris, in which the three principals (the third is a militaristic Kay Thompson) are separated by a divided screen, their repetitions do not express their capacities for inspiration and inflection from one another, but an underlying regimentation of emotion. The magic of individuality is replaced by social glamour.

52 (p. 140). As the prose of novels is an extension of the prose of news. The teller of news must let what happens dictate what is worth telling; he fails his responsibility when he will not trace the story to its roots in the world as it stands. The novelist must let himself dictate what is worth telling; he fails his responsibility when he will not trace the story to its roots in story itself, to its source in his wish to tell it and our capacity to hear it, to the human need for news and our poor position for knowing what is news (which is about us) and what is gossip (which is about others).

Orson Welles's use of the imitation *March of Time* at the start of *Citizen Kane,* for all its Lisztian virtuosity, is a more limited device than the literal newsreel. It is in the line of those uses or references within movies to other movies which are supposed to suggest that the film you are watching is the real thing happening. Here, it accounts, I think, for the untrue ending of the film. Rosebud in flames is the *March of Time*'s conclusion to the life of Kane, or Kane's view of his life (which perhaps comes to the same), not the conclusion of Welles's film about him. As it stands, it suggests that the mystery of a man's life is only accidentally unsolved; its irony is that the solution is right under the nose of the reporter. Whereas the irony is that we should think so. It may be that Welles meant us to see this, to feel the triviality of this apocalypse, to recognize that the reporter was from the beginning on the wrong track. But then we should have known that from the beginning. Depriving us of the meaning (i.e., the reference) of "Rosebud" until the end, and depriving the reporter of it forever, reduces the suspense to a gimmick.

53 (p. 144). I do not wish to take away the goodness of a good work by appalling it with a great one. The times of their making are also part of these films. *Grand Illusion* is about the First World War, and came after it, in the waste and hopelessness of it. *The Mortal Storm* occurs between the beginning of the Second World War and America's entry into it, which men of good will were hoping for.

54 (p. 144). The inanition of the Swiss-border motif is achieved at the end of *The Sound of Music,* in which the operetta family under an operetta sun tramp gaily to freedom and fame across the welcoming Alps, the camera nowhere in particular, secure in its mindless insult to the motif it copies. It's artistically integrated, though; the opening of the film was also of Julie Andrews singing through the Alps.

55 (p. 145). While it goes without saying that I have had no intention of making an exhaustive list of techniques, I should mention some which I have not even exemplified, namely those common devices that have passed out of use and seem not to be under exploration now, e.g., the dissolve, accelerated motion, reverse motion, stop motion. Do these devices entail assertions that movies no longer wish to assume? Or is their comic effect so special or limited that its depth could be sounded once for all? Has anyone imagined a more perfect comic or technical use of certain of these tricks than Méliès and Émile Cohl had already achieved before the First World War? (I have just seen for the first time Vigo's *À propos de Nice,* in which a funeral procession is shot in accelerated motion. The point of the device here—cited explicitly, at the screening of the film I attended, by the film's cameraman, Boris Kaufman—is to comment upon the desire, at fashionable seaside resorts, to hurry death out of sight.)

56 (p. 152). Isolation is a quality Welles invariably projects as an actor. It comes from an air of inner preoccupation, together with that voice—for which mere words can seem inadequate things, which seems to know, and yet care, that it will not be understood by the mind to which its words appear to be directed, which seeks to release a lyricism apparently denied the ordinary male in modern society. Welles should have been, when not making his movies, an opera singer. Or radio should not have died, in which the voice is the character, not a disembodiment of it. An actor of genius can achieve at once the distraction and the lyricism that bypasses the range of his hearer, in Heathcliff as well as in Hamlet. The dandy also expects not to be understood, but his distinction is not to care. A man capable of this sound, who at the same time was not too mysteriously preoccupied to care about what is being said to him, for whom another human voice could still matter to him, would have to know how to listen, to be penetrated by a word said to him, or unsaid. The American star best at this, I think, was Spencer Tracy.

What is, I gather, taken as staginess in the speech of actors in early talkies seems to me rather the sound of high radio drama, say, in the voices of the young Katharine Hepburn and the dreamy apostrophes of Ronald Colman, though perhaps radio drama itself derived from the Broadway melodrama of the time. The greatest use of radio's lyricism, or incantation, is what I hear in Polonsky's *Force of Evil,* whose brilliance and stylishness seem no longer to be a pet secret of my own.

57 (p. 152). The other day in Harvard Square a graffito was declaring, "King Kong died for your sins." Was this the idea of an inglorious movie-maker? Or have I again missed something that everyone else knows is common knowledge?

58 (p. 154). "The Modern Theatre Is the Epic Theatre," in *Brecht on Brecht,* ed. and trans. by John Willett (New York: Hill and Wang, 1964).

59 (p. 155). "The Avoidance of Love: A Reading of *King Lear,"* in *Must We Mean What We Say?*

60 (p. 157). Music also exercises an absolute control of our attention; it justifies this by continuously rewarding it. Painting allows attention an absolute freedom; nothing will happen that is not before your eyes. The novel can neither command absolute control nor afford absolute freedom; it operates in the weave between them, as lives do. Its permanent responsibility is to the act of conversing with us.

61 (p. 201). William Rothman, in his doctoral dissertation on aesthetics and cinema (Harvard, 1973), argues, to my mind convincingly, that a particular relation between the shown and the unshown is central to Hitchcock's narrative style, and that this relation develops in a consistent direction throughout his *oeuvre*. His comments on a late draft of the present essay caused me at half a dozen points to correct or qualify or expand what I had said, for each of which I am grateful.

62 (p. 203). The terms I associate with "the end of romance," together with the earlier terms I associated with what I called "secular mysteries," especially the idea of "the mismatch between the depth to which an ordinary human life requires expression and the surface of ordinary means through which that life must express itself," provide terms in which I would like to describe Terrence Malick's *Badlands*. Whatever the objections to trusting one's responses to a friend's film, particularly, I suppose, after just one viewing, the objections to keeping still can grow no less grave. For the moment I simply raise my hand in favor of the film, prepared to say this much: It is a film that invokes and deserves the medium's great and natural power for giving expression to the inexpressive, in everything from the enforced social silence, or shyness, of Chaplin and Keaton to the enforceable personal silence, or reserve, of Bogart and Cooper. It presses questions we ought to have made ourselves answer. What is the faith that understands silent strength to be in service of the good? What words would such strength find in which to express itself? For in the end something must be *said* for our lives. We are saying something now, always, or allowing it to be said. When someone is born, or dies, or marries, or graduates, or has a birthday, millions still allow an ordinary drug store card to express their sentiments. Fewer millions, I guess, are more sophisticated and entrust their sentiments only to a more expensive comic drug store card. I do not deny that in such events it is better to see that something is said than to care overly about what is said. But if it is the spirit that counts, what happens when we no longer understand the spirit? —In what spirit does the killer in *Badlands* say that he "has a lot to say"? In what spirit does Malick baffle this claim by showing the boy unable even to fill a sixty-second recording in a vandalized Record-Your-Own-Voice booth? In what spirit does the girl entrust the narration of her life to the rack of phrases picked from magazine shelves? Which shelves would you

recommend? To have company under whatever sky, you will have to entrust its conformation to whichever booth of expression you can occupy. One might hear a resemblance between this girl's voice and the occasional voices in recent years taped from some place of violent secession. Patricia Hearst's message of June 1974, concerning the shootout in Los Angeles the month before, is the latest instance I am aware of. (A not entirely unrelated dissociation occurred in Nixon's farewell speech on the morning of August 9, 1974, concerning the death of Theodore Roosevelt's young wife.) Then one should ask whether the words of the narrator in *Badlands,* or her tone or spirit, would have been different, or hearable by us differently, if she had been narrating events we could find good. Is one prepared to say that if the events had been good then the message had not required taping? To whom, from where, does one address a letter to the world? To what end does one wish to leave one's mark upon the world?

63 (p. 216). I am assuming that an accommodation can be made with certain of the views of Annette Michelson in "Film and the Radical Aspiration." This issue is broached in the introduction to *Film Theory and Criticism,* an anthology edited by Gerald Mast and Marshall Cohen (Oxford University Press, 1974).

64 (p. 220). There is a good presentation of an English translation of the script in the Classic Film Scripts series published by Simon and Schuster.

Index